OCS Study MMS 2005-O61

FINAL REPORT

VOLUME I

Alternative Oil Spill Occurrence Estimators and their Variability for the Beaufort Sea – Fault Tree Method

MMS Contract Number 1435-01-04-PO-336507

January, 2006

By

Bercha International Inc.
Calgary, Alberta, Canada

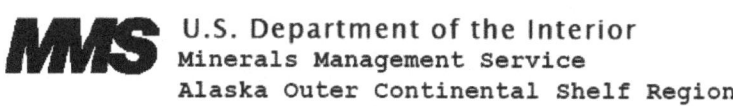

U.S. Department of the Interior
Minerals Management Service
Alaska Outer Continental Shelf Region

OCS Study MMS 2005-O61

FINAL REPORT

VOLUME I

Alternative Oil Spill Occurrence Estimators and their Variability for the Beaufort Sea – Fault Tree Method

January, 2006

Principal Investigator: Dr. Frank G. Bercha, P.Eng.

Bercha International Inc.
2926 Parkdale Boulevard N.W.
Calgary, Alberta, T2N 3S9, Canada
Email: berchaf@berchagroup.com

This study was funded by the U.S. Department of the Interior, Minerals Management Service (MMS), Alaska Outer Continental Shelf Region, Anchorage, under Contract No. 1435-01-04-PO-336507, as part of the MMS Alaska Environmental Studies Program.

ABSTRACT

Oil spill occurrence estimates were generated for several expected future oil and gas development scenarios (including exploration, production, and abandonment) in the Beaufort Sea Offshore Continental Shelf (OCS) lease sale regions. Because sufficient historical data on offshore oil spills for these regions do not exist, an oil spill occurrence model based on fault tree methodology was developed and applied. Using the fault trees, base data from the Gulf of Mexico including the variability of the data, were modified and augmented to represent expected Arctic offshore oil spillage frequencies. Three principal spill occurrence indicators, as follows, were quantified:

- Spill frequency
- Spill frequency per barrel produced
- Spill index, the product of spill size and spill frequency

These indicators were quantified for the following spill sizes:

- Small (S):   =50 to <100 bbl
- Medium (M):   =100 to <1,000 bbl
- Large (L):   =1,000 to <10,000 bbl
- Huge (H):   = 10,000 bbl

Quantification was carried out for each future year for four different Beaufort Sea development scenarios, ranging in duration up to 38 years. In addition, a comparative scenario for non-Arctic locations was formulated and analyzed for oil spill occurrence. Generally, it was found that the non-Arctic spill indicators were likely to be significantly higher than those for similar scenarios in the Arctic. The computations were carried out using a Monte Carlo process to permit the inclusion of estimated uncertainties in the base data and Arctic effects. A wide range of details for each scenario was generated, including the following:

- Expected time history of spill occurrences over the scenario life.
- Spill occurrence variations by spill volumes in the above spill size ranges.
- Spill occurrence variation by spill cause such as boat anchoring or ice gouging.
- Spill occurrence contribution from each main facility type, including pipelines, platforms, and wells.
- Comparison of spill occurrence predictions between Arctic and non-Arctic scenarios.
- Life of field averages of spill occurrence estimators.
- The variability in the results due to uncertainties in the base data and in the Arctic effects was expressed as cumulative distribution functions and statistical measures.

In the final report, a detailed description of the methodology, results, and conclusions and recommendations is given, as well as a section on limitations of the study.

ACKNOWLEDGEMENTS

Grateful acknowledgement for funding and direction is made to MMS Alaska OCS Region. In particular, the following MMS personnel are acknowledged together with their roles:

- Dr. Dick Prentki, Contracting Officer's Technical Representative
- Jim Craig, Resource Evaluation Section
- Caryn Smith, Oil-Spill-Risk-Analysis Coordinator
- Cheryl Anderson, MMS Spill Database Coordinator
- Debra M. Bridge, Contracting Officer
- Warren Horowitz, Environmental Studies GIS Coordinator
- Dennis Hinnah, Office of Field Operations

This work was carried out by Bercha International Inc. Key Bercha personnel on the project team were as follows:

- Dr. Frank G. Bercha, Project Manager and Principal Engineer
- Milan Cerovšek, Reliability Engineering Specialist
- Edmund A. Yasinko, Offshore Pipeline Specialist
- Wesley Abel, Offshore Engineering Specialist
- Susan Charlton, Editorial and Word Processing Manager

EXECUTIVE SUMMARY

A.   Summary of Work Done

Oil spill occurrence estimators were generated for several expected future oil and gas development scenarios (including exploration, production, and abandonment) in the Beaufort and Chukchi Seas Offshore Continental Shelf (OCS) lease sale regions. Because sufficient historical data on offshore oil spills for these regions do not exist, an oil spill occurrence model based on fault tree methodology was developed and applied. Using the fault trees, base data from the Gulf of Mexico, including their variability, were modified and augmented to represent expected Arctic offshore oil spillage frequencies. Three principal spill occurrence indicators, as follows, were quantified for each year of each scenario, as well as for each scenario life of field averages:

- Spill frequency

- Spill frequency per barrel produced

- Spill index, the product of spill size and spill frequency

Fractional spill sizes were rounded up or down to the nearest whole number, with rounding up for any decimal ending in 5.

These indicators were quantified for the following spill sizes:

- Small (S):   =50 to <100 bbl

- Medium (M):   =100 to <1,000 bbl

- Large (L):   =1,000 to <10,000 bbl

- Huge (H):   = 10,000 bbl

Quantification was carried out for each future year for four different Beaufort Sea exploration and development scenarios, ranging in duration up to 38 years. Three scenarios represented developments associated with three different sales (Sales 1, 2, and 3), and the fourth was for a composite scenario: "Sale All", consisting of composite developments from all three sales. In addition, a comparative scenario for non-Arctic locations was formulated and analyzed for oil spill occurrence for the composite development. Generally, it was found that the non-Arctic spill indicators were likely to be higher than those for similar scenarios in the Arctic. The computations were carried out using a Monte Carlo process to permit the inclusion of estimated uncertainties in the input data. A wide range of details for each scenario was generated, including the following:

- Expected time history of spill occurrences over the scenario life.

- Spill occurrence variations by spill volumes in the above spill size ranges.

- Spill occurrence variation by spill cause such as boat anchoring or ice gouging.

- Spill occurrence contribution from each main facility type, including pipelines, platforms, and wells.

- Comparison of spill occurrence predictions between Arctic and non-Arctic scenarios.

- The variability in the results due to uncertainties in the input data is expressed as cumulative distribution functions and statistical measures.

In the final report, a detailed description of the methodology, results, and conclusions and recommendations is given, as well as a section on limitations of the study.

B.   Conclusions

B.1   General Conclusions

Oil spill occurrence indicators were quantified for future offshore development scenarios in the south Beaufort Sea in the area of MMS jurisdiction. The quantification included the consideration of the variability of historical data as well as the expected variability of Arctic effects on oil spill occurrence indicators. Consideration of the variability of all input data yields both higher variability and higher expected value of the spill occurrence indicators. The three types of spill occurrence indicators were: annual oil spill frequency, annual oil spill frequency per barrel produced, and annual spill index – and, additionally, the life of field averages for each of these three oil spill indicators were assessed.

B.2   Oil Spill Occurrence Indicators by Spill Size

How do spill indicators for the different scenarios and for their non-Arctic counterparts vary by spill size and source? Table1 summarizes the Life of Field (LOF) average spill indicator values. Figure 1 illustrates these for Sale 1, 2, and 3. The following can be observed from Table 1.

- Each spill indicator for Sale 1, 2, and 3 is similar in value. The indicators are higher for the composite "Sale All" scenario.

- Spill frequency per year and per barrel decreases significantly with increasing spill size for all scenarios.

- The spill index increases dramatically with spill size for all scenarios.

- All non-Arctic scenario spill indicators are greater than their Arctic counterparts. Non-Arctic spill indicators are approximately 40% greater.

Table 1
Summary of Average Spill Indicators for All Scenarios

Spill Indicators Life of Field Average	SALE 1			SALE 2			SALE 3			SALE All			SALE All non Arctic		
	Spill Frequency per 10^3 years	Spill Frequency per 10^9 bbl produced	Spill Index [bbl]	Spill Frequency per 10^3 years	Spill Frequency per 10^9 bbl produced	Spill Index [bbl]	Spill Frequency per 10^3 years	Spill Frequency per 10^9 bbl produced	Spill Index [bbl]	Spill Frequency per 10^3 years	Spill Frequency per 10^9 bbl produced	Spill Index [bbl]	Spill Frequency per 10^3 years	Spill Frequency per 10^9 bbl produced	Spill Index [bbl]
Small and Medium Spills 50-999 bbl	9.404 / 56%	0.612 / 56%	4 / 1%	9.586 / 57%	0.674 / 57%	4 / 1%	11.320 / 57%	0.714 / 57%	5 / 1%	26.204 / 57%	0.667 / 57%	11 / 1%	38.900 / 58%	0.990 / 58%	15 / 1%
Large Spills 1000-9999 bbl	4.099 / 24%	0.267 / 24%	31 / 10%	3.989 / 24%	0.281 / 24%	30 / 10%	4.575 / 23%	0.289 / 23%	35 / 10%	10.951 / 24%	0.279 / 24%	82 / 10%	15.653 / 23%	0.398 / 23%	117 / 10%
Huge Spills =>10000 bbl	3.369 / 20%	0.219 / 20%	270 / 89%	3.323 / 20%	0.234 / 20%	268 / 89%	3.901 / 20%	0.246 / 20%	317 / 89%	9.158 / 20%	0.233 / 20%	740 / 89%	12.956 / 19%	0.330 / 19%	1048 / 89%
Significant Spills =>1000 bbl	7.468 / 44%	0.486 / 44%	300 / 99%	7.312 / 43%	0.514 / 43%	298 / 99%	8.476 / 43%	0.535 / 43%	352 / 99%	20.109 / 43%	0.512 / 43%	822 / 99%	28.608 / 42%	0.728 / 42%	1165 / 99%
All Spills	16.872 / 100%	1.098 / 100%	304 / 100%	16.897 / 100%	1.188 / 100%	302 / 100%	19.796 / 100%	1.249 / 100%	357 / 100%	46.313 / 100%	1.178 / 100%	833 / 100%	67.508 / 100%	1.718 / 100%	1180 / 100%
Pipeline Spills	5.953 / 35%	0.388 / 35%	25 / 8%	5.899 / 35%	0.415 / 35%	23 / 8%	6.551 / 33%	0.413 / 33%	26 / 7%	15.925 / 34%	0.405 / 34%	64 / 8%	27.192 / 40%	0.692 / 40%	96 / 8%
Platform Spills	7.122 / 42%	0.464 / 42%	9 / 3%	7.210 / 43%	0.507 / 43%	9 / 3%	8.751 / 44%	0.552 / 44%	11 / 3%	19.947 / 43%	0.508 / 43%	24 / 3%	25.562 / 38%	0.650 / 38%	30 / 3%
Well Spills	3.797 / 23%	0.247 / 23%	271 / 89%	3.787 / 22%	0.266 / 22%	271 / 89%	4.494 / 23%	0.283 / 23%	321 / 90%	10.441 / 23%	0.266 / 23%	746 / 89%	14.755 / 22%	0.375 / 22%	1054 / 89%
Platform and Well Spills	10.918 / 65%	0.711 / 65%	280 / 92%	10.998 / 65%	0.773 / 65%	279 / 92%	13.245 / 67%	0.835 / 67%	331 / 93%	30.388 / 66%	0.773 / 66%	770 / 92%	40.317 / 60%	1.026 / 60%	1084 / 92%
All Spills	16.872 / 100%	1.098 / 100%	304 / 100%	16.897 / 100%	1.188 / 100%	302 / 100%	19.796 / 100%	1.249 / 100%	357 / 100%	46.313 / 100%	1.178 / 100%	833 / 100%	67.508 / 100%	1.718 / 100%	1180 / 100%

January, 2006

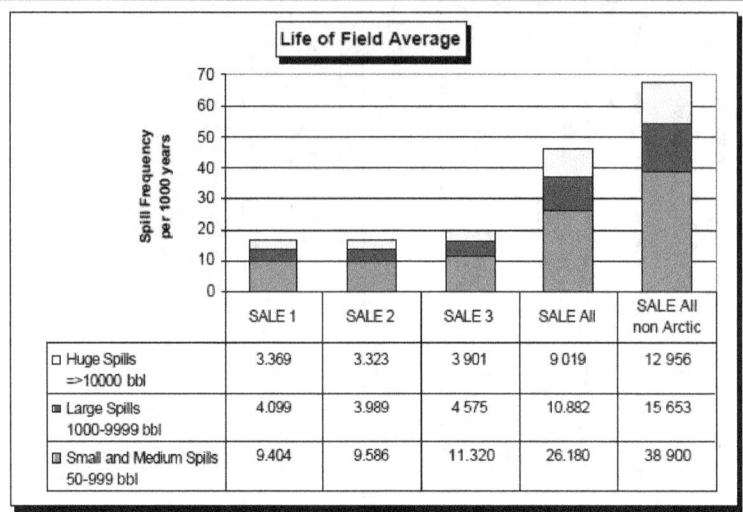

Life of Field Average	SALE 1	SALE 2	SALE 3	SALE All	SALE All non Arctic
☐ Huge Spills =>10000 bbl	3.369	3.323	3 901	9 019	12 956
▣ Large Spills 1000-9999 bbl	4.099	3.989	4 575	10.882	15 653
▣ Small and Medium Spills 50-999 bbl	9.404	9.586	11.320	26.180	38 900

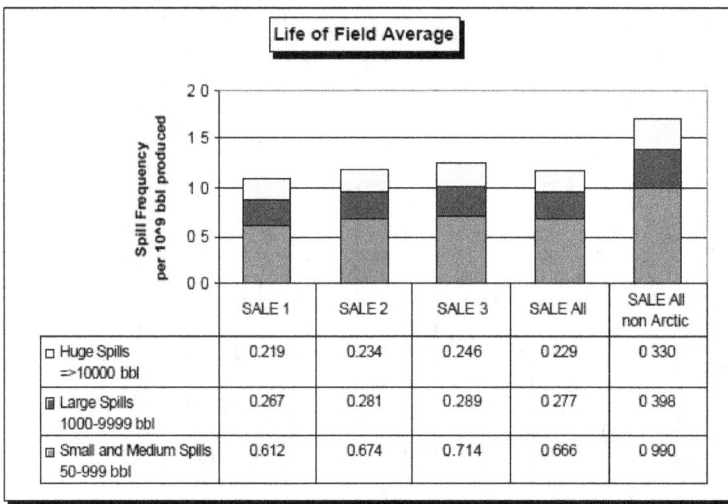

Life of Field Average	SALE 1	SALE 2	SALE 3	SALE All	SALE All non Arctic
☐ Huge Spills =>10000 bbl	0.219	0.234	0.246	0 229	0 330
▣ Large Spills 1000-9999 bbl	0.267	0.281	0.289	0 277	0 398
▣ Small and Medium Spills 50-999 bbl	0.612	0.674	0.714	0 666	0 990

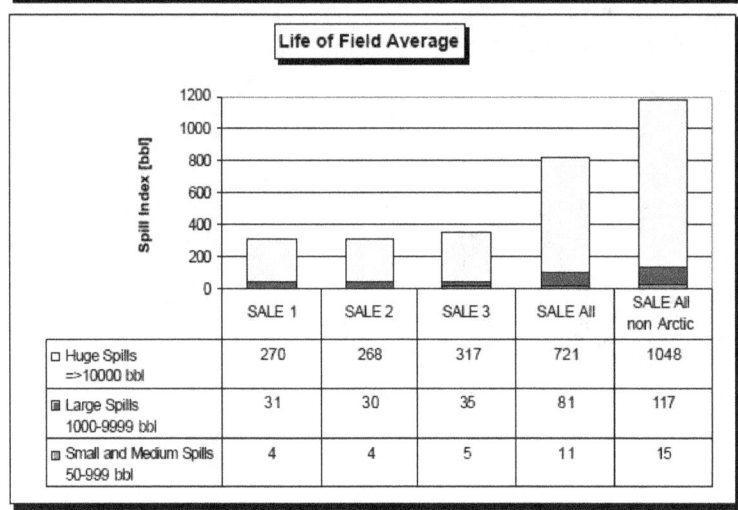

Life of Field Average	SALE 1	SALE 2	SALE 3	SALE All	SALE All non Arctic
☐ Huge Spills =>10000 bbl	270	268	317	721	1048
▣ Large Spills 1000-9999 bbl	31	30	35	81	117
▣ Small and Medium Spills 50-999 bbl	4	4	5	11	15

Figure 1
Life of Field Spill Indicators – By Spill Size

B.3   Oil Spill Occurrence Indicators by Spill Source

How do the spill indicators vary by spill source facility type for representative scenarios? The contributions of spill indicators by source facility have been summarized by representative scenario years, again, in Table 1 and also in Figure 2. Table 1 and Figure 2 give the component contributions, in absolute value and percent, for each of the main facility types; namely, pipelines (P/L), platforms, and wells. The following may be noted from Table 1:

- Platforms contribute the most (43%) to the two spill frequency indicators, but the least (3%) to the spill index.

- Pipelines are next in relative contribution to spill frequencies (34%) and intermediate in contribution to spill index (8%).

- Wells are by far (at 89%) the highest contributors to spill index.

- It can be concluded that platforms are likely to have the most, but smaller spills, while wells will have the least number, but largest spills. Pipelines will be in between, with a tendency towards more spills than wells, but less or about the same number as platforms.

Figures 3 and 4 show relative contributions by facility and spill size to the maximum production year 2024 and Life of Field average spill indicators, respectively. Although Life of Field average spill indicator absolute values are significantly smaller than the maximum production year values, the proportional contributions by spill facility source and spill size are almost identical.

B.4   Variability of Oil Spill Occurrence Indicators

Figures 5, 6, and 7 show the Cumulative Distribution Functions for each of the Beaufort Sea Sale All Life of Field average spill indicators by spill size and source. The variability of these indicators is fairly representative of the trends in variability for spill indicators for all scenarios modeled. Generally, the following can be observed from the figures:

- The variance of the frequency spill indicators (Figures 5 and 6) decreases as spill size increases. In other words, small and medium spills illustrate the largest variability; huge spills show the least variability for facilities.

- The variability of the spill index (Figure 7) shows the same trend for pipelines and platforms, but the opposite trend for wells.

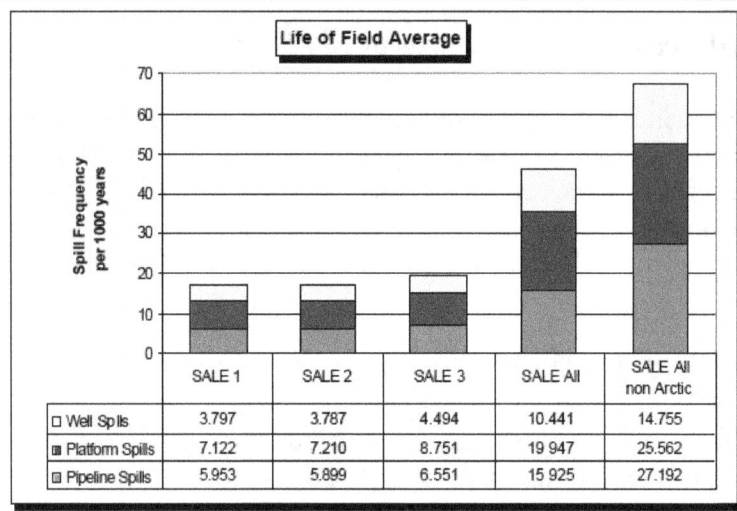

	SALE 1	SALE 2	SALE 3	SALE All	SALE All non Arctic
☐ Well Spills	3.797	3.787	4.494	10.441	14.755
▨ Platform Spills	7.122	7.210	8.751	19 947	25.562
▨ Pipeline Spills	5.953	5.899	6.551	15 925	27.192

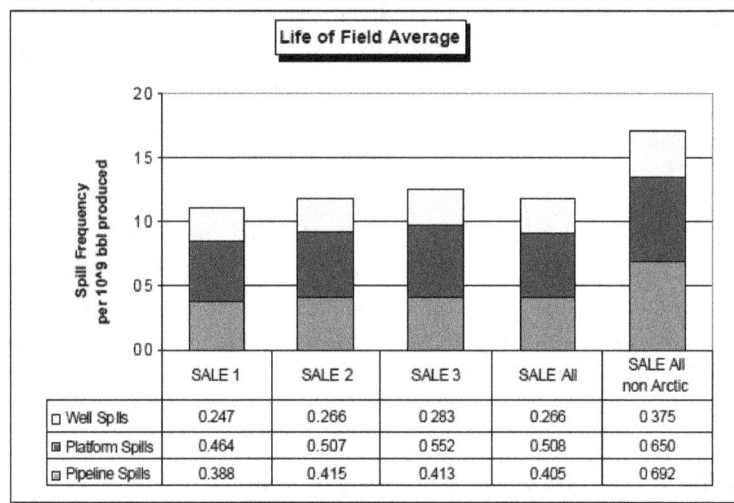

	SALE 1	SALE 2	SALE 3	SALE All	SALE All non Arctic
☐ Well Spills	0.247	0.266	0 283	0.266	0 375
▨ Platform Spills	0.464	0.507	0 552	0.508	0 650
▨ Pipeline Spills	0.388	0.415	0.413	0.405	0 692

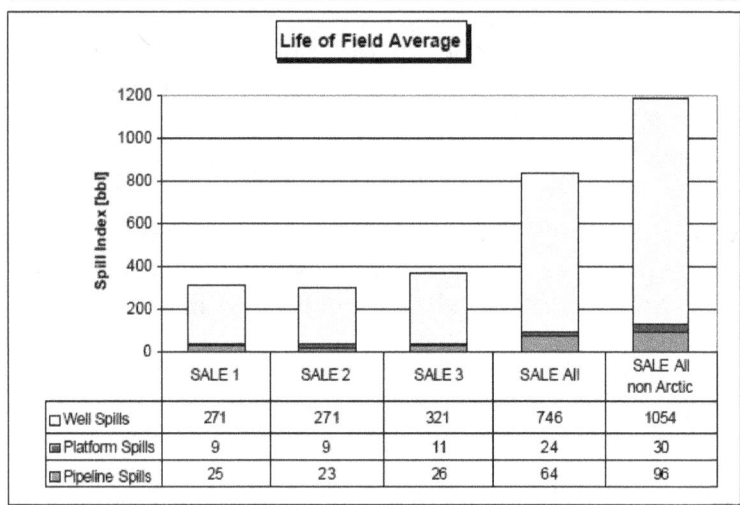

	SALE 1	SALE 2	SALE 3	SALE All	SALE All non Arctic
☐ Well Spills	271	271	321	746	1054
▨ Platform Spills	9	9	11	24	30
▨ Pipeline Spills	25	23	26	64	96

Figure 2
Life of Field Spill Indicators – By Source Composition

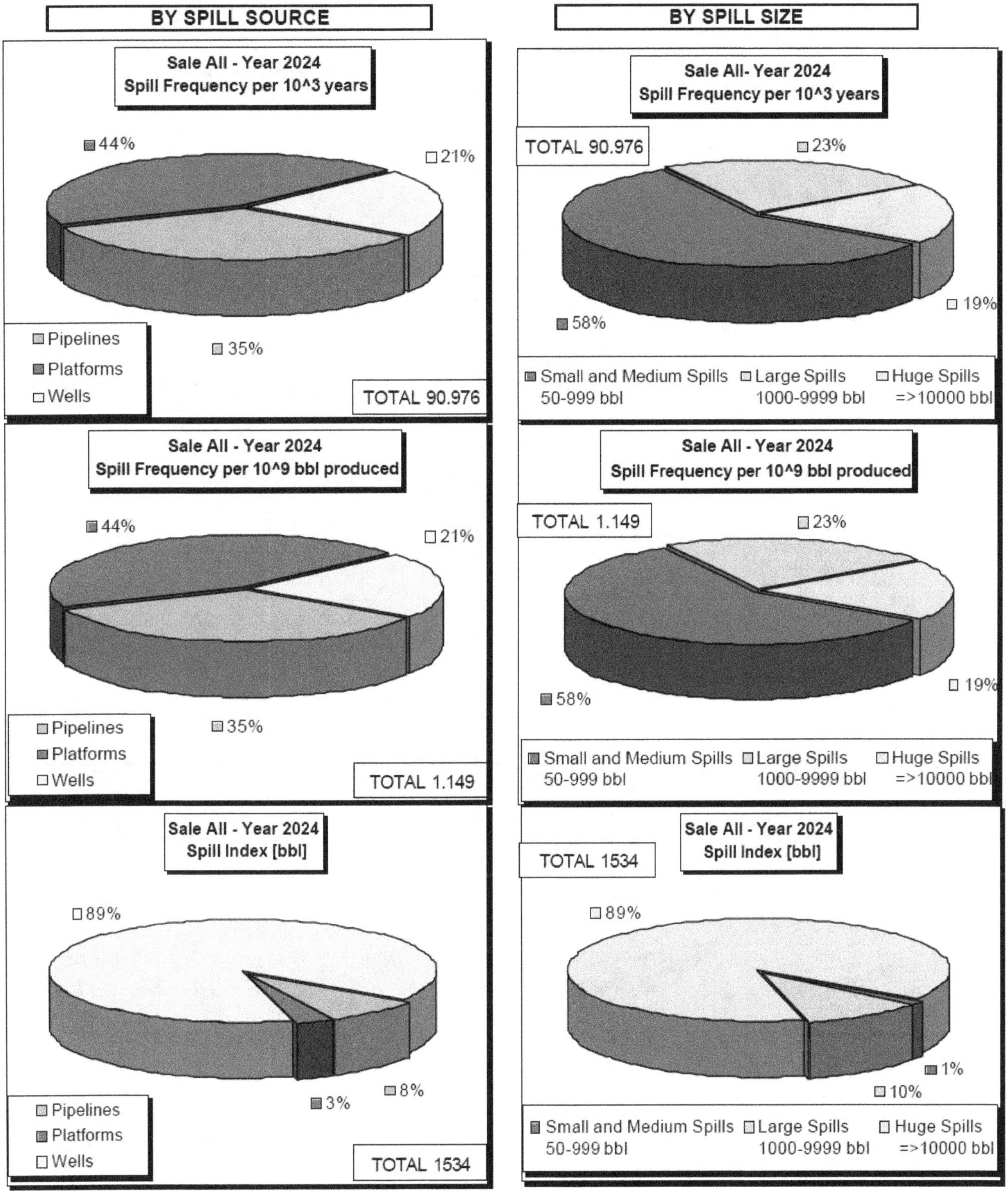

BY SPILL SOURCE

Sale All - Year 2024
Spill Frequency per 10^3 years

■ 44%   □ 21%

□ Pipelines
■ Platforms   □ 35%
□ Wells

TOTAL 90.976

Sale All - Year 2024
Spill Frequency per 10^9 bbl produced

■ 44%   □ 21%

□ Pipelines
■ Platforms   □ 35%
□ Wells

TOTAL 1.149

Sale All - Year 2024
Spill Index [bbl]

□ 89%

□ Pipelines
■ Platforms   ■ 8%
□ Wells   ■ 3%

TOTAL 1534

BY SPILL SIZE

Sale All- Year 2024
Spill Frequency per 10^3 years

TOTAL 90.976   □ 23%

■ 58%   □ 19%

■ Small and Medium Spills   □ Large Spills   □ Huge Spills
50-999 bbl   1000-9999 bbl   =>10000 bbl

Sale All - Year 2024
Spill Frequency per 10^9 bbl produced

TOTAL 1.149   □ 23%

■ 58%   □ 19%

■ Small and Medium Spills   □ Large Spills   □ Huge Spills
50-999 bbl   1000-9999 bbl   =>10000 bbl

Sale All - Year 2024
Spill Index [bbl]

TOTAL 1534   □ 89%

■ 1%
□ 10%

■ Small and Medium Spills   □ Large Spills   □ Huge Spills
50-999 bbl   1000-9999 bbl   =>10000 bbl

Figure 3
Sale All – Year 2024 – Spill Indicator Composition by Source and Spill Size

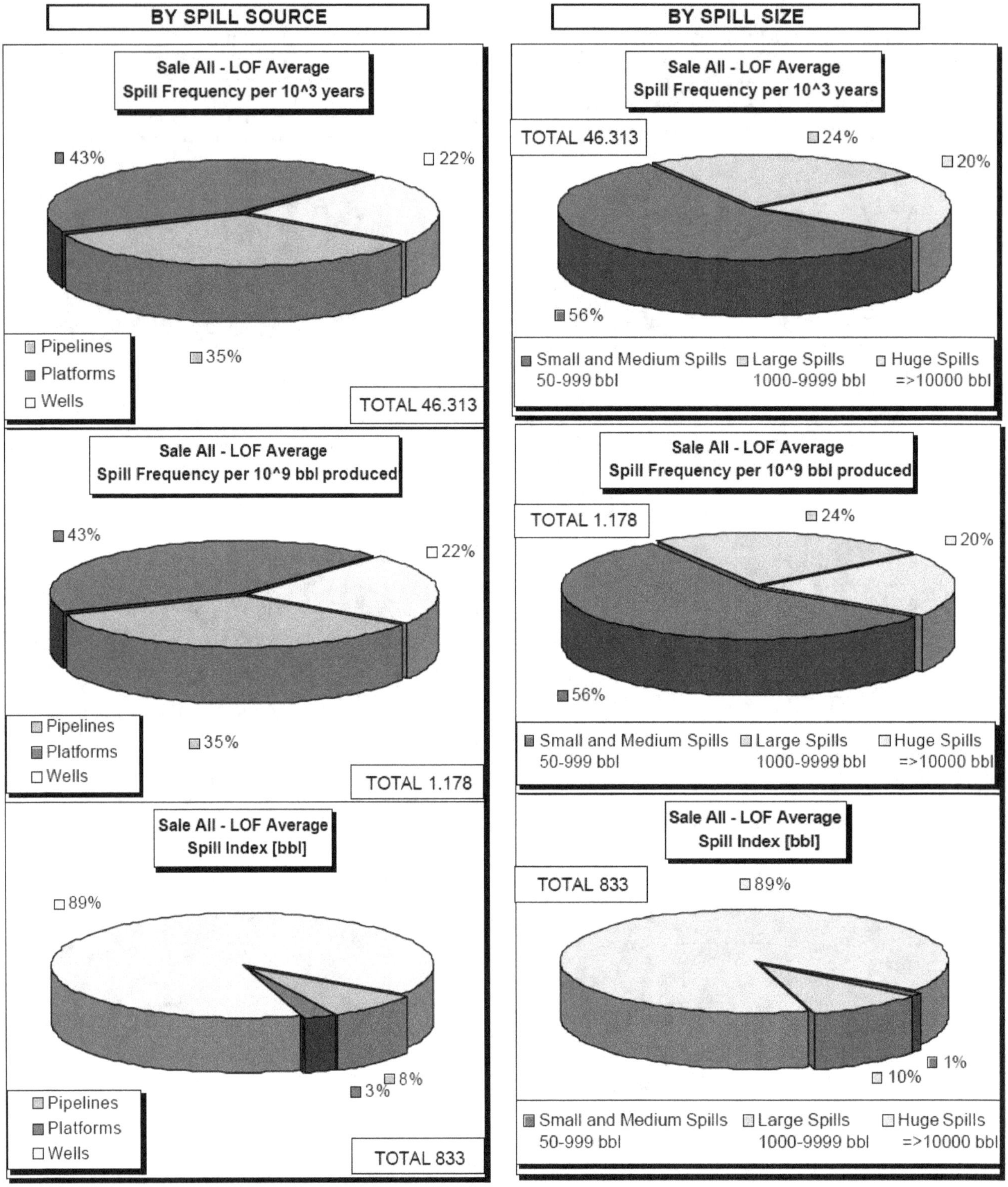

BY SPILL SOURCE	BY SPILL SIZE

Sale All - LOF Average
Spill Frequency per 10^3 years

☐ 43%   ☐ 22%

☐ 35%

☐ Pipelines
☐ Platforms
☐ Wells

TOTAL 46.313

Sale All - LOF Average
Spill Frequency per 10^3 years

TOTAL 46.313   ☐ 24%   ☐ 20%

☐ 56%

☐ Small and Medium Spills   ☐ Large Spills   ☐ Huge Spills
  50-999 bbl   1000-9999 bbl   =>10000 bbl

Sale All - LOF Average
Spill Frequency per 10^9 bbl produced

☐ 43%   ☐ 22%

☐ 35%

☐ Pipelines
☐ Platforms
☐ Wells

TOTAL 1.178

Sale All - LOF Average
Spill Frequency per 10^9 bbl produced

TOTAL 1.178   ☐ 24%   ☐ 20%

☐ 56%

☐ Small and Medium Spills   ☐ Large Spills   ☐ Huge Spills
  50-999 bbl   1000-9999 bbl   =>10000 bbl

Sale All - LOF Average
Spill Index [bbl]

☐ 89%

☐ 8%
☐ 3%

☐ Pipelines
☐ Platforms
☐ Wells

TOTAL 833

Sale All - LOF Average
Spill Index [bbl]

TOTAL 833   ☐ 89%

☐ 1%
☐ 10%

☐ Small and Medium Spills   ☐ Large Spills   ☐ Huge Spills
  50-999 bbl   1000-9999 bbl   =>10000 bbl

Figure 4
Sale All – Life of Field Average Spill Indicator Composition by Source and Spill Size

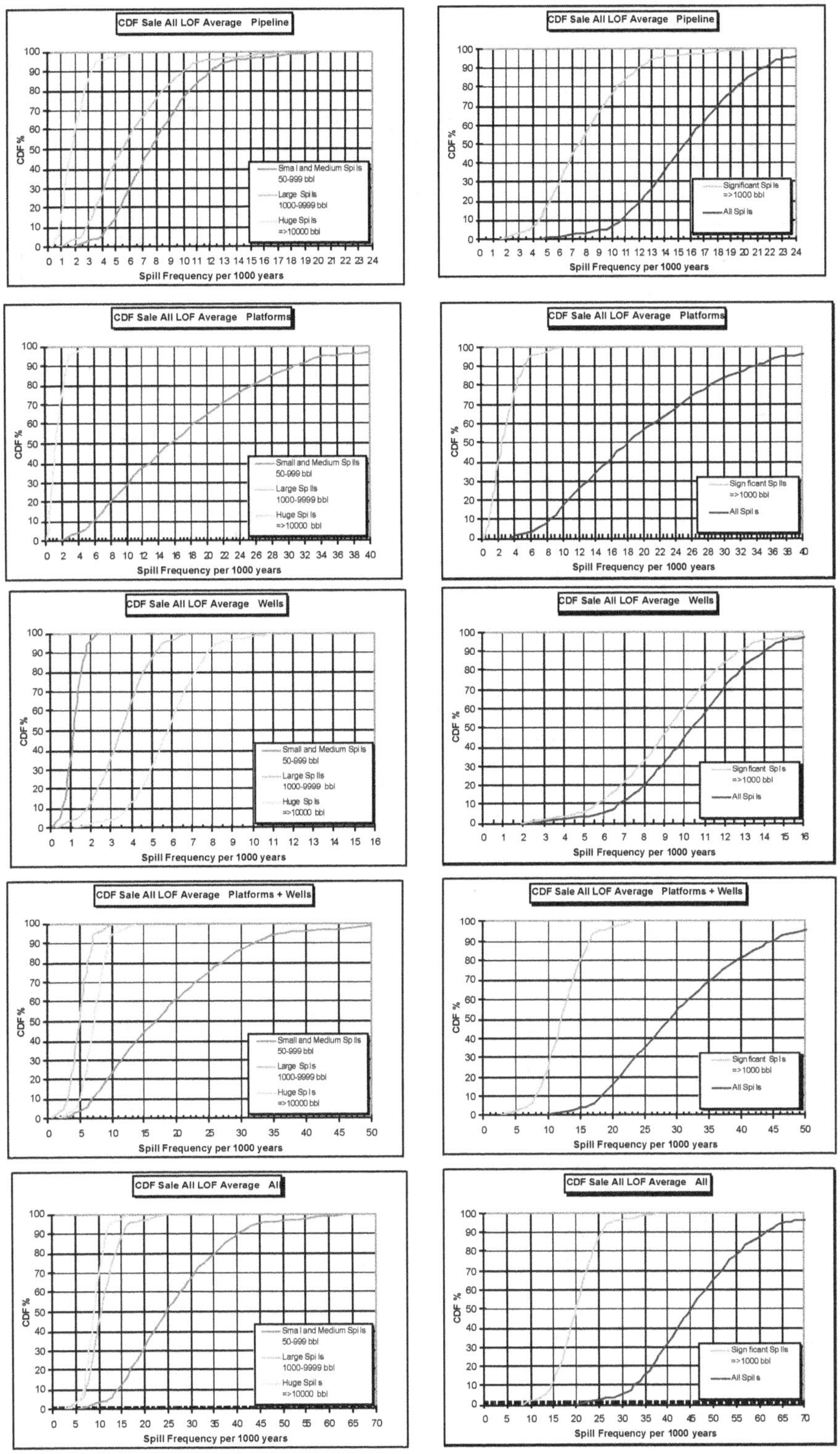

Figure 5
Life of Field Average Spill Frequency – Cumulative Distribution Functions – Sale All

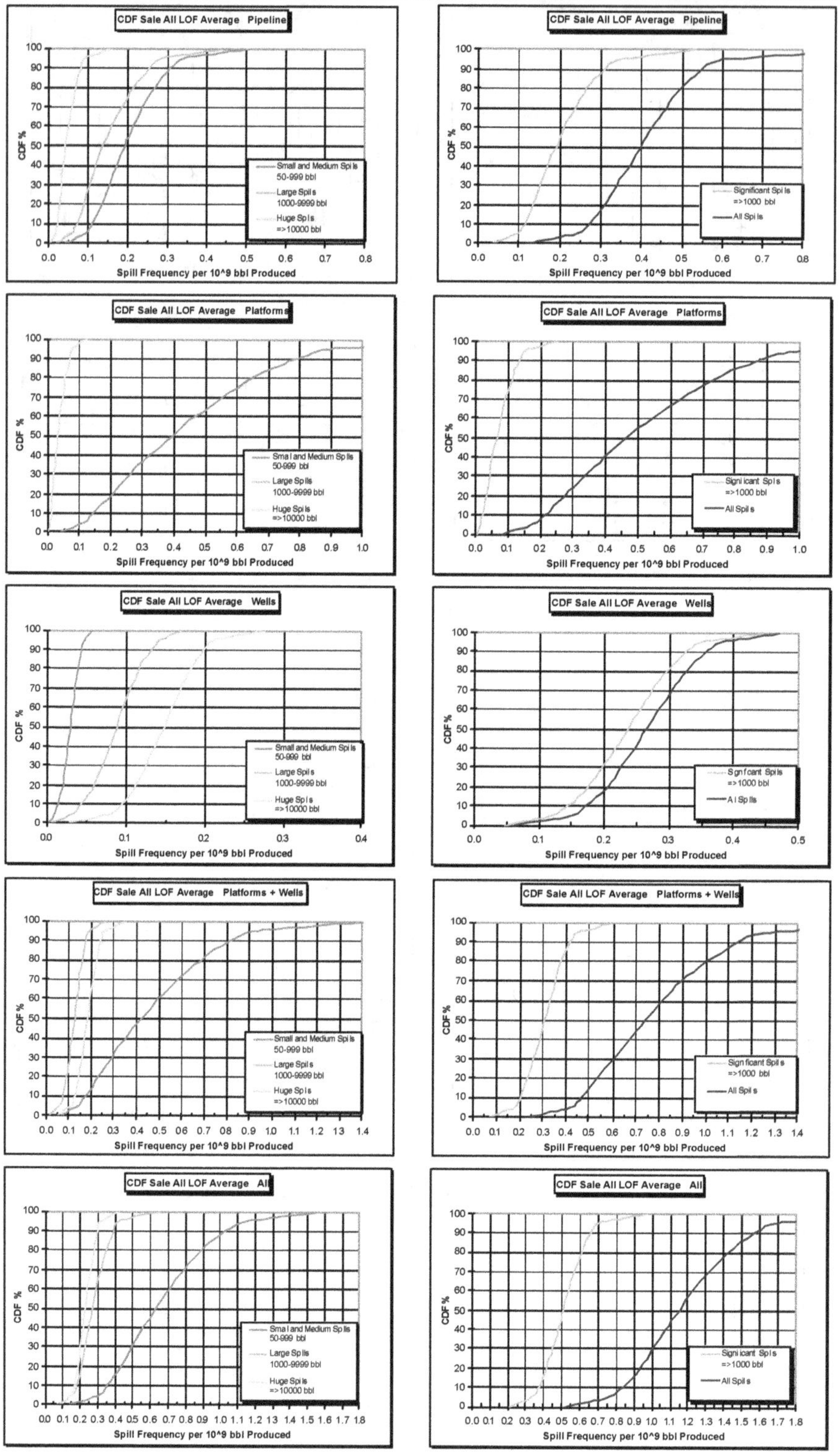

Figure 6
Life of Field Average Spill Frequency per Barrel Produced – Cumulative
Distribution Functions – Sale All

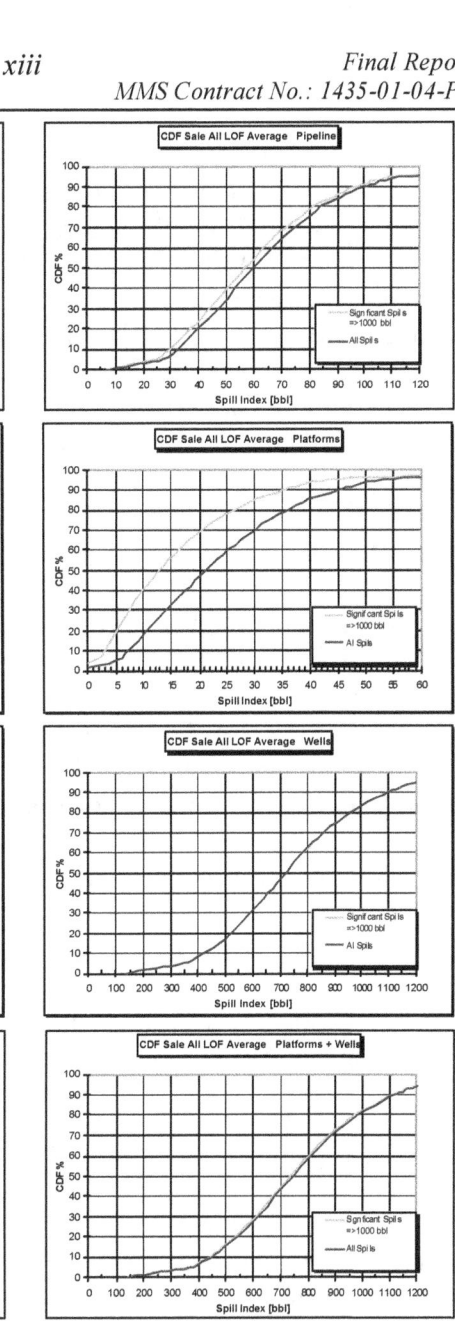
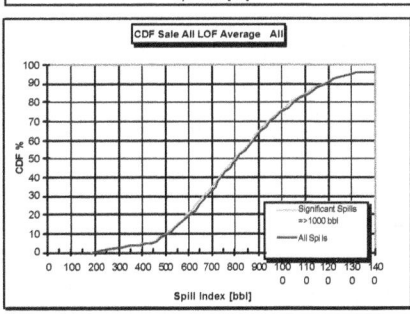

Figure 7
Life of Field Average Spill Index (bbl) – Cumulative Distribution Functions – Sale All

The Cumulative Distribution Functions contain extensive information on the statistical properties of the spill indicators. For example, from Figure 5, it can be seen, for significant spills, that the Life of Field average mean (50%) value of 20 (spills per 1,000 years) ranges between 30 and 12 at the upper and lower 95% confidence intervals. A similar percentage variation is shown for the Life of Field average spill frequency per barrel produced in Figure 6. The spill index variability shown in Figure 7 is proportionally higher. For example, in Figure 7, the mean value of the significant spills index of 800 per billion barrels produced ranges from 1,300 to 400 – a somewhat larger proportion of mean than that of the spill frequency indicators.

C.   Conclusions on the Methodology and its Applicability

An analytical tool for the prediction of oil spill occurrence indicators for systems without history has been developed based on the utilization of fault tree methodology. Although the results generated are voluminous, they are essentially transparent, simple, and easy to understand. The analytical tool developed is also quite transparent, very efficient in terms of computer time and input-output capability. In addition, the basic model is setup so that any input variables can be entered as distributions.

A wealth of information that can be utilized for the optimal planning and regulation of future developments is generated by the analytical tool. Key aspects of the analytical tool capability may be summarized as follows:

- Ability to generate expected and mean values as well as their variability in rigorous numerical statistical format.

- Use of verifiable input data based on MMS or other historical spill data and statistics.

- Ability to independently vary the impacts of different causes on the spill occurrences as well as add new causes such as some of those that may be expected for the Arctic or other new environments.

- Ability to generate spill occurrence indicator characteristics such as annual variations, facility contributions, spill size distributions, and spill causes, and life of field (Life of Field) averages.

- Ability to generate comparative spill occurrence indicators such as those of comparable scenarios in more temperate regions. The model developed provides a basis for estimating each Arctic effect's importance through sensitivity analysis as well as propagation of uncertainties.

- Capability to quantify uncertainties rigorously, together with their measures of variability.

D.   Limitations of the Methodology and Results

During the work, a number of limitations in the input data, the scenarios, the application of the fault tree methodology, and finally the oil spill occurrence indicators themselves have been identified. These shortcomings are summarized in the following paragraphs.

Two categories of input data were used; namely the historical spill data and the Arctic effect data. Although a verifiable and optimal historical spill data set has been used, the following shortcomings may be noted:

- Gulf of Mexico (OCS) historical data bases were provided by MMS for pipelines and facilities, and were used as a starting point for the fault tree analysis. Although these data are adequate, a broader population base would give more robust statistics. Unfortunately, data from a broader population base, such as the North Sea, do not contain the level of detail provided in the GOM data.

- The Arctic effects include modifications in causes associated with the historical data set as well as additions of spill causes unique to the Arctic environment. Quantification of existing causes for Arctic effects was done in a relative cursory way restricted to engineering judgment.

- Upheaval buckling and thaw settlement effect assessments were included on the basis of an educated guess; no engineering analysis was carried out for the assessment of frequencies to be expected for these effects.

- A reproducible but relatively elementary analysis of gouging and scour effects was carried out.

The scenarios are those developed for use in the MMS Alaska OCS Region Environmental Impact Statements for Oil and Gas Lease Sales. As estimated they appear reasonable and were incorporated in the form provided. There are two possible shortcomings of the scenarios as follows:

- Distributed values for the key quantities were not provided, thus precluding their incorporation as distributions in the Monte Carlo analysis.

- The facility abandonment rate appears to be significantly lower than the rate of decline in production.

Generally, the fault tree methodology was limited primarily by the shortcomings in input data discussed above.

The following comments can be made on limitations associated with the indicators that have been generated.

- The indicators have inherited the deficiencies of the input and scenario data noted above.

- The model generating the indicators is fundamentally a linear model which ignores the effects of scale, of time variations such as the learning and wear-out curves (Bathtub curve), and production volume non-linear effects.

E.   Recommendations

The following recommendations based on the work may be made:

- Continue to utilize the Monte Carlo spill occurrence indicator model for new scenarios to support MMS needs, as it is currently the best predictive spill occurrence model available.

- Utilize the oil spill occurrence indicator model to generate additional model validation information, including direct application to specific non-Arctic scenarios, such as GOM projects, which have an oil spill statistical history.

- Utilize the oil spill occurrence indicator model in a sensitivity mode to identify the importance of different Arctic effect variables introduced to provide a prioritized list of those items having the highest potential impact on Arctic oil spills. These effects are incorporated to the extent that they are represented in spill databases used.

- Generalize the model so that it can be run both in an adjusted expected value and a distributed value (Monte Carlo) form with the intent that expected value form can be utilized without the Monte Carlo add-in for preliminary estimates and sensitivity analyses, while for more comprehensive rigorous studies, the Monte Carlo version can be used.

- Develop an adjusted expected value oil spill occurrence indicator model as a user friendly software package, which can be used for the assessment of oil spill occurrence indicators and their characteristics for any designated scenario. The software package should include the following:
  - Modular structure
  - User manual
  - Online help
  - Password protected parameters and algorithms
  - Extensive tabular and graphical outputs

TABLE OF CONTENTS

VOLUME I

CHAPTER   **PAGE**

LIST OF APPENDICES
(VOLUME II – APPENDICES)

LIST OF TABLES

LIST OF FIGURES

FIGURE   **PAGE**

GLOSSARY OF TERMS AND ACRONYMS

Acute Risk	Risk that has an immediate adverse effect due to a single accident such as an oil blowout.
ALARP	**A**s **L**ow **a**s **R**easonably **P**racticable
API	**A**merican **P**etroleum **I**nstitute
ARM	**A**vailability, **R**eliability and **M**aintainability
BOP	**B**lowout **P**reventer
CDF	**C**umulative **D**istribution **F**requency
Chronic Risk	Risk that has an adverse effect only after long-term or repeated occurrences.
Consequence	The direct effect of an accidental event.
DJU	**D**rilling **J**ack-**U**p
ESD	**E**mergency **S**hut**d**own
ESDV	**E**mergency **S**hut**d**own **V**alve
FPSO	**F**loating **P**roduction and **S**torage **O**peration
GBS	**G**ravity **B**ase **S**tructure
GOM	**G**ulf **o**f **M**exico
H$_2$S	**H**ydrogen **S**ulfide
Hazard	A condition with a potential to create risks such as accidental leakage of natural gas from a pressurized vessel.
HSE	**H**ealth and **S**afety **E**xecutive (United Kingdom)
HT	**H**igh **T**emperature
HTHP	**H**igh **T**emperature, **H**igh **P**ressure
LFL	**L**ower **F**lammability **L**imit
LOF	**L**ife of **F**ield
MAOP	**M**aximum **A**llowable **O**perating **P**ressure. The highest pressure at which a pipeline or vessel can be operated considering design and regulatory conditions.
MMS	**M**inerals **M**anagement **S**ervice, Department of the Interior
Monte Carlo	A numerical method for evaluating algebraic combinations of statistical distributions.
MSL	**M**ean **S**ea **L**evel
NOP	**N**ormal **O**perating **P**ressure. The highest pressure at which a pipeline or vessel can be operated considering design conditions.

NPD	Norwegian Petroleum Directorate
OCS	Offshore Continental Shelf
OIM	Offshore Installation Manager
QRA	Quantitative Risk Assessment
Risk	A compound measure of the probability and magnitude of adverse effect.
ROV	Remotely Operated Vehicle
SINTEF	The Foundation of Scientific and Industrial Research at the Norwegian Institute of Technology
Spill Frequency	The number of spills of a given spill size range per year. Usually expressed as spills per 1,000 years (and so indicated).
Spill Frequency per Barrel Produced	The number of spills of a given spill size range per barrel produced. Usually expressed as spills per billion barrels produced (and so indicated).
Spill Index	The product of spill frequency for a given spill size range and the mean spill size for that spill size range.
Spill Occurrence	Characterization of an oil spill as an annual frequency and associated spill size or spill size range.
Spill Occurrence Indicator	Any of the oil spill occurrence characteristics; namely, spill frequency, spill frequency per barrel produced, or spill index (defined above).
Spill Sizes	Small (S): 50 - 99 bbl Medium (M): 100 - 999 bbl Large (L): 1,000 - 9,999 bbl Huge (H): = 10,000 bbl Significant (SG): = 1,000 bbl
SPM	Single Point Mooring
SSIV	Sub-Sea Isolation Valve
SSSV	Subsurface Safety Valve
UFL	Upper Flammability Limit
UKCS	UK Continental Shelf

CHAPTER 1

INTRODUCTION

1.1   General Introduction

The MMS Alaska Offshore Continental Shelf (OCS) Region uses oil spill occurrence predictions for National Environmental Protection Act assessments for all parts of their area of jurisdiction, ranging from the shore through shallow water, to deeper water. Although land to 3 miles is not within MMS jurisdiction, it is included in the MMS environmental impact analysis; hence it is also included in the study area here. In 2000 to 2002, a study was carried out by Bercha International Inc. [12] [*] (OCS Study MMS 2002-047) to assess and quantify oil spill occurrence indicators for the Beaufort and Chukchi Seas. In this study, methodologies based on fault tree analysis were developed for the assessment of oil spill rates associated with exploration and production facilities and operations in deeper waters in the Chukchi and Beaufort Seas.

The prediction of the reliability (or failure) of systems without history can be approached through a variety of mathematical techniques, the most preferable and accepted being fault trees [7, 10, 11, 14, 15, 18, 23, 26, 45, 51, 65], and their combination with numerical distribution methods such as Monte Carlo simulation [1]. In the previous study [12], fault tree methodology was applied to the prediction of oil spill rates for oil and gas developments such as those now operational or contemplated for the Beaufort and Chukchi Seas in the Alaska OCS, and used to generate predictions of oil spill occurrence indicators.

As there is a paucity of offshore Arctic oil spill occurrences, associated data worldwide and from the Gulf of Mexico (GOM) were used as a starting point to develop a simulation model of oil spill occurrence probabilities. The model for non-Arctic occurrence probabilities was then modified to include Arctic effects and their variabilities. Because variability information for the non-Arctic data was not available at the time of the previous study [12], the resultant spill occurrence probabilities only reflected the variability associated with Arctic effects. The shortcoming in the estimate of the variability and consequently, in most cases, also in the expected value, was noted in the previous study [12] and tabled for future consideration. In 2004, following internal discussions and discussions with stakeholders, the present study – which is to include both the variability of the non-Arctic database used as a starting point and the variability of Arctic effects – was initiated.

---

[*] Numbers in square brackets refer to citations listed in the "References" section of this report.

1.2   Study Objectives

The objectives of this study are as follows:

- Assimilate and analyze world-wide and US OCS oil spill statistics and evaluate their applicability to deeper lease tracts which could be offered in the upcoming Beaufort Sea sales.

- Develop the fault tree method for estimating oil spill occurrences from Beaufort Sea developments associated with spills of different size categories.

- Using the fault tree approach, develop alternative oil spill indicators and assess their variability.

- Provide statistical support to MMS in evaluation of statistical issues in estimation of oil spill rates.

- One of the specific objectives of this study was to add the variability of the non-Arctic factors.

1.3   Study Area Definition

The geographical study area is the offshore continental shelf in the U.S. Beaufort Sea, as generally illustrated in Figure 1.1. Of interest is the offshore area from landfall to approximately the 60-meter isobath. This area is selected due to the possibility of future oil and gas development within it, based on potential leases. Although a depth greater than 60 meters was originally contemplated as part of the study area, the analysis of development scenarios has indicated that it is highly unlikely that any oil and gas developments will take place in depths greater than 60 meters. More details on the leases and the geology of the study area are described in several MMS publications [35, 36, 37, 38, 39].

Temporally, the study scenarios investigated span into the future from the present to Year 2038.

1.4   General Background

The final report, dated August 2002 [12], described the methodology and results of applying the fault tree method to the evaluation of oil spill occurrence estimators for the Beaufort and Chukchi Seas. The focus of this report was on the development of a fault tree method to model both non-Arctic GOM spill causes as well as Arctic causes and effects that would be encountered in the Beaufort and Chukchi Seas OCS Regions. The variability of the parameters associated with Arctic effects was developed in order to provide an estimate of the variance in the spill occurrence predictions resulting directly from variances in the Arctic effects. These variances were numerically incorporated through the use of Monte Carlo simulation for the fault tree model numerical predictions.

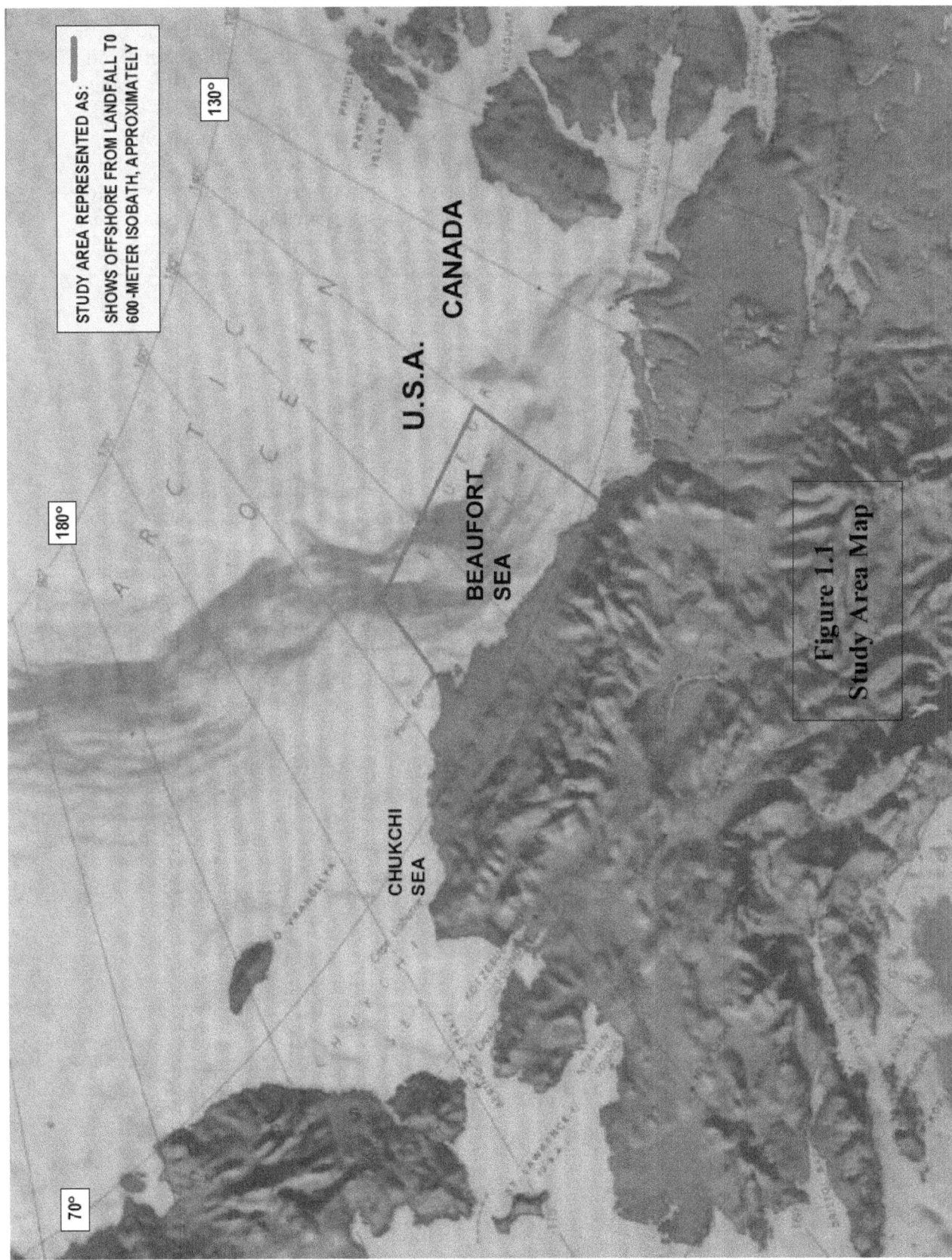

STUDY AREA REPRESENTED AS:
SHOWS OFFSHORE FROM LANDFALL TO
600-METER ISOBATH, APPROXIMATELY

130°

180°

70°

CANADA

U.S.A.

BEAUFORT
SEA

CHUKCHI
SEA

ARCTIC OCEAN

Figure 1.1
Study Area Map

MMS

BERCHA GROUP

The lack of variance of non-Arctic effects was clearly identified in the final report as a possible limitation, but justified because the focus of the work was on the Arctic spill causes. Recent discussions with stakeholders from the North Slope indicate a strong interest in extending the study to include not only effects of variations in the Arctic parameters, but also of variations in non-Arctic parameters. During meetings and discussions at the Information Transfer Meeting #9 in Anchorage (March 2003), the matter of including variability of non-Arctic effects was discussed between the contractor and Minerals Management Service (MMS) as well as stakeholder representatives. Following these meetings, as well as further discussion, proposal preparation and submission, and contract award, the present study was initiated in 2004.

1.5   Technical Approaches

1.5.1   General Technical Discussion

Uncertainties in the results of oil spill occurrence predictions generated in the subject study can be attributed to uncertainties in input data, scenario characterization, and the occurrence model. In the original study, uncertainties in input data were quantified for the Arctic effects only. Uncertainties in the scenario were included through the choice of scenarios representing the expected and maximum development levels. The uncertainty and occurrence model chosen was a numerical one which incorporates the maximum and minimum bounds of the input parameters. Thus the principal source of uncertainty in the occurrence results is that caused by uncertainties in the input parameters themselves. As noted earlier, the uncertainties from the Arctic input parameters were quantified; however, only discrete values of the non-Arctic input parameters were used.

The non-Arctic input parameters fall under two principal categories as follows:

- Spill frequencies
- Spill volumes

These spill frequencies and volumes as used in the study were derived from the following principal sources:

- Pipeline spills – GOM data
- Platform spills – GOM data
- Well (drilling and production) blowout spills – Worldwide data

The precise sources of the data are described in detail in Chapter 2 of this report.

1.5.2 Spill Frequencies

There are two main approaches, as follows, for evaluating the variance in the in the spill frequencies:

- **First Order Approaches** – A high level approach based on the incorporation of Arctic effects in direct proportion to historical data variability.

- **Second Order Approaches** – A more detailed approach in which Arctic effects and their variances are directly incorporated into the analysis.

The two approaches can be applied in a complementary manner, as explained in Section 4.3.

1.5.3 Spill Volumes

In regard to the second general area, the volume distributions, a frequency distribution of the likely spill volumes in each spill size category was developed from the spill data records. This frequency distribution was then transformed to a cumulative distribution function and combined with the appropriate spill frequency to provide a distribution of the spill index (product of spill frequency and spill volume), which includes both Arctic and non-Arctic variability. The computation of the spill index through the multiplication of two probability densities was carried out using the Monte Carlo method.

1.6 Scope of Work

Task 1:   *Data Assimilation*

       a)   Update of GOM pipeline and platform spill data.

       b)   Identification of alternative data sources including the Foundation of Scientific and Industrial Research at the Norwegian Institute of Technoloty (SINTEF), United Kingdom Health & Safety Executive (HSE), and others.

       c)   Assimilation and analysis of additional blowout data (SINTEF).

       d)   Beaufort Sea scenario updates from MMS information.

Task 2:   *Development of Non-Arctic Total Annual Spill Frequency and Volume Probability Distributions*

       a)   Development of non-Arctic total annual spill frequency and volume distribution for pipelines.

       b)   Development of non-Arctic total annual spill frequency and volume distribution for platforms.

    c)   Development of non-Arctic total annual spill frequency and volume distribution for well drilling and production wells.

Task 3:   *Development of Arctic Spill Frequency Causal Event and Total Probability Distributions*

    a)   Development of Arctic spill frequency causal event probability distributions associated with pipeline spills.

    b)   Development of Arctic spill frequency causal event probability distributions associated with platform spills.

    c)   Development of Arctic spill frequency causal event probability distributions associated with well drilling and production well blowouts.

Task 4:   *Generation of Oil Spill Occurrence Estimator Probability Distributions*

    a)   Modification of model to accommodate variability in non-Arctic effects, new spill size categories (>1000bbl), and life-of-field (LOF) results.

    b)   Model runs for all (four) Beaufort Sea scenarios.

    c)   Model runs as required for other (e.g., non-Arctic) scenarios.

Task 5:   *Reporting*

    a)   Progress Report #1 following completion of Tasks 1 and 2.

    b)   Draft Final Report and Final Report.

1.7   Work Organization

The present study consisted of statistical and engineering investigations, followed by extensive numerical analysis. Although the assimilation of historical and future scenario data is of indisputable significance to the work, the salient contribution consisted primarily of the analytical work involving fault trees and oil spill occurrence indicator generation. Although the individual calculations are relatively simple, the subdivision of the calculations into realistic representative categories of facilities, spill sizes, and water depth for several development scenarios resulted in a relatively complex mix of computations, generally illustrated in the flow chart in Figure 1.2.

The flow chart in Figure 1.2, of course, does not show all the different combinations and permutations; rather, it indicates the typical calculations for one case, and suggests the balance by dotted lines. Moving from left to right; initially historical data were obtained for each of three principal facility categories, pipelines, platforms, and wells. Pipelines were further subdivided among < 10 inch and = 10 inch diameter lines. Wells were categorized in two ways: according to producing (production) wells and the drilling (D) of exploration and development wells. For each of the above facility subcategories, spill causes were analyzed for small, medium, large, and huge spills, defined as follows:

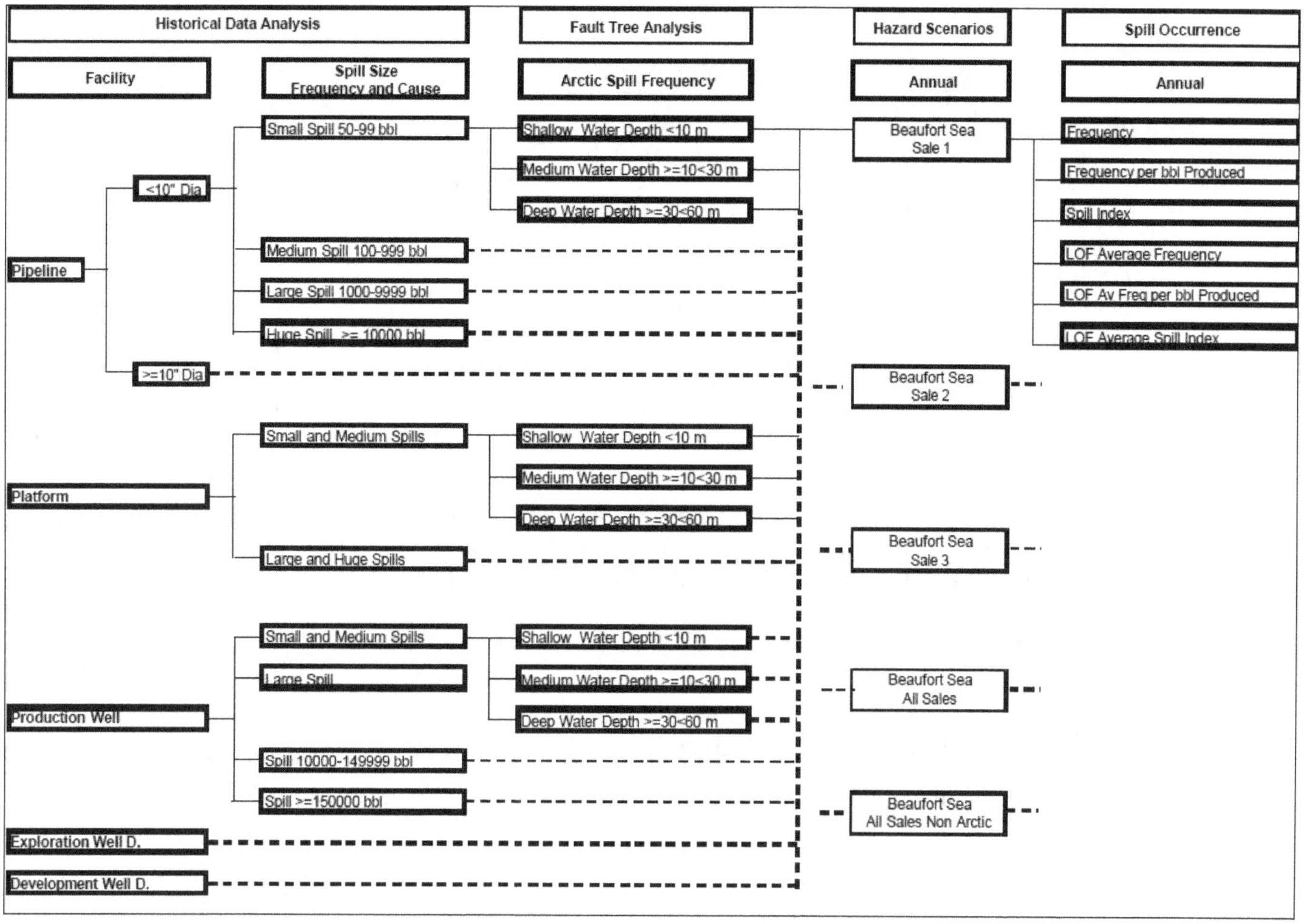

Historical Data Analysis		Fault Tree Analysis	Hazard Scenarios	Spill Occurrence
Facility	Spill Size Frequency and Cause	Arctic Spill Frequency	Annual	Annual

Pipeline

<10" Dia
- Small Spill 50-99 bbl
  - Shallow Water Depth <10 m
  - Medium Water Depth >=10<30 m
  - Deep Water Depth >=30<60 m
- Medium Spill 100-999 bbl
- Large Spill 1000-9999 bbl
- Huge Spill >= 10000 bbl

>=10" Dia

Beaufort Sea Sale 1
- Frequency
- Frequency per bbl Produced
- Spill Index
- LOF Average Frequency
- LOF Av Freq per bbl Produced
- LOF Average Spill Index

Beaufort Sea Sale 2

Platform
- Small and Medium Spills
  - Shallow Water Depth <10 m
  - Medium Water Depth >=10<30 m
  - Deep Water Depth >=30<60 m
- Large and Huge Spills

Beaufort Sea Sale 3

Production Well
- Small and Medium Spills
  - Shallow Water Depth <10 m
- Large Spill
  - Medium Water Depth >=10<30 m
  - Deep Water Depth >=30<60 m
- Spill 10000-149999 bbl
- Spill >=150000 bbl

Beaufort Sea All Sales

Beaufort Sea All Sales Non Arctic

Exploration Well D.

Development Well D.

Figure 1.2
Calculation Flow Chart

- Small (S)   -   50 to 99 bbl
- Medium (M)   -   100 to 999 bbl
- Large (L)   -   1,000 to 9,999 bbl
- Huge (H)   -   = 10,000 bbl

For those spills of 10,000 bbl or more, the term 'huge spill' has been introduced to permit unique designation of each spill category by one letter, rather than the more customary terminology of 'very large' which would require two letters. Significant spills, which are spills of 1,000 bbl or more (Large and Huge) are also identified. Fractional spill sizes were rounded up or down to the nearest whole number, with rounding up for any decimal ending in 5.

In the interests of conciseness and clarity, the above four categories of spill sizes will generally be designated by either their name (small, medium, large, huge) or, when space is limited, by their acronym (S, M, L, H), in the balance of this report.

Next, in the frequency analysis utilizing fault trees, each of three representative water depth ranges was assessed as follows:

- Shallow   -   < 10 meters
- Medium   -   10 to 29 meters
- Deep   -   30 to 60 meters

Although originally it was anticipated that 'very deep' water would be considered, it was found that none of the development scenarios anticipated by MMS extended beyond the 60-meter isobath.

A total of five different future development scenarios were defined for the Beaufort Sea, termed Sales 1, 2, and 3, Sale All (which is the composite of the three sales), and non-Arctic (a hypothetical scenario). Each scenario was described for each year in its development history, as far as the year 2038 for the longest duration scenarios. In addition, the hypothetical non-Arctic scenario was developed for comparative purposes on the assumption that it was located in a non-Arctic area. This permitted the comparison of the spill indicator results with and without the application of the fault tree analysis to account for Arctic effects.

Finally, for each of the combinations considered, four Arctic oil spill occurrence indicators were generated, as follows:

- Oil spill frequency
- Oil spill frequency per barrel produced
- Spill index, which is the product of the oil spill frequency and the mean spill size (for the particular category under consideration)

- Life of Field Indices

The total number of spill indicator quantifications conducted was approximately 60,000, as detailed in Section 5.1.

1.8   Outline of Report

Following this brief introductory chapter, Volume I of the final report addresses each of the principal tasks and subtasks in its logical sequence. Accordingly, Chapter 2 describes the historical data assimilation and analysis, Chapter 3 defines the future development scenarios to be utilized, Chapter 4 deals with the fault tree analysis to obtain Arctic oil spill frequencies, while Chapter 5 summarizes the results of the oil spill occurrence indicator computations and their distributions. Chapter 6 summarizes conclusions and recommendations including a section on the benefits and shortcomings of the present study. Extensive references and bibliography are given in the References.

The appendices given in Volume II form an integral part of the work for the reader who wishes to learn about background and calculation details. Accordingly, Appendix 1 summarizes the historical data assimilated and analyzed. Because Chapter 2, on historical data, is restricted to the data actually utilized in the present computations, Appendix 1 will be of interest to readers wanting a more comprehensive view of oil spill occurrence statistics including those from other parts of the world. Appendix 2 gives details of the fault tree analysis. Appendix 3 gives details on the future development scenarios utilized as a basis for the study. Appendix 4 gives a printout of all the calculation steps, including results, utilized in the development of the Arctic oil spill occurrence indicators using the Monte Carlo approach. Appendix 5 gives general conclusions and results.

CHAPTER 2

HISTORICAL DATA

2.1   Approaches to Historical Data

Historical data on offshore oil spills were utilized as a numerical starting point for predicting Arctic offshore oil spill characteristics. Because a statistical history on Arctic offshore oil spills does not exist, oil spill histories for temperate offshore locations were utilized. Although Arctic offshore exploration and production was started in the early 1970s, operations have been sporadic, with very few spills, so that a statistical history cannot be generated.

The following data sets or databases were utilized:

(a) Gulf of Mexico (GOM) Offshore Continental Shelf (OCS) Pipeline Spills (1972-1999)

(b) GOM OCS Platform Spills (1972-1999)

(c) Oil Blowouts, Worldwide (1955-1995)

The above categories of data are discussed and summarized in Appendix 1. The contents of the balance of this chapter are restricted to the presentation and discussion of only those data sets utilized in the present study.

2.2   Pipeline Oil Spill Data

The MMS database called *PPL_REPAIRS* was used as a basis for the assessment of subsea pipeline oil spills. This database contains records of all reported spills in the GOM. The database was used to obtain spill records for spills of 50 bbl or more between January 1st, 1972 and December 31st, 1999. The 31 spills reported in this date range were further subdivided into volume, pipeline diameter, pipeline segment length, and pipeline segment depth ranges as summarized in Table 2.1.

Next, 31 GOM OCS pipeline spill records were reviewed and analyzed for causal and spill size distributions. Table 2.2 shows the summary of the causal record information, while Table 2.3 summarizes the spill cause distributions for two spill size ranges (small and medium, large and huge). Finally, Table 2.4 gives the principal parameters of the spill population for pipelines. The "Historical" value is the historical average value from Table 2.1; the low value is the most common annual low value (0 spills), and the high value is the approximate 90% confidence interval value. The high and low values were obtained by multiplying the Historical value by the high and low factors respectively. These factors were obtained from the total population database to correspond to the upper and lower 90% confidence interval data points.

Table 2.1
GOM OCS Pipeline Spills Statistics Summary (1972-1999)

GOM OCS Pipeline Spills, Categorized 1972-99			Spill Statistics	Exposure**	Frequency
			Number of Spills	km-years	Spills per 10^5 km-years
By Pipe Diameter*		< 10"	16	105,336	15.1894
		>= 10"	15	81,847	18.3270
By Spill Size		Small 50-99 bbl	6	187,183	3.2054
		Medium 100 - 999 bbl	12	187,183	6.4108
		Large 1000 - 9999 bbl	10	187,183	5.3424
		Huge >=10000 bbl	3	187,183	1.6027
By Diameter, By Spill Size	< 10"	Small 50-99 bbl	4	105,336	3.7974
		Medium 100 - 999 bbl	7	105,336	6.6454
		Large 1000 - 9999 bbl	4	105,336	3.7974
		Huge >=10000 bbl	1	105,336	0.9493
	>= 10"	Small <100 bbl	2	81,847	2.4436
		Medium 100 - 999 bbl	5	81,847	6.1090
		Large 1000 - 9999 bbl	6	81,847	7.3308
		Huge >=10000 bbl	2	81,847	2.4436

*14 of the 31 records have both MIN_WATER_DEPTH and MAX_WATER_DEPTH set to "0".
**Exposure comes from an analysis of PPL_MASTERS database as published on Feb 15, 2001.
　Ratio for <10"/>10"=1.287

Table 2.2
Analysis of GOM OCS Pipeline Spill Data for Causal Distribution and Spill Size

CAUSE CLASSIFICATION	# OF SPILLS	SPILL SIZE BBL										NUMBER OF SPILLS					
		1	2	3	4	5	6	7	8	9	10	S	M	L	H	SM	LH
CORROSION	4											1	2	1		3	1
External	1	80										1				1	
nternal	3	100	5000	414									2	1		2	1
THIRD PARTY IMPACT	16											2	5	6	3	7	9
Anchor Impact	10	19833	65	50	300	900	323	15576	2000	800	1211	2	4	2	2	6	4
Jackup Rig or Spud Barge	1	3200												1			1
Trawl/Fishing Net	5	4000	100	14423	4569	4533							1	3	1	1	4
OPERATION IMPACT	4											3		1		3	1
Rig Anchoring	1	50										1				1	
Work Boat Anchoring	3	50	5100	50								2		1		2	1
MECHANICAL	2												2			2	
Connection Failure	1	135											1			1	
Material Failure	1	210											1			1	
NATURAL HAZARD	4											1	1	2		2	2
Mud Slide	3	250	80	8212								1	1	1		2	1
Storm/ Hurricane	1	3500												1			1
ARCTIC																	
ce Gouging																	
Strudel Scour																	
Upheaval Buckling																	
Thaw Settlement																	
Other																	
UNKNOWN	1	119											1			1	
TOTALS	31											7	11	10	3	18	13

Table 2.3
Distribution and Frequency of Historical Spills – Pipeline

CAUSE CLASSIFICATION	Small and Medium Spills 50-999 bbl				Large and Huge Spills >=1000 bbl			
	HISTORICAL DISTRI-BUTION %	NUMBER OF SPILLS	EXPOSURE [km-years]	FREQUENCY spill per 10⁵km-year	HISTORICAL DISTRI-BUTION %	NUMBER OF SPILLS	EXPOSURE [km-years]	FREQUENCY spill per 10⁵ km-year
CORROSION	16.67	3		1.6027	7.69	1		0.5342
External	5.56	1		0.5342				
Internal	11.11	2		1.0685	7.69	1		0.5342
THIRD PARTY IMPACT	38.89	7		3.7397	69.23	9		4.8081
Anchor Impact	33.33	6		3.2054	30.77	4		2.1369
Jackup Rig or Spud Barge					7.69	1		0.5342
Trawl/Fishing Net	5.56	1		0.5342	30.77	4		2.1369
OPERATION IMPACT	16.67	3		1.6027	7.69	1		0.5342
Rig Anchoring	5.56	1		0.5342				
Work Boat Anchoring	11.11	2		1.0685	7.69	1		0.5342
MECHANICAL	11.11	2		1.0685				
Connection Failure	5.56	1	187183	0.5342			187183	
Material Failure	5.56	1		0.5342				
NATURAL HAZARD	11.11	2		1.0685	15.38	2		1.0685
Mud Slide	11.11	2		1.0685	7.69	1		0.5342
Storm/ Hurricane					7.69	1		0.5342
ARCTIC								
Ice Gouging								
Strudel Scour								
Upheaval Buckling								
Thaw Settlement								
Other								
UNKNOWN	5.56	1		0.5342				
TOTALS	100.00	18		9.6163	100.00	13		6.9451

Table 2.4
Pipeline Historical Spill Frequency Variability

GOM OCS Pipeline Spills, Categorized 1972-99		Low Factor	High Factor	Frequency spill per 10⁵ km-years			
				Historical	Low	Mode	High
By Diameter, By Spill Size							
< 10"	Small	0	2.57	3.7974	0	1.6329	9.7592
	Medium	0	2.57	6.6454	0	2.8575	17.0786
	Large	0	2.57	3.7974	0	1.6329	9.7592
	Huge	0	2.57	0.9493	0	0.4082	2.4398
= 10"	Small	0	2.57	2.4436	0	1.0507	6.2800
	Medium	0	2.57	6.1090	0	2.6269	15.7001
	Large	0	2.57	7.3308	0	3.1522	18.8401
	Huge	0	2.57	2.4436	0	1.0507	6.2800

For example, if there were 30 data points, the upper 90% (or high value) was the third highest, while the lower 90% (or low value) was selected as the third lowest, which was invariably zero, as numerous years had no spills. Next, the third highest value was divided by the historical value to get the high factor. Finally, the high factor was used to obtain the high value by multiplying the applicable historical frequency by this high factor. The mode was then calculated from the triangular distribution relationship [13], as follows:

$$Mode = 3 \; x \; Historical - High - Low \qquad (2.1)$$

2.3   Platform Spill Data

Platform spills in the MMS database are given for the period from 1972 to 1999. The platform spill data are given with an exposure of producing well-years. As for pipelines, the spill records themselves were accessed in order to obtain the correlation between spill cause and spill size. Table 2.5 shows the results of the causal and spill size distribution analysis, while Table 2.6 gives the causal distribution as well as the spill frequency per 10,000 well-years. Finally, Table 2.7 gives the principal parameters of the spill population for platforms. The high values were chosen as the annual spill rates closest to the upper and lower 90% confidence interval (and calculated as described in Section 2.2); the low value is usually zero.

In order to assess spill occurrence from platform facilities, using the above per well-year frequency, it is necessary to estimate the number of wells per platform. The number of production wells given in each scenario was distributed equally among the production platforms specified (by MMS) for this study.

2.4   Oil Well Blowout Data

The development scenarios considered under this study include both the drilling of exploratory and development wells, and the process of producing oil from production wells [69]. The basis for the non-Arctic historical oil well blowout statistics, a number of sources were reviewed including the North Star and Liberty oil development project reports [52], and the cumulative distribution function for oil blowout releases [59], as well as the book by Per Holland entitled "Offshore Blowouts", which gives risk analysis data from the SINTEF worldwide offshore blowout database [25]. The most comprehensive historical information was found in the latter reference [25], which not only gives the results of database analyses for the North Sea and the Gulf of Mexico, but also provides confidence intervals calculated from these databases. Table 2.8 gives a summary of the historical data analysis by Per Holland [25] for production wells and the drilling of exploratory and development wells. The combination of these statistics together with the cumulative distribution function for oil blowout release volumes given in [59], generated in support of the Northstar project, permits the blowout spill volume frequency distribution as summarized in Table 2.9. Finally, combining the population parameters of oil well blowouts from Table 2.8 with the size distribution factors – which can be derived from Table 2.9 – one arrives at the historical oil spill blowout distribution characteristics by spill size and well type, summarized in Table 2.10.

Table 2.5
Analysis of GOM OCS Platform Spill Data for Causal Distribution and Spill Size (1972-1999)

CAUSE CLASSIFICATION	# OF SPILLS	SPILL SIZE BBL													NUMBER OF SPILLS					
		1	2	3	4	5	6	7	8	9	10	11	12	13	S	M	L	H	SM	LH
PROCESS FACILITY RLS.	13	130	50	120	104	60	1456	125	50	50	55	400	280	75	6	6	1		12	1
STORAGE TANK RLS.	3	9935	7000	435												1	2		1	2
STRUCTURAL FAILURE	1	58													1				1	
HURRICANE/STORM	2	75	66												2				2	
COLLISION	2	600	108													2			2	
TOTALS	21														9	9	3		18	3

Table 2.6
Causal and Spill Size Distribution of GOM OCS Platform Spills (1972-1999)

CAUSE CLASSIFICATION	Small and Medium Spills				Large and Huge Spills			
	HIST. DISTRI-BUTION (%)	# OF SPILLS	EXPOSURE (well-yr)	FREQUENCY (spill per 10^4 well-yr)	HIST. DISTRI-BUTION (%)	# OF SPILLS	EXPOSURE (well-yr)	FREQUENCY (spill per 10^4 well-yr)
PROCESS FACILITY RLS.	66.67	12		1.0024	33.33	1		0.0835
STORAGE TANK RLS.	5.56	1		0.0835	66.67	2		0.1671
STRUCTURAL FAILURE	5.56	1	119714	0.0835			119714	
HURRICANE/STORM	11.11	2		0.1671				
COLLISION	11.11	2		0.1671				
TOTALS	100.00	18		1.5036	100.00	3		0.2506

Table 2.7
Platform Historical Spill Frequency Variability

Spill Size	Frequency Unit	Low Factor	High Factor	Historical	Low	Mode	High
Small and Medium Spills 50-999 bbl	spill per 10^4well-year	0	2.88	1.5036	0.0000	0.1804	4.3303
Large and Huge Spills >=1000 bbl	spill per 10^4well-year	0	2.88	0.2506	0.0000	0.0301	0.7217

Table 2.8
Summary of North Sea and Gulf of Mexico
(Holland, 1997)

Well Type	Unit	Low 90% CI	Average	High 90% CI
Production Well	Spills per 10^4 well-year	0.86	1.91	2.95
Exploration Well Drilling	Spills per 10^4 wells	11.00	25.05	51.00
Development Well Drilling		4.00	9.15	16.10

Table 2.9
Well Blowout Historical Spill Size Distribution
(ScanPower, 2001)

EVENT	FREQUENCY UNIT	Small and Medium Spills 50-999 bbl	Large Spills 1000-9999 bbl	Small, Medium, and Large Spills 50-9999 bbl	Spills 10000-149999 bbl	Spills >=150000 bbl	All spills
		HISTORICAL FREQUENCY					
PRODUCTION WELL	spills per 10^4 well-year	0.15	1.03	1.18	0.44	0.29	1.91
EXPLORATION WELL DRILLING	spills per 10^4 wells	1.97	13.75	15.72	5.91	3.42	25.05
DEVELOPMENT WELL DRILLING	spills per 10^4 wells	0.65	4.57	5.22	1.96	1.96	9.15

Table 2.10
Well Blowout Historical Spill Probability and Size Variability

EVENT	FREQUENCY UNIT	Low Factor	High Factor	Frequencies			
				Historical	Low	Mode	High
				Small and Medium Spills 50-999 bbl			
PRODUCTION WELL	spill per 10⁴well-year	0.448	1.545	0.147	0.066	0.148	0.227
EXPLORATION WELL DRILLING	spill per 10⁴wells	0.439	2.036	1.966	0.863	1.032	4.002
DEVELOPMENT WELL DRILLING	spill per 10⁴wells	0.437	1.760	0.654	0.286	0.526	1.151
				Large Spills 1000-9999 bbl			
PRODUCTION WELL	spill per 10⁴well-year	0.448	1.545	1.028	0.460	1.037	1.588
EXPLORATION WELL DRILLING	spill per 10⁴wells	0.439	2.036	13.754	6.039	7.220	28.001
DEVELOPMENT WELL DRILLING	spill per 10⁴wells	0.437	1.760	4.570	1.998	3.671	8.041
				Small, Medium and Large Spills 50-9999 bbl			
PRODUCTION WELL	spill per 10⁴well-year	0.448	1.545	1.175	0.526	1.185	1.815
EXPLORATION WELL DRILLING	spill per 10⁴wells	0.439	2.036	15.719	6.903	8.252	32.003
DEVELOPMENT WELL DRILLING	spill per 10⁴wells	0.437	1.760	5.224	2.284	4.197	9.192
				Spill 10000-149999 bbl			
PRODUCTION WELL	spill per 10⁴well-year	0.448	1.545	0.441	0.197	0.444	0.681
EXPLORATION WELL DRILLING	spill per 10⁴wells	0.439	2.036	5.909	2.595	3.102	12.031
DEVELOPMENT WELL DRILLING	spill per 10⁴wells	0.437	1.760	1.963	0.858	1.577	3.454
				Spill >=150000 bbl			
PRODUCTION WELL	spill per 10⁴well-year	0.448	1.545	0.294	0.132	0.296	0.454
EXPLORATION WELL DRILLING	spill per 10⁴wells	0.439	2.036	3.421	1.502	1.796	6.965
DEVELOPMENT WELL DRILLING	spill per 10⁴wells	0.437	1.760	1.963	0.858	1.577	3.454

2.5   Arctic Effects Historical Data

2.5.1   General Approaches to the Quantification of Arctic Effects

There are essentially two main categories of Arctic effects; namely, those that are unique to the Arctic, such as marine ice effects, and those that are the same types of effects as those in temperate areas, but occurring with a different frequency, such as anchor impacts on subsea pipelines. The first will be termed "unique" effects; the second, "modified" effects. Modified Arctic effects are dealt with in conjunction with the fault tree analysis described in Chapter 4. Only those Arctic effects or hazards unique to the Arctic, and potentially having a historical occurrence database, such as ice gouging, are discussed in the balance of this section.

2.5.2   Ice Gouging

Ice gouging occurs when a moving ice feature contacts the sea bottom and penetrates into it, generally as it moves against a positive sea bottom slope. The ice feature can be a multiyear ridge, a hummock, or ice rafting formation. Various studies have been conducted on the frequency and depth distribution of ice gouges [8, 27, 29, 30, 46, 67, 68], and a number of assessments of the likelihood of resultant subsea pipeline failure [8, 29] have also been carried out. Pipeline failure frequencies at different water depth regimes as a result of ice gouging in this study have been estimated on the basis of the historical ice gouge characteristics [29] together with an analytical assessment [8, 68] of their likelihood to damage a pipeline.

According to Weeks [67, 68], a relationship between the expected probability of pipeline failure from ice gouging and ice gouging local characteristics may be expressed as follows:

$$N = e^{-kx} \ H_S \ ? \ F \ ? \ T \ ? \ L_P \ ? \ sin? \qquad\qquad (2.2)$$

Where:

N = Number of pipeline failures at burial depth of cover x (meters)

k = Inverse of mean scour depth (m^{-1})

x = Depth of cover (m)

H_S = Probability of pipeline failure given ice gouge impact or hit

F = Scour flux per km-yr

L_P = Length of pipeline (km)

$?$ = Gouge orientation (degrees) from pipeline centerline

For the Northstar project, according to [30], the mean scour depth is 0.2 m giving a **k** factor of 5.0. In addition, a good estimate of scour flux for shallow water is 2 gouges/km-yr. Using an average pipeline depth of cover of 2.5 m, an average directional angle of 45°, a conditional failure probability (H_S) of 0.8, gives a frequency of 5.23 x 10^{-6}/km-yr. For the purposes of the analysis, this frequency must be distributed among different spill size consequences. Due to the difficulty of detecting spills under ice, one can expect that the majority of spills would be in the large and huge categories. However, huge spills would be limited by segment length. Thus, a conditional probability (given a spill) of 50% has been assigned to large spills, and one of 14% to huge spills. Least likely are small spills, and accordingly they have been given a probability of 13%. The remaining probability of 23% has been assigned to medium sized spills. The resultant distribution of expected frequencies of spill sizes associated with ice gouging is given in Table 2.11.

Also, high and low values have been assigned in order to permit an analysis of the likely distribution of the effects. Essentially, these variations in effect probability were obtained through a parametric sensitivity analysis using Equation 2.1 for a range of likely values of depth of cover from 2.0 m to 3.0 m (with an expected value of 2.5 m). These resultant low and high values are also summarized in Table 2.11. For medium water depth, an analogous process was carried out with a reduced gouge flux of 1.5 gouges/km-yr. For deep water (= 30 m) no gouging is expected.

2.5.3 Strudel Scour

When fresh water collecting on top of the ice sheet generally from rivers running into the Arctic seas, and drains through a hole in the ice, its hydrodynamic effect on the ocean floor below forms a depression which is called a strudel scour. Numerous studies have been conducted on strudel scour [29, 30], so that a prediction on the number of strudel scours per unit area can be made on the basis of historical data. Strudel scours are restricted to shallow water. With an average strudel scour frequency of 4 scours/mi^2 (1.5 scours/km^2) [30], the methodology in [30] can be utilized to predict a possible failure rate of subsea pipelines in shallow waters due to strudel scour of approximately 8.9 x 10^{-8}/km-yr. Using reasoning similar to that for the distribution of spill sizes for ice gouging, and assigning limits based on parametric sensitivity studies, the distribution of strudel scour frequencies for shallow water as shown in Table 2.11 can be derived. Strudel scours are not expected in water depths greater than 10 m.

Table 2.11
Summary of Pipeline Unique Arctic Effect Inputs

Cause Classification	Spill Size	Water Depth								
		Shallow			Medium			Deep		
		Frequency Increment per 10^5 km-year								
		Min	Mode	Max	Min	Mode	Max	Min	Mode	Max
Ice Gouging	S	0.0060	0.0680	0.8290	0.0048	0.0544	0.6632			
	M	0.0090	0.1210	1.4670	0.0072	0.0968	1.1736			
	L	0.0210	0.2610	3.1900	0.0168	0.2088	2.5520			
	H	0.0060	0.0730	0.8930	0.0048	0.0584	0.7144			
Strudel Scour	S	0.0004	0.0012	0.0044						
	M	0.0006	0.0020	0.0078						
	L	0.0014	0.0045	0.0170						
	H	0.0004	0.0012	0.0048						
Upheaval Buckling	S	0.00007	0.00023	0.00088	0.00007	0.00023	0.00088	0.00007	0.00023	0.00088
	M	0.00013	0.00041	0.00156	0.00013	0.00041	0.00156	0.00013	0.00041	0.00156
	L	0.00028	0.00089	0.00340	0.00028	0.00089	0.00340	0.00028	0.00089	0.00340
	H	0.00008	0.00025	0.00095	0.00008	0.00025	0.00095	0.00008	0.00025	0.00095
Thaw Settlement	S	0.00004	0.00012	0.00044	0.00004	0.00012	0.00044	0.00004	0.00012	0.00044
	M	0.00006	0.00020	0.00078	0.00006	0.00020	0.00078	0.00006	0.00020	0.00078
	L	0.00014	0.00045	0.00170	0.00014	0.00045	0.00170	0.00014	0.00045	0.00170
	H	0.00004	0.00012	0.00048	0.00004	0.00012	0.00048	0.00004	0.00012	0.00048
Other	S	0.00162	0.01738	0.20869	0.00123	0.01369	0.16613	0.00003	0.00009	0.00033
	M	0.00246	0.03092	0.36929	0.00185	0.02435	0.29399	0.00005	0.00015	0.00059
	L	0.00571	0.06670	0.80303	0.00431	0.05253	0.63928	0.00011	0.00033	0.00128
	H	0.00163	0.01865	0.22480	0.00123	0.01469	0.17896	0.00003	0.00009	0.00036

2.5.4 Upheaval Buckling

Upheaval buckling occurs in a pipeline as a result of its thermal expansion which causes it to buckle upwards to accommodate the extra length generated from thermal effects. Unfortunately, there appears to be no defensible analytical method for calculating the probability of upheaval buckling of Arctic subsea pipelines in general. Accordingly, upheaval buckling has been taken simply as a percentage of the strudel scour effects. Assuming that a upheaval buckling occurs 20% as often as strudel scour, the distribution shown in Table 2.9 can be derived. Upheaval buckling is expected to be independent of water depth; accordingly, the same values have been used for each water depth range.

2.5.5 Thaw Settlement

Thaw settlement occurs when a permafrost lens or formation over which the pipeline was installed melts as a result of the heat generated by the pipeline and ceases to support the pipeline so that the pipeline overburden loads the pipeline and causes it to deflect downwards. As for the case of upheaval buckling, writers are not aware of any method for defensibly calculating the probability of pipeline failures from thaw settlement. Accordingly, resort is again made to the percentage of a known phenomenon approach and thaw settlement has been assumed to occur at a rate equal to 10% of that associated with strudel scour. The resultant distribution is shown in Table 2.11. Like upheaval buckling, thaw settlement is expected to be independent of water depth.

2.5.6 Platform Arctic Unique Effects

Potential causes of platform spills (other than blowouts, which are included under wells) that are uniquely associated with the Arctic are ice forces and low temperature effects. Although the possibility that ice forces will cause spills varies greatly from facility to facility, some broad assumptions have been made in regards to the likelihood of spills being caused by ice force effects. Specifically, it was assumed that the platforms are designed for a 10,000 year return period, with a reliability level of 96%. That is, 4% of the time, the 10,000 year return period ice force can cause a spill. Further, it was assumed that 85% of spills so caused are small and medium, with large and huge spills associated with the other 15%. In regards to facility low temperature, a percentage of historical facility releases was taken. Specifically, it was assumed that the facility low temperature effects will cause medium spills at a rate of 6% of that of total historical small and medium spills, and large and huge spills at a rate of 3% of that associated with large and huge historical spills. Finally, other Arctic unique causes were assumed to constitute another 10% of the sum of the above spill rates in each of the spill categories. Table 2.12 summarizes the resultant Arctic unique effect frequencies derived for platforms on a per-well year basis.

Table 2.12
Summary of Platform Unique Arctic Effect Inputs

CAUSE	SPILL SIZE	FREQUENCY INCREMENT PER 10^4 well-year (Mode)			REASON
		Shallow	Medium	Deep	
Ice Force	Small, Medium	0.0340	0.0510	0.0765	Assumed 10,000 year return period ice force causes spill 4% occurrences (96% reliability). 85% of the spills are Small/Medium.
	Large, Huge	0.0060	0.0090	0.0135	
Facility Low Temperature	Small, Medium	0.1000	0.1000	0.1000	Assumed fraction of Historical Process Facilities release frequency with 6% for Small/Medium and 3% for Large/Huge spill sizes.
	Large, Huge	0.0080	0.0080	0.0080	
Other	Small, Medium	0.0134	0.0151	0.0177	10% of sum of above.
	Large, Huge	0.0014	0.0017	0.0022	

2.6　Historical Spill Size Distribution

Table 2.13 gives the historical spill size distributions obtained from the available historical data. Here, the mode was taken as the historical average spill size in each spill size category, while the high and low values were taken to be the upper and lower bounds of each spill size category. The Huge spill high values were chosen on the basis of the upper 90% confidence interval spill volumes in the databases.

Table 2.13
Summary of Historical Spill Size Distribution Parameters

	Spill Size	Small Spills (50-99 bbl)			Medium Spills (100-999 bbl)			Large Spills (1,000-9,999 bbl)			Huge Spills (= 10,000 bbl)		
PIPELINE SPILL VOLUMES	Spill Expectation	Low	Mode	High	Low	Mode	High	Low	Mode	High	Low	Mode	High
	Pipeline (Diameter <10") Spill	50	58	99	100	226	999	1000	4436	9999	10000	14423	20000
	Pipeline (Diameter >10") Spill	50	58	99	100	387	999	1000	3932	9999	10000	17705	20000
	Spill Size	Small and Medium Spills (50-999 bbl)			Large and Huge Spills (= 1,000 bbl)								
PLATFORM SPILL VOLUMES	Spill Expectation	Low	Mode	High	Low	Mode	High						
	Platform Spill	50	158	999	1000	6130	10000						
	Spill Size	Small and Medium Spills (50-999 bbl)			Large Spills (1,000-9,999 bbl)			Spills (10,000-149,999 bbl)			Spills (= 150,000 bbl)		
WELL SPILL VOLUMES	Spill Expectation	Low	Mode	High	Low	Mode	High	Low	Mode	High	Low	Mode	High
	Well Spill	50	500	999	1000	4500	9999	10000	20000	149999	150000	200000	250000

CHAPTER 3

FUTURE DEVELOPMENT SCENARIOS

3.1   Approaches to Future Development Scenarios

For the purposes of the fault tree analysis utilized in this study, future offshore oil and gas development scenarios need to include the following characteristics:

- Water depth range, particularly for pipelines
- Physical quantities of individual facilities (e.g., production wells, pipelines) on an annual basis in correspondence with the baseline data exposure factors (e.g., per well year or per km-yr)
- Associated oil production volumes
- Other characteristics such as pipeline diameter or type of well drilled

Table 3.1 shows the Classification of Development Scenarios by water depth range and operation type. The salient aspect of this classification is subdivision into water depth ranges among which Arctic hazard characteristics (such as ice gouging rates) may change. The following water depth categories have been used:

- Shallow   -   < 10 meters
- Medium   -   10 to 29 meters
- Deep   -   30 to 60 meters
- Very Deep   -   > 60 meters

In Table 3.1, an indication is given of the types of facilities that might be utilized in each of the principal types of oil and gas activities, exploration, production, or transportation. As will be seen in this chapter, current forecasts for development scenarios over the next 40 years exclude very deep locations, in excess of 60 m. Accordingly, any suggestions for facilities under the very deep scenario would be speculative and will not be used in the current study.

In general, the scenarios described in this chapter were developed to an appropriate level and type of detail to match the type of unit spill data and statistics available as a basis for the oil spill occurrence indicator quantification.

The principal regions of interest within the study area are the Beaufort Sea Lease Areas shown in Figure 3.1.

Table 3.1
Classification of Development Scenarios

PRINCIPAL ACTIVITY	WATER DEPTH (m)			
	SHALLOW (< 10)	**MEDIUM** (10 to 29)	**DEEP** (30 to 60)	**VERY DEEP** (> 60)
EXPLORATION	▪ Artificial island ▪ Drill barge ▪ Ice island	▪ Artificial island ▪ Drill ship (summer) ▪ Caisson	▪ Drill ship (summer) ▪ Semisubmersible (summer)	▪ Drill ship (summer) ▪ Semisubmersible (summer)
PRODUCTION	▪ Artificial island ▪ Caisson island	▪ Caisson island ▪ Gravity Base Structure (GBS)	▪ Caisson island ▪ Gravity Base Structure (GBS)	▪ New design structure ▪ Submarine habitat
TRANSPORT	▪ Subsea pipeline	▪ Subsea pipeline	▪ Subsea pipeline ▪ Storage & tankers	▪ Subsea pipeline ▪ Submarine storage ▪ Icebreaking tankers ▪ Submarine tankers

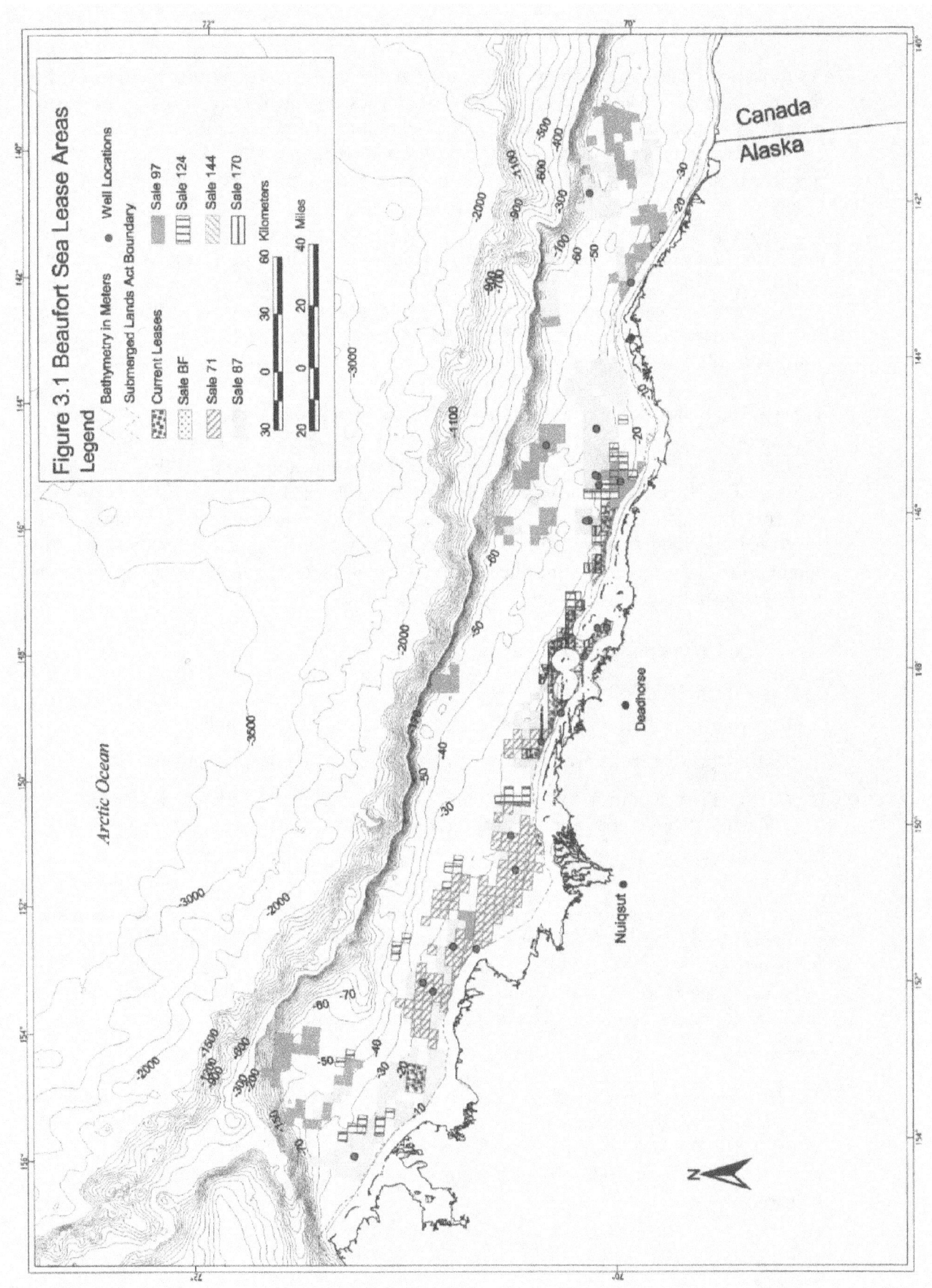

3.2   Beaufort Sea Development Scenarios

As a basis for the current analysis, the geographic and water depth distribution of the facilities and its variation over the life of the development is required in order to effectively incorporate the effects of Arctic operations on the oil spill occurrences. The obvious way to approach this, at least for an initial scenario, is to sketch a map of the possible geographic configuration of the facilities. Such a map, based on the composite Beaufort Sea (All Sale) scenario is shown in Figure 3.2. The facility quantities and locations shown are hypothetical, and not based on any operator's plan. This location map also shows the four water depth zones – shallow, medium, deep, and very deep. As can be seen, no facilities are predicted in the very deep region. The details of the development scenarios, given in Appendix 2, were generated by Alaska MMS personnel for three different Beaufort Sea Lease Sale alternatives, Sales 1, 2, and 3, and for a composite of all sales.

Table 3.2 summarizes the complete Beaufort Sea composite (Sale All) scenario including its temporal development from 2004 to Year 2038, at which time it is forecast to cease production. For items such as exploration and field delineation well drilling, the actual number of wells drilled in a given year were needed, since the statistics of well spill (blowouts) are on a per well drilled exposure unit. For items that continue from year to year, such as production wells or subsea pipelines, both the annual incremental and the cumulative total are needed. Specifically, the following facility quantities by water depth zone were estimated and distributed as shown in Table 3.2:

- Exploration wells drilled – annual

- Delineation wells drilled – annual

- Production platforms – annual increment and cumulative number

- Production/service wells – annual increment and cumulative number

- Pipeline quantities for < 10", and = 10", and total – annual increment and cumulative number of pipeline length in service

- Oil production volumes – annual

As noted above, these quantities match the type of unit spill data that can be made available through the analysis. For example, we have spill data by pipeline diameter only for lines < and = 10", so a full spectrum of pipeline diameters would be redundant. The important aspect of the information in Table 3.2, however, is the distribution of the facilities by water depth, as there is a significant variation in Arctic hazards by water depth.

Similar tables were developed for Lease Sales 1, 2, and 3. These are given in detail in Appendix 2. Peak production for the composite scenario occurs in Year 2020. Accordingly, Table 3.3 summarizes the quantities of facilities and their distribution by water depth for Year 2020, the maximum production year of the composite (Sale All) scenario.

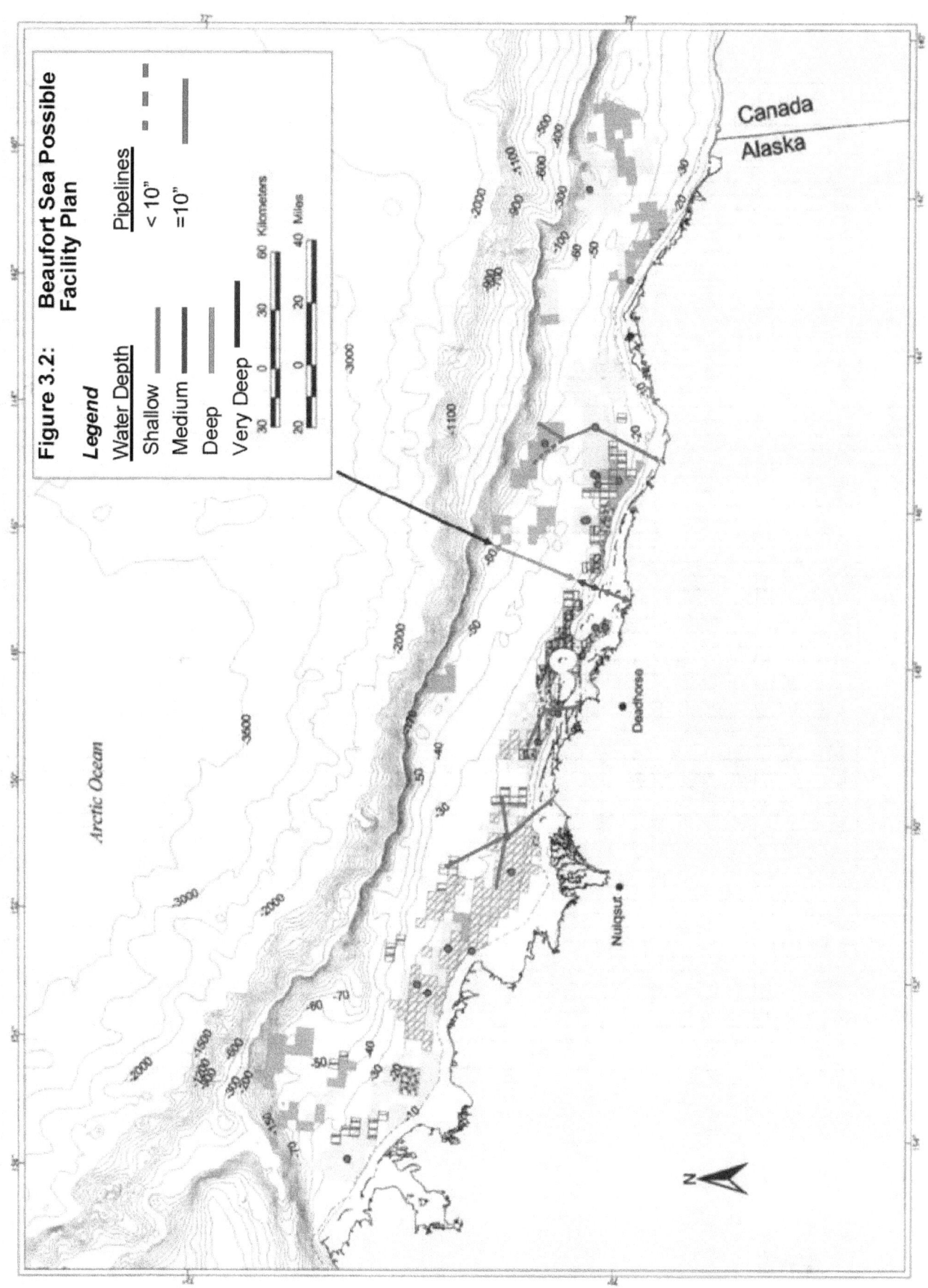

Figure 3.2: Beaufort Sea Possible Facility Plan

Table 3.2
Beaufort Sea All Sales (2004 – 2038)

Year	Water Depth	Exploration Wells	Delineation Wells	Production Platforms Incr.	Production Platforms Cum.	Production Wells Incr.	Production Wells Cum.	Sum<10" Incr.	Sum<10" Cum.	Sum >=10" Incr.	Sum >=10" Cum.	Sum All Incr.	Sum All Cum.	Production MMbbl
2004	Shallow	1												
	Medium													
	Deep													
	Total	1												
2005	Shallow	1												
	Medium													
	Deep													
	Total	1												
2006	Shallow	1	2											
	Medium													
	Deep													
	Total	1	2											
2007	Shallow	2												
	Medium													
	Deep													
	Total	2												
2008	Shallow	1	2											
	Medium	1												
	Deep													
	Total	2	2											
2009	Shallow		2	1	1	3	3							
	Medium	1												
	Deep													
	Total	1	2	1	1	3	3							
2010	Shallow	1			1	10	13			10	10	10	10	7.9
	Medium	1	2											
	Deep													
	Total	2	2		1	10	13			10	10	10	10	7.9
2011	Shallow			1	2	13	26				10		10	15.7
	Medium													
	Deep													
	Total			1	2	13	26				10		10	15.7
2012	Shallow			1	3	13	39			10	20	10	20	23.6
	Medium	2												
	Deep	1												
	Total	3		1	3	13	39			10	20	10	20	23.6
2013	Shallow				3	20	59			10	30	10	30	39.4
	Medium	1	3											
	Deep	1												
	Total	2	3		3	20	59			10	30	10	30	39.4
2014	Shallow				3	10	69				30		30	44.4
	Medium		4	1	1	3	3							
	Deep													
	Total		4	1	4	13	72				30		30	44.4
2015	Shallow				3		69			10	40	10	40	42.1
	Medium		2		1	10	13			10	10	10	10	13.2
	Deep	1												
	Total	1	2		4	10	82			20	50	20	50	55.3
2016	Shallow				3		69				40		40	37.5
	Medium			1	2	13	26				10		10	22.0
	Deep													
	Total			1	5	13	95				50		50	59.5
2017	Shallow				3		69			10	50	10	50	31.0
	Medium			1	3	13	39	5	5	15	25	20	30	43.5
	Deep	1												
	Total	1		1	6	13	108	5	5	25	75	30	80	74.5
2018	Shallow				3		69				50		50	25.5
	Medium			1	4	24	63		5		25		30	50.6
	Deep	1												
	Total	1		1	7	24	132		5		75		80	76.1
2019	Shallow				3		69			15	65	15	65	21.1
	Medium			1	5	24	87	5	10	15	40	20	50	81.4
	Deep													
	Total			1	8	24	156	5	10	30	105	35	115	102.5
2020	Shallow				3		69				65		65	17.4
	Medium				5	20	107		10		40		50	86.1
	Deep													
	Total				8	20	176		10		105		115	103.5

Table 3.2 - *continued*

Year	Water Depth	Exploration Wells	Delineation Wells	Production Platforms Incr.	Production Platforms Cum.	Production Wells Incr.	Production Wells Cum.	Sum<10" Incr.	Sum<10" Cum.	Sum >=10" Incr.	Sum >=10" Cum.	Sum All Incr.	Sum All Cum.	Production MMbbl
2021	Shallow				3		69				65		65	14.4
	Medium				5	20	127		10		40		50	83.5
	Deep													
	Total				8	20	196		10		105		115	97.9
2022	Shallow				3		69				65		65	11.9
	Medium				5	10	137		10		40		50	81.2
	Deep													
	Total				8	10	206		10		105		115	93.1
2023	Shallow				3		69				65		65	9.8
	Medium				5		137		10		40		50	75.8
	Deep													
	Total				8		206		10		105		115	85.6
2024	Shallow				3		69				65		65	8.1
	Medium				5		137		10		40		50	71.1
	Deep													
	Total				8		206		10		105		115	79.2
2025	Shallow			-1	2	-23	46			-10	55	-10	55	5.1
	Medium				5		137		10		40		50	62.4
	Deep													
	Total			-1	7	-23	183		10	-10	95	-10	105	67.5
2026	Shallow				2		46				55		55	4.2
	Medium				5		137		10		40		50	54.8
	Deep													
	Total				7		183		10		95		105	59.0
2027	Shallow			-1	1	-23	23			-10	45	-10	45	1.9
	Medium				5		137		10		40		50	48.0
	Deep													
	Total			-1	6	-23	160		10	-10	85	-10	95	49.9
2028	Shallow			-1		-23				-15	30	-15	30	
	Medium				5		137		10		40		50	42.2
	Deep													
	Total			-1	5	-23	137		10	-15	70	-15	80	42.2
2029	Shallow										30		30	
	Medium				5		137		10		40		50	37.0
	Deep													
	Total				5		137		10		70		80	37.0
2030	Shallow									-10	20	-10	20	
	Medium				5		137		10		40		50	32.4
	Deep													
	Total				5		137		10	-10	60	-10	70	32.4
2031	Shallow										20		20	
	Medium				5		137		10		40		50	28.5
	Deep													
	Total				5		137		10		60		70	28.5
2032	Shallow										20		20	
	Medium				5		137		10		40		50	25.0
	Deep													
	Total				5		137		10		60		70	25.0
2033	Shallow										20		20	
	Medium				5		137		10		40		50	21.9
	Deep													
	Total				5		137		10		60		70	21.9
2034	Shallow										20		20	
	Medium			-1	4	-23	114		10	-10	30	-10	40	17.0
	Deep													
	Total			-1	4	-23	114		10	-10	50	-10	60	17.0
2035	Shallow										20		20	
	Medium				4		114		10		30		40	14.9
	Deep													
	Total				4		114		10		50		60	14.9
2036	Shallow									-5	15	-5	15	
	Medium			-2	2	-46	68	-5	5	-10	20	-15	25	13.1
	Deep													
	Total			-2	2	-46	68	-5	5	-15	35	-20	40	8.3
2037	Shallow										15		15	
	Medium				2		68		5		20		25	7.3
	Deep													
	Total				2		68		5		35		40	7.3
2038	Shallow										15		15	
	Medium				2		68		5		20		25	6.5
	Deep													
	Total				2		68		5		35		40	6.5

Table 3.3
Summary of Development Scenarios for Year 2020[1]

Sale	Year	Water Depth	Exploration Wells	Delineation Wells	Production Platforms Incr.	Production Platforms Cum.	Production Wells Incr.	Prod./Serv. Wells Cum.	Sum<10" Incr.	Sum<10" Cum.	Sum >=10" Incr.	Sum >=10" Cum.	Sum All Incr.	Sum All Cum.	Production [MMbbl]
1	2020	Shallow				2		46				30		30	10.1
		Medium				1		23				10		10	18.9
		Deep													
		Total				3		69				40		40	29.0
2	2020	Shallow				1		23				20		20	7.3
		Medium				2		46		5		15		20	28.6
		Deep													
		Total				3		69		5		35		40	35.9
3	2020	Shallow										15		15	
		Medium				2	20	38		5		15		20	38.6
		Deep													
		Total				2	20	38		5		30		35	38.6
ALL	2020	Shallow				3		69				65		65	17.4
		Medium				5	20	107		10		40		50	86.1
		Deep													
		Total				8	20	176		10		105		115	103.5

---

[1] Year 2020 is the maximum production year for All Sale scenario.

MMS

CHAPTER 4

FAULT TREE ANALYSIS FOR
ARCTIC OIL SPILL FREQUENCIES

4.1   General Description of Fault Tree Analysis

Fault trees are a method for modeling the occurrence of failures. They are used when an adequate history to provide failure statistics is not available. Developed initially by Rasmussen for the US Nuclear Regulatory Commission in the early 1970s [65, 51], fault trees have become a popular risk analytic tool for predicting risks, assessing relative risks, and quantifying comparative risks [7, 9, 14, 15, 18, 23, 26, 45]. In 1976, we first used fault trees to quantify oil spill probabilities in the Canadian Beaufort Sea for the Canadian Department of the Environment [10, 11]. In the present study they are used for the transformation of historical spill statistics for non-Arctic regions to predictive spill statistics for Arctic regions in the study area.

4.2   Fault Tree Methodology

4.2.1   Fault Tree Analysis Basics

The basic symbols used in the graphic depiction of simple (as used here) fault tree networks are illustrated in Figure 4.1(a). As may be seen, the two types of symbols designate logic gates and event types. The basic fault tree building blocks are the events and associated sub-events, which form a causal network. The elements linking events are the AND and OR gates, which define the logical relationship among events in the network. The output event from an OR gate occurs if any one or more of the input events to the gate occurs. The output event from an AND gate occurs only if all the input events occur simultaneously.

The basic structure of a fault tree is illustrated in Figure 4.1(b). Because of their connection through an AND gate, Event D and Event E must both occur for the resultant Event B to occur. An OR gate connects Events B and C; therefore, the occurrence of either one or both of Events B and C results in the occurrence of the resultant Event A. As may be seen, the principal fault tree structures are easy to apply; however, the representation of complex problems often requires very large fault trees, which become more difficult to analyze and require more advanced techniques such as minimal cut-set analysis [2, 14, 18, 23, 51]. For the present application, a simple system connected through OR gates only will used.

SYMBOL	DESCRIPTION
A. LOGIC	
	EITHER / OR GATE
	AND GATE
B. EVENT	
	RESULTANT EVENT
	BASIC EVENT

(a) Basic Fault Tree Symbols

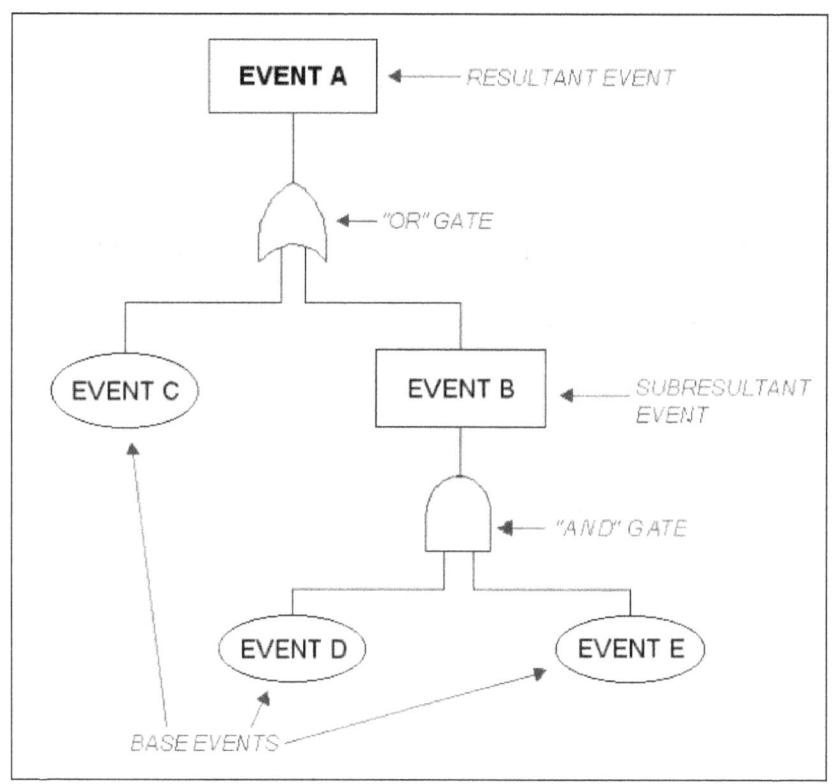

(b) Basic Fault Tree Structure

Figure 4.1
Fault Tree Basics

Computationally, the probability of input events joined through an AND gate are multiplied to calculate the probabilities of the output event. The probabilities of input events joined through an OR gate are added to calculate the probability of the output event. The relevant equations and associated assumptions may be summarized as follows:

For   AND Gate:

$$P = \prod_{n}^{i=1} P_i \qquad (4.1a)$$

Example: Output Event Probability = P_x
Input Events failure probabilities, P_1, P_2, ...

$$P_x = P_1(P_2)(P_3) \qquad (4.1b)$$

For   OR Gate:

$$P = 1 - \prod_{n}^{i=1}(1 - P_i) \qquad (4.2a)$$

Example: Output Event Probability = P_y
Input Event failure probabilities, P_1, P_2, ...

$$P_y = 1 - \prod_{n}(1 - P_1)(1 - P_2)(1 - P_3)$$

$$P_y = P_1 + P_2 + P_3; \; for \; P_i \leq 0.1 \qquad (4.2b)$$

In more complex fault trees, it is necessary to assure that base events which affect more than one fault tree branch are not numerically duplicated. This is done through the use of minimal cut-set theory [14, 18, 23, 51]. However, as indicated earlier, the fault trees used in this study are sufficiently simple in structure and level of detail to exclude the requirement of using minimal cut-set theory in their computation algorithms.

4.2.2   *Current Application of Fault Trees*

Figure 4.2 illustrates a two-tier fault tree that can be used to develop pipeline large spill frequencies for the Arctic study area from the historical frequencies. Note that this example is illustrative of the process only, and does not correspond to the same numerical values used in computations later. The type of fault tree shown, to be used extensively later, is a relatively simple fault tree showing the resultant event, the spill, generated from a series of subresultant events corresponding to the pipeline spill causal classification, such as that shown in Table 2.3. The upper tier of numbers (marked "H") below each of the events in the fault tree represents the historical frequency (per 100,000 km-yr) while the lower one (marked "A") represents the modified frequency for Arctic operations. As these fault trees are composed entirely of OR gates, the computation of resultant events is quite simple – consisting of the addition of the probabilities of events at each level of the fault tree to obtain the resultant probability at the next higher value.

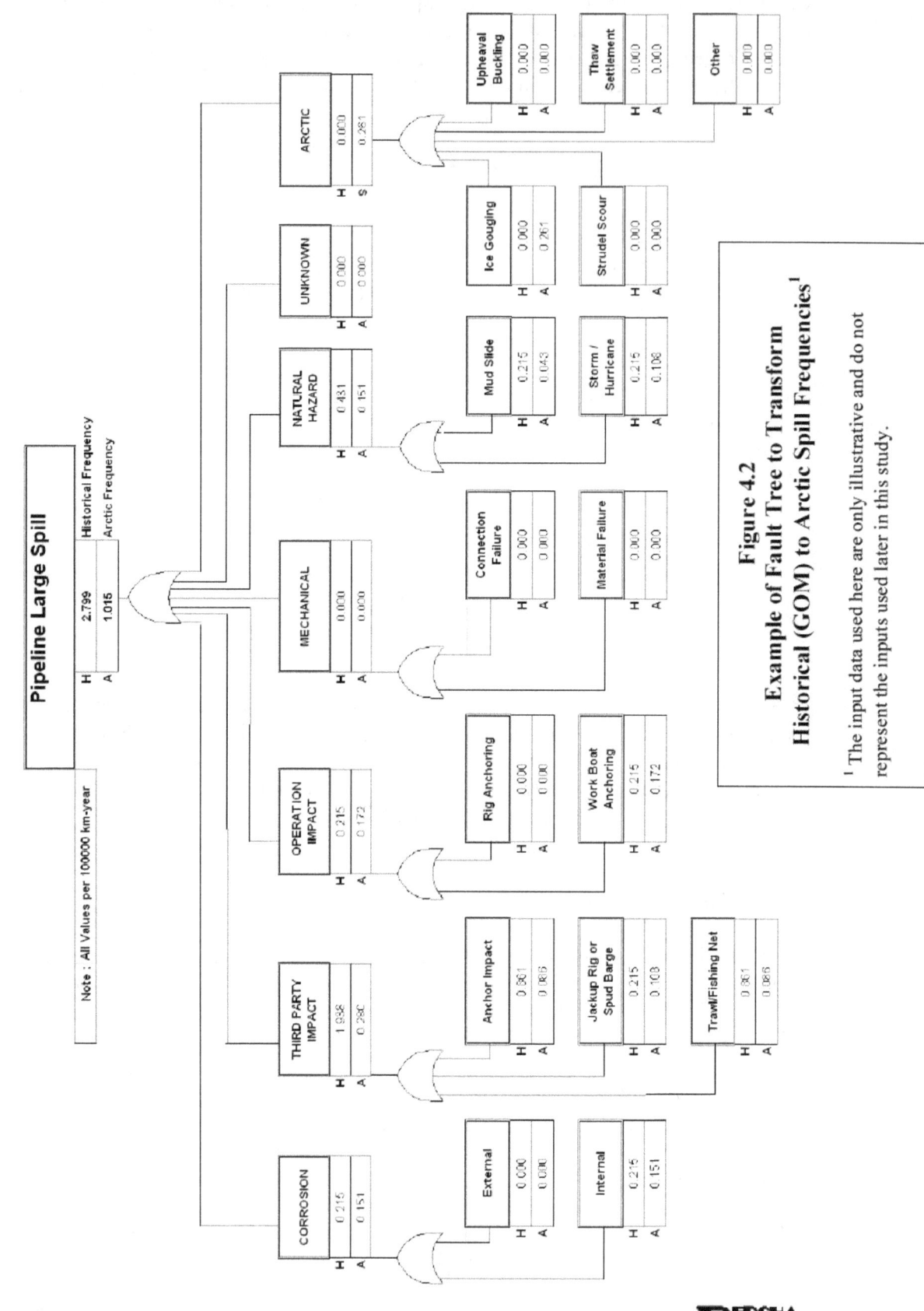

Figure 4.2
Example of Fault Tree to Transform
Historical (GOM) to Arctic Spill Frequencies[1]

[1] The input data used here are only illustrative and do not represent the inputs used later in this study.

For example, to obtain the "Natural Hazard" Arctic ("A") probability of 0.151, add 0.043 and 0.108. Essentially, the fault tree resultant (top event) shows that the Arctic frequency of spills (for the example pipeline category, location, and spill size) is approximately 1 in 100,000 km-yr or 1.015×10^{-5}/km-yr. The non-Arctic historical frequency for this spill size, by comparison, is 2.799×10^{-5}/km-yr, or approximately 2.8 times higher. Both frequencies are for illustrative purposes only.

4.2.3 Monte Carlo Simulation

A type of numerical simulation, called Monte Carlo simulation [9] can be used to obtain the outcome of a set of interactions for equations in which the independent variables are described by distributions of any arbitrary form. The Monte Carlo simulation is a systematic method for selecting values from each of the independent variable distributions and computing all valid combinations of these values to obtain the distribution of the dependent variable. Naturally, this is done utilizing a computer, so that thousands of combinations can be rapidly computed and assembled to give the output distribution.

Consider the example of the following equation:

$$X = X_1 + X_2 \tag{4.4}$$

Where X is the dependent variable (such as the resultant spill frequency) and X_1 and X_2 are base event probabilities joined through an "and" gate. Suppose now that X_1 and X_2 are some arbitrary distributions that can be described by a collection of values x_1 and x_2. What we do in the Monte Carlo process, figuratively, is to put the collection of the X_1 values into one hat, the X_1 hat, and the same for the X_2 values – into an X_2 hat. We then randomly draw one value from each of the hats and compute the resultant value of the dependent variable, X, using equation 4.4. This is done several thousand times. Thus, a resultant or dependent variable distribution, X, is estimated from the computations of all valid combinations of the independent variables (X_1 and X_2).

Generally, the resultant can be viewed as a cumulative distribution function as illustrated in Figure 4.3. Such a cumulative distribution function (CDF) is also a measure of the accuracy or, conversely, the variance of the distribution. As can be seen from this figure, if the distribution is a vertical line, no matter where one draws on the vertical axis, the same value of the variable will result – that is, the variable is a constant. At the other extreme, if the variable is completely random then the distribution will be represented as a diagonal straight line between the minimum and maximum value. Intermediate qualitative descriptions of the randomness of the variable follow from inspection of the CDF in Figure 4.3.

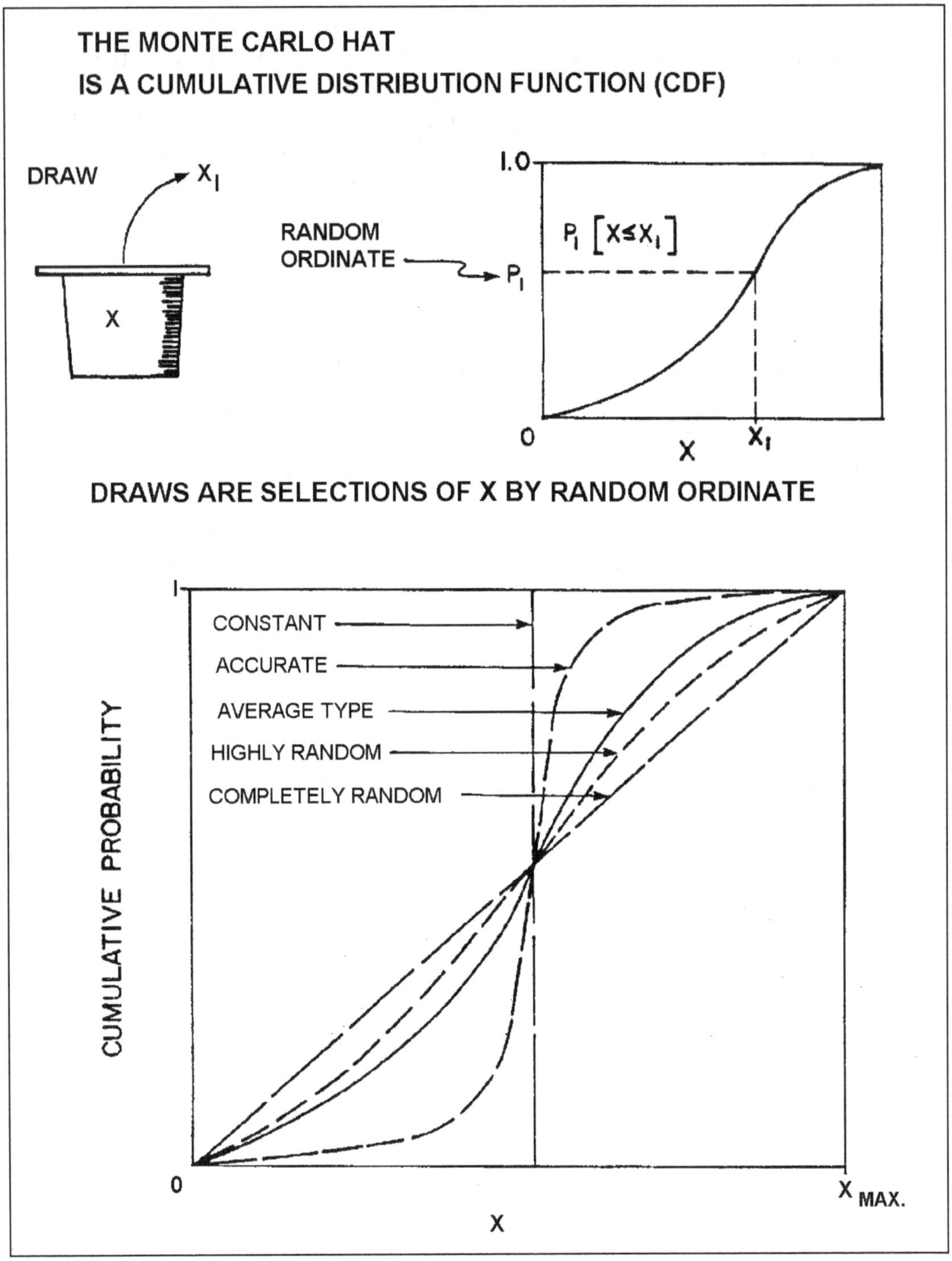

THE MONTE CARLO HAT
IS A CUMULATIVE DISTRIBUTION FUNCTION (CDF)

DRAW　　→ X_I

RANDOM
ORDINATE　→ P_I

$P_I \left[X \leq X_I \right]$

1.0

0　　X　　X_I

DRAWS ARE SELECTIONS OF X BY RANDOM ORDINATE

CUMULATIVE PROBABILITY

CONSTANT
ACCURATE
AVERAGE TYPE
HIGHLY RANDOM
COMPLETELY RANDOM

0　　X　　$X_{MAX.}$

Figure 4.3
Monte Carlo Technique Schematic

There are two other important concepts related to the CDF enter into Monte Carlo modeling: auto-correlation and cross-correlation. Suppose the variables X_1 can vary only within a specified interval over the simulation time increment. Then, after the first random draw, the next draw would be restricted within certain limits of the initial draw simply as a result of the physical restrictions of the problem. Such a restriction is represented as an auto-correlation coefficient. Now, suppose that not only are the X_1 restricted, but also the X_2. Suppose further, however, that given a certain X_1, a restriction were placed on the range of X_2 associated with that X_1. Say, only small X_1 could associate with the full range of X_2, while large X_1 could only be associated with certain lower X_2. Then, such a relationship would be expressed as a cross-correlation factor and certain limits would be imposed for the drawing on both X_1 and associated X_2. In the present analysis, all distributed variables are considered to be independent – so that auto and cross-correlations need not be invoked.

4.2.4 *Distribution Derived from Historical Data for Monte Carlo Analysis*

In order to model the variability of the base data and its distribution through the Arctic effects, using the Monte Carlo approach, an appropriate distribution needs to be derived. As in the previous study [12], a Triangular Distribution was selected.

According to [13], the Triangular Distribution is typically used as a descriptor of a population for which there is only limited sample data, as is the current case. The distribution is based on a knowledge of a minimum and maximum, which was derived from the historical data here, and an educated guess as to what the modal value might be. Here, the modal value was chosen to be a function of the average historical value, as given in Equation 2.1. Despite being a simplistic description of a population, the Triangular Distribution is a very useful one for modeling processes where the relationship between variables is understood, but data are scarce.

Also, when combining several variables in a functional relationship utilizing numerical methods, as is done in Monte Carlo Simulation, the Triangular Distribution is a preferred one due to its simplicity and relatively accurate probabilistic resultant when evaluated by a large number of random draws, as occurs in the Monte Carlo process. The data used here typifies sparse data with a preferred or modal value and an easily identifiable maximum and minimum. Then, for the case of the simple upper and lower 100% confidence interval (called High and Low), the expected value *E* (or mean value) of the Triangular Distribution can be expressed as:

$$E = (High + Mode + Low) / 3 \tag{4.3}$$

For maximum and minimum which are not at the 100% confidence interval level – such as those at 90% confidence levels – a Monte Carlo computation is used to evaluate the expected value of each distribution, giving results somewhat different from Equation 4.3. Based on the historical data earlier presented in Tables 2.4, 2.7, and 2.10, the Triangular Distribution expected value computed from the low, average, and high values at 90% confidence intervals are given in Tables 4.1, 4.2, and 4.3, for pipelines, platforms, and wells respectively.

Table 4.1
Pipeline Spill Frequency Triangular Distribution Properties

GOM OCS Pipeline Spills, Categorized 1972-99		Low Factor	High Factor	Frequency spill per 10^5 km-years				
				Historical	Low	Mode	High	Expected
By Diameter, By Spill Size								
<10"	Small	0	2.57	3.7974	0	1.6329	9.7592	5.1720
	Medium	0	2.57	6.6454	0	2.8575	17.0786	9.0510
	Large	0	2.57	3.7974	0	1.6329	9.7592	5.1720
	Huge	0	2.57	0.9493	0	0.4082	2.4398	1.2930
=10"	Small	0	2.57	2.4436	0	1.0507	6.2800	3.3282
	Medium	0	2.57	6.1090	0	2.6269	15.7001	8.3205
	Large	0	2.57	7.3308	0	3.1522	18.8401	9.9846
	Huge	0	2.57	2.4436	0	1.0507	6.2800	3.3282

Table 4.2
Platform Spill Frequency Triangular Distribution Properties

Spill Size	Frequency Unit	Low Factor	High Factor	Historical	Low	Mode	High	Expected
Small and Medium Spills 50-999 bbl	spill per 10^4 well-year	0	2.88	1.5036	0.0000	0.1804	4.3303	2.1571
Large and Huge Spills =1000 bbl	spill per 10^4 well-year	0	2.88	0.2506	0.0000	0.0301	0.7217	0.3595

MMS

Table 4.3
Well Blowout Frequency Triangular Distribution Properties

EVENT	FREQUENCY UNIT	Low Factor	High Factor	Frequencies				
				Historical	Low	Mode	High	Expected
				Small and Medium Spills 50-999 bbl				
PRODUCTION WELL	spill per 10^4 well-year	0.448	1.545	0.147	0.066	0.148	0.227	0.147
EXPLORATION WELL DRILLING	spill per 10^4 wells	0.439	2.036	1.966	0.863	1.032	4.002	2.262
DEVELOPMENT WELL DRILLING	spill per 10^4 wells	0.437	1.760	0.654	0.286	0.526	1.151	0.692
				Large Spills 1000-9999 bbl				
PRODUCTION WELL	spill per 10^4 well-year	0.448	1.545	1.028	0.460	1.037	1.588	1.026
EXPLORATION WELL DRILLING	spill per 10^4 wells	0.439	2.036	13.754	6.039	7.220	28.001	15.824
DEVELOPMENT WELL DRILLING	spill per 10^4 wells	0.437	1.760	4.570	1.998	3.671	8.041	4.833
				Small, Medium and Large Spills 50-9999 bbl				
PRODUCTION WELL	spill per 10^4 well-year	0.448	1.545	1.175	0.526	1.185	1.815	1.173
EXPLORATION WELL DRILLING	spill per 10^4 wells	0.439	2.036	15.719	6.903	8.252	32.003	18.086
DEVELOPMENT WELL DRILLING	spill per 10^4 wells	0.437	1.760	5.224	2.284	4.197	9.192	5.525
				Spill 10000-149999 bbl				
PRODUCTION WELL	spill per 10^4 well-year	0.448	1.545	0.441	0.197	0.444	0.681	0.440
EXPLORATION WELL DRILLING	spill per 10^4 wells	0.439	2.036	5.909	2.595	3.102	12.031	6.799
DEVELOPMENT WELL DRILLING	spill per 10^4 wells	0.437	1.760	1.963	0.858	1.577	3.454	2.076
				Spill =150000 bbl				
PRODUCTION WELL	spill per 10^4 well-year	0.448	1.545	0.294	0.132	0.296	0.454	0.293
EXPLORATION WELL DRILLING	spill per 10^4 wells	0.439	2.036	3.421	1.502	1.796	6.965	3.936
DEVELOPMENT WELL DRILLING	spill per 10^4 wells	0.437	1.760	1.963	0.858	1.577	3.454	2.076

4.2.5   Approaches to Assessment of Arctic Spill Frequency Variability

There are two basic approaches to the assessment of the variability of non-Arctic spill rates, and consequently the Arctic spill rates, using the fault tree method. The first method utilizes the historical variability of the non-Arctic base data and distributes it in direct proportion throughout the Arctic fault tree. This method is a relatively high level, approximate method, and is called the First Order Approach. In this method, the non-Arctic variable distribution is multiplied by a point value to obtain the Arctic variable distribution. The second method consists of systematically perturbing the variability of all the causal events, plus that of the Arctic unique effects. This method is more detailed and specific, and is termed the Second Order Approach. In the Second Order Approach, the non-Arctic variable distribution is multiplied by an adjustment or correction distribution to obtain the Arctic variable distribution. The First Order Approach, when used individually, did not adequately represent trends in the variability of the Arctic effects. The Second Order Approach, if not used in conjunction with the First Order Approach, resulted in arbitrary mean or expected values, because it was not tied directly to any real historical data. The optimal approach was to use the two methods, with the First Order Approach utilized to give the initial level of first order variability, and the Second Order Approach utilized to better reflect Arctic effects on the variability of causal events. In what follows, the discussion is based on the use of both methods in a complimentary fashion.

4.3   Pipeline Fault Tree Analysis

4.3.1   Pipeline First Order Arctic Effects

The effects of the Arctic environment and operations are reflected in the effect on facility failure rates in two ways; namely, through "Modified Effects", those changing the frequency component of certain fault contributions such as anchor impacts which are common in both Arctic and temperate zones, and through "Unique Effects" or additive elements such as ice gouging which are unique to the Arctic offshore environment. Table 4.4 shows the frequency modifications (in %) and frequency increment additions (per 10^5 km-yr)developed for Arctic pipelines for different spill sizes throughout the three relevant water depth ranges. The right hand column of the table gives a summary of the reasoning behind the effects. For the Arctic unique effects, both the expected value (from Table 2.9) and the median value, determined through the Monte Carlo analysis, are given. The median values differ from the expected values due to skewness of the distributions introduced through the assigned values of the upper and lower bounds (Table 2.9). The following comments can be made for each of the causes described:

- *External corrosion* – Due to the low temperature, limited biological and lowered chemical effects are expected. Coatings will be state of art and high level of quality control will be used during pipeline installation resulting in high integrity levels of coating to prevent external corrosion.

Table 4.4
Pipeline First Order Arctic Effect Summary

CAUSE CLASSIFICATION	Spill Size	Shallow	Medium	Deep	Reason
		Historical Expected Frequency Change %			
CORROSION					
External	All	(30)	(30)	(30)	Low temperature and bio effects. Extra smart pigging.
Internal	All	(30)	(30)	(30)	Extra smart pigging.
THIRD PARTY IMPACT					
Anchor Impact	All	(50)	(50)	(50)	Low traffic.
Jackup Rig or Spud Barge	All	(50)	(50)	(50)	Low facility density.
Trawl/Fishing Net	All	(50)	(60)	(70)	Low fishing activity. Less bottom fishing in deeper water.
OPERATION IMPACT					
Rig Anchoring	All	(20)	(20)	(20)	Low marine traffic during ice season (8 months).
Work Boat Anchoring	All	(20)	(20)	(20)	Low work boat traffic during ice season (8 months).
MECHANICAL					
Connection Failure	All				
Material Failure	All				
NATURAL HAZARD					
Mud Slide	All	(60)	(50)	(40)	Gradient low. Mud slide potential (gradient) increases with water depth.
Storm/ Hurricane	All	(50)	(50)	(50)	Fewer severe storms.

CAUSE CLASSIFICATION	Spill Size	Freq. Increment per 10^5 km-year			
		Expected Mode	Expected Mode	Expected Mode	
ARCTIC					
Ice Gouging	S	0.3495	0.2796		Ice gouge failure rate calculated using exponential failure distribution for 2.5-m cover, 0.2-m average gouge depth, 2 gouges per km-yr flux. Spill size Distribution explained in text Section 2.5.2. Medium depth has 0.8 as many gouges as shallow.
		0.0680	0.0544		
	M	0.6178	0.4943		
		0.1210	0.0968		
	L	1.3438	1.0750		
		0.2610	0.2088		
	H	0.3762	0.3010		
		0.0730	0.0584		
Strudel Scour	S	0.0021			Only in shallow water. Average frequency of 4 scours/mile² and 100 ft of bridge length with 10% conditional Pipelines failure probability. The same spill size distribution as above.
		0.0012			
	M	0.0038			
		0.0020			
	L	0.0082			
		0.0045			
	H	0.0023			
		0.0012			
Upheaval Buckling	S	0.0004	0.0004	0.0004	All water depth. The failure frequency is 20% of that of Strudel Scour.
		0.0002	0.0002	0.0002	
	M	0.0008	0.0008	0.0008	
		0.0004	0.0004	0.0004	
	L	0.0016	0.0016	0.0016	
		0.0009	0.0009	0.0009	
	H	0.0005	0.0005	0.0005	
		0.0002	0.0002	0.0002	
Thaw Settlement	S	0.0002	0.0002	0.0002	All water depth. The failure frequency is 10% of that of Strudel Scour.
		0.0001	0.0001	0.0001	
	M	0.0004	0.0004	0.0004	
		0.0002	0.0002	0.0002	
	L	0.0008	0.0008	0.0008	
		0.0004	0.0004	0.0004	
	H	0.0002	0.0002	0.0002	
		0.0001	0.0001	0.0001	
Other	S	0.0881	0.0701	0.0002	25% of sum of above.
		0.0174	0.0137	0.0001	
	M	0.1557	0.1238	0.0003	
		0.0309	0.0244	0.0002	
	L	0.3386	0.2694	0.0006	
		0.0667	0.0525	0.0003	
	H	0.0948	0.0754	0.0002	
		0.0187	0.0147	0.0001	

- *Internal corrosion* – Additional (above historical levels) inspection or smart pigging is anticipated.

- *Anchor impact* – The very low traffic densities of third party shipping in the area justify a 50% reduction in anchor impact expectations on the pipeline.

- *Jack-up rig or spud barges* – Associated or other operations are going to be substantially more limited than they are in the historical data population in the Gulf of Mexico.

- *Trawl/Fishing net* – Very limited fishing is expected in the Beaufort Sea.

- *Rig anchoring* – Although it is anticipated that no marine traffic except possibly icebreakers will occur during the ice season, an increased traffic density during the four month open water season to resupply the platforms is expected, justifying only a 20% decrease in this failure cause.

- *Workboat anchoring* – The same applies to workboat anchoring as to rig anchoring.

- *Mechanical connection failure or material failure* – No change was made to account for Arctic effects.

- *Mudslide* – A relatively low gradient resulting in limited mudslide potential is anticipated. A gradual increase in the mudslide potential (reflected by smaller decreases in failure frequency) ranging from 60% for shallow water to only 40% in deep water was included to account for the anticipated increase in gradient as deeper waters are encountered.

- *Storms* – Considerably fewer severe storms are anticipated on an annual basis in the Arctic than in GOM, due to damping of the ocean surface by ice cover.

- *Arctic effects* – Arctic effects are effects which are unique to the Arctic and are not reflected in the historical fault tree itself. Arctic effects were discussed in detail in Chapter 2, Section 2.5. The discussion in that section is summarized in the right hand column of Table 4.1. The frequency increments in this table are given as both the "expected" values and the "mode" values. The mode values are the mode values given in Table 2.9. The median values, however, are those calculated using the Monte Carlo method with the low, mode, and high values from Table 2.9, as inputs to the Monte Carlo. The expected or median values are clearly considerably higher than the mode or most likely values. This lack of coincidence between expected and mode values is due to the skewness of the distribution.

4.3.2   Pipeline Second Order Arctic Effect Variations

The second order effects are incorporated through the construction of a secondary triangular distribution by which the historical causal frequency distributions are multiplied to provide the resultant Arctic effect distribution. This secondary distribution utilizes the value of the first order effect reduction as its mode, with appropriate second order perturbations for the upper and lower 90% confidence interval bounds. Table 4.5 summarizes these second order effect distributions. For the Arctic modified effects, given in the top of the table, the secondary distribution is simply the first order effect frequency change used as the mode of the distribution, and 90% upper and lower confidence interval changes given under the Min and Max column. For the Arctic unique effects, total frequency increments are given, with the upper confidence interval value at approximately 12 times the mode, and the lower bound value at approximately $^1/_{10}$ of the modal value.

4.3.3   Arctic Pipeline Fault Tree Frequency Calculations

Incorporation of the frequency effects as variations in and additions to the historical frequencies can be represented in a fault tree, as shown for the large spill size for Arctic pipelines in Figure 4.4. In this figure, the historical frequency as well as that associated with small, medium, and deep-water zones are shown under each of the event boxes. Each box is further split into two, for pipelines = 10" diameter as represented in the historical database. Such fault trees were developed for all of the pipeline spill sizes, and these additional spill size fault trees, for small, medium, large, and huge spills are presented in Appendix 3, where the complete calculations are given.

Of greatest importance, however, are the pipeline failure frequencies or failure rates per km-yr calculated from the first and second order input distributions using Monte Carlo simulation. These failure rates for the entire range of spill sizes, small, medium, large, and huge, are given in Tables 4.6, 4.7, 4.8, and 4.9, respectively.

Indeed, a huge array of numbers is shown in these tables. Consider Table 4.8, which is the frequency calculation corresponding to the large spill size fault tree shown in Figure 4.8. Consider the bottom line opposite totals. What the table tells us is that the total spill frequency for pipelines < 10" diameter was 5.172 (per 10^5 km-yr) historically. With the first and second order frequency changes attributable to Arctic effects, this frequency is reduced to 4.375 for shallow water, to 4.004 for medium depth water, and to 2.636 for deep water. A similar trend in the reduction of failure frequencies with increasing water depth for pipelines = 10" is manifested in the right hand side of the table. Because the frequencies per unit pipeline length and operating year are the key drivers in the balance of the analysis, they have been given in the body of the report (in Tables 4.6 to 4.9) for each of the spill sizes for pipelines. Finally, Table 4.10 summarizes the expected values of the pipeline spill frequencies.

Table 4.5
Pipeline First and Second Order Arctic Effect Distribution Summary

CAUSE CLASSIFICATION	Spill Size	Shallow			Medium			Deep		
		Frequency Change %								
		Min	Mode	Max	Min	Mode	Max	Min	Mode	Max
CORROSION										
External	All	(90)	(30)	(10)	(90)	(30)	(10)	(90)	(30)	(10)
Internal	All	(90)	(30)	(10)	(90)	(30)	(10)	(90)	(30)	(10)
THIRD PARTY IMPACT										
Anchor Impact	All	(90)	(50)	(10)	(90)	(50)	(10)	(90)	(50)	(10)
Jackup Rig or Spud Barge	All	(90)	(50)	(10)	(90)	(50)	(10)	(90)	(50)	(10)
Trawl/Fishing Net	All	(90)	(50)	(10)	(90)	(60)	(10)	(90)	(70)	(10)
OPERATION IMPACT										
Rig Anchoring	All	(50)	(20)	(10)	(50)	(20)	(10)	(50)	(20)	(10)
Work Boat Anchoring	All	(50)	(20)	(10)	(50)	(20)	(10)	(50)	(20)	(10)
MECHANICAL										
Connection Failure	All									
Material Failure	All									
NATURAL HAZARD										
Mud Slide	All	(90)	(60)	(10)	(90)	(50)	(10)	(90)	(40)	(10)
Storm/ Hurricane	All	(90)	(50)	(10)	(90)	(50)	(10)	(90)	(50)	(10)
		Frequency Increment per 10⁵ km-year								

		Min	Mode	Max	Min	Mode	Max	Min	Mode	Max
ARCTIC										
Ice Gouging	S	0.0060	0.0680	0.8290	0.0048	0.0544	0.6632			
	M	0.0090	0.1210	1.4670	0.0072	0.0968	1.1736			
	L	0.0210	0.2610	3.1900	0.0168	0.2088	2.5520			
	H	0.0060	0.0730	0.8930	0.0048	0.0584	0.7144			
Strudel Scour	S	0.0004	0.0012	0.0044						
	M	0.0006	0.0020	0.0078						
	L	0.0014	0.0045	0.0170						
	H	0.0004	0.0012	0.0048						
Upheaval Buckling	S	0.00007	0.00023	0.00088	0.00007	0.00023	0.00088	0.00007	0.00023	0.00088
	M	0.00013	0.00041	0.00156	0.00013	0.00041	0.00156	0.00013	0.00041	0.00156
	L	0.00028	0.00089	0.00340	0.00028	0.00089	0.00340	0.00028	0.00089	0.00340
	H	0.00008	0.00025	0.00095	0.00008	0.00025	0.00095	0.00008	0.00025	0.00095
Thaw Settlement	S	0.00004	0.00012	0.00044	0.00004	0.00012	0.00044	0.00004	0.00012	0.00044
	M	0.00006	0.00020	0.00078	0.00006	0.00020	0.00078	0.00006	0.00020	0.00078
	L	0.00014	0.00045	0.00170	0.00014	0.00045	0.00170	0.00014	0.00045	0.00170
	H	0.00004	0.00012	0.00048	0.00004	0.00012	0.00048	0.00004	0.00012	0.00048
Other	S	0.00162	0.01738	0.20869	0.00123	0.01369	0.16613	0.00003	0.00009	0.00033
	M	0.00246	0.03092	0.36929	0.00185	0.02435	0.29399	0.00005	0.00015	0.00059
	L	0.00571	0.06670	0.80303	0.00431	0.05253	0.63928	0.00011	0.00033	0.00128
	H	0.00163	0.01865	0.22480	0.00123	0.01469	0.17896	0.00003	0.00009	0.00036

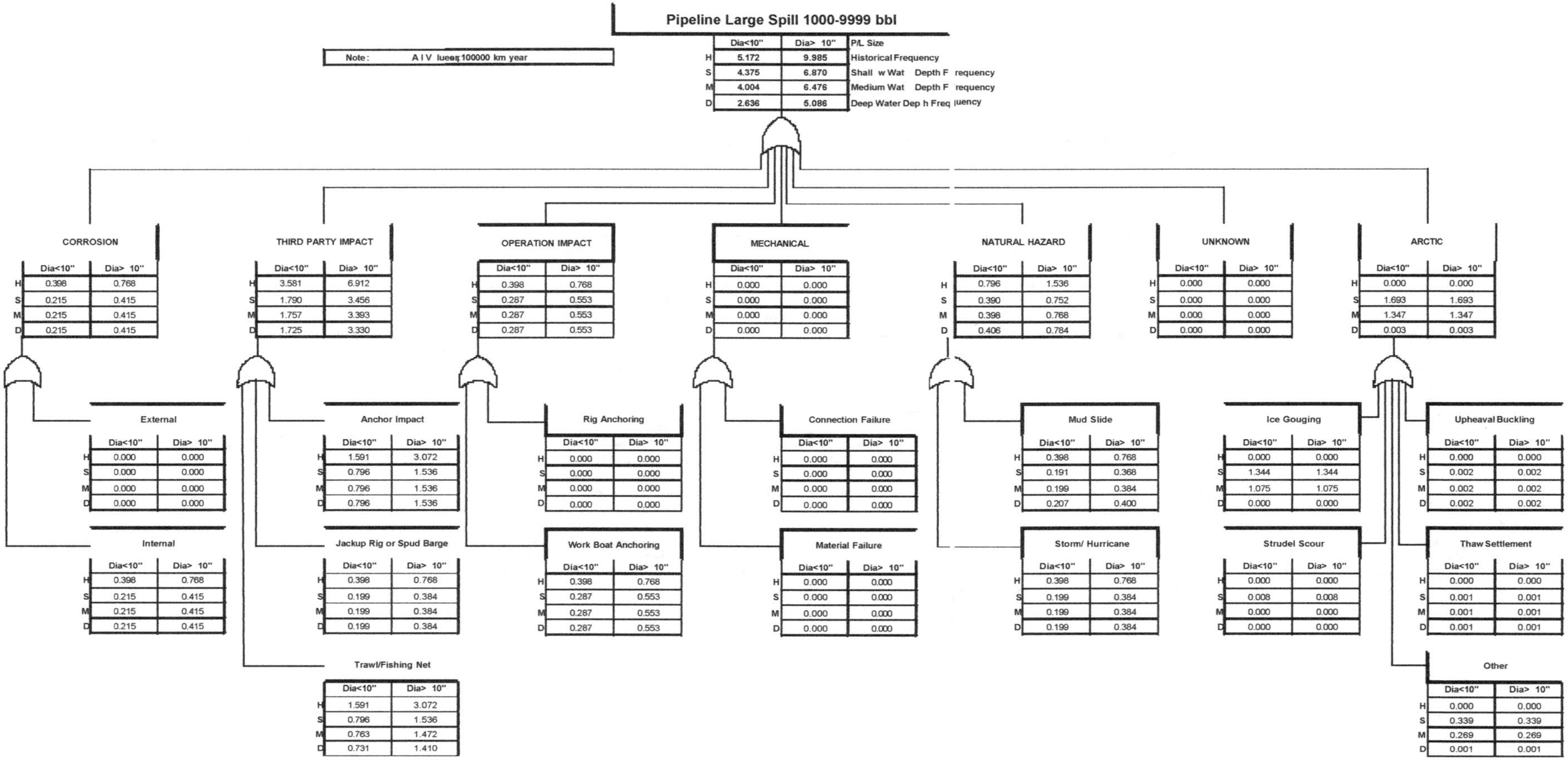

Pipeline Large Spill 1000-9999 bbl

	Dia<10"	Dia> 10"	P/L Size
H	5.172	9.985	Historical Frequency
S	4.375	6.870	Shall w Wat Depth F requency
M	4.004	6.476	Medium Wat Depth F requency
D	2.636	5.086	Deep Water Dep h Freq uency

Note: A l V l ueseq 100000 km year

CORROSION

	Dia<10"	Dia> 10"
H	0.396	0.768
S	0.215	0.415
M	0.215	0.415
D	0.215	0.415

External

	Dia<10"	Dia> 10"
H	0.000	0.000
S	0.000	0.000
M	0.000	0.000
D	0.000	0.000

Internal

	Dia<10"	Dia> 10"
H	0.396	0.768
S	0.215	0.415
M	0.215	0.415
D	0.215	0.415

THIRD PARTY IMPACT

	Dia<10"	Dia> 10"
H	3.581	6.912
S	1.790	3.456
M	1.757	3.393
D	1.725	3.330

Anchor Impact

	Dia<10"	Dia> 10"
H	1.591	3.072
S	0.796	1.536
M	0.796	1.536
D	0.796	1.536

Jackup Rig or Spud Barge

	Dia<10"	Dia> 10"
H	0.396	0.768
S	0.199	0.384
M	0.199	0.384
D	0.199	0.384

Trawl/Fishing Net

	Dia<10"	Dia> 10"
H	1.591	3.072
S	0.796	1.536
M	0.763	1.472
D	0.731	1.410

OPERATION IMPACT

	Dia<10"	Dia> 10"
H	0.396	0.768
S	0.287	0.553
M	0.287	0.553
D	0.287	0.553

Rig Anchoring

	Dia<10"	Dia> 10"
H	0.000	0.000
S	0.000	0.000
M	0.000	0.000
D	0.000	0.000

Work Boat Anchoring

	Dia<10"	Dia> 10"
H	0.396	0.768
S	0.287	0.553
M	0.287	0.553
D	0.287	0.553

MECHANICAL

	Dia<10"	Dia> 10"
H	0.000	0.000
S	0.000	0.000
M	0.000	0.000
D	0.000	0.000

Connection Failure

	Dia<10"	Dia> 10"
H	0.000	0.000
S	0.000	0.000
M	0.000	0.000
D	0.000	0.000

Material Failure

	Dia<10"	Dia> 10"
H	0.000	0.000
S	0.000	0.000
M	0.000	0.000
D	0.000	0.000

NATURAL HAZARD

	Dia<10"	Dia> 10"
H	0.796	1.536
S	0.390	0.752
M	0.396	0.768
D	0.406	0.784

Mud Slide

	Dia<10"	Dia> 10"
H	0.396	0.768
S	0.191	0.368
M	0.199	0.384
D	0.207	0.400

Storm/ Hurricane

	Dia<10"	Dia> 10"
H	0.396	0.768
S	0.199	0.384
M	0.199	0.384
D	0.199	0.384

UNKNOWN

	Dia<10"	Dia> 10"
H	0.000	0.000
S	0.000	0.000
M	0.000	0.000
D	0.000	0.000

ARCTIC

	Dia<10"	Dia> 10"
H	0.000	0.000
S	1.693	1.693
M	1.347	1.347
D	0.003	0.003

Ice Gouging

	Dia<10"	Dia> 10"
H	0.000	0.000
S	1.344	1.344
M	1.075	1.075
D	0.000	0.000

Strudel Scour

	Dia<10"	Dia> 10"
H	0.000	0.000
S	0.008	0.008
M	0.000	0.000
D	0.000	0.000

Upheaval Buckling

	Dia<10"	Dia> 10"
H	0.000	0.000
S	0.002	0.002
M	0.002	0.002
D	0.002	0.002

Thaw Settlement

	Dia<10"	Dia> 10"
H	0.000	0.000
S	0.001	0.001
M	0.001	0.001
D	0.001	0.001

Other

	Dia<10"	Dia> 10"
H	0.000	0.000
S	0.339	0.339
M	0.269	0.269
D	0.001	0.001

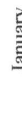

**Figure 4.4
Large Spill Frequencies for Pipeline**

January, 2006

Table 4.6
Arctic Pipeline Small Spill Frequencies

SMALL SPILLS 50-99 bbl

CAUSE CLASSIFICATION	% HISTORICAL DISTRIBUTION	Pipelines Diameter<10" FREQUENCY spills per 10⁴km-year	Shallow Frequency Change	Shallow New Frequency	Shallow % New Distribution	Medium Frequency Change	Medium New Frequency	Medium % New Distribution	Deep Frequency Change	Deep New Frequency	Deep % New Distribution	Pipelines Diameter =10" FREQUENCY spills per 10⁴km-year	Shallow Frequency Change	Shallow New Frequency	Shallow % New Distribution	Medium Frequency Change	Medium New Frequency	Medium % New Distribution	Deep Frequency Change	Deep New Frequency	Deep % New Distribution
CORROSION	16.67	0.862	(0.396)	0.466	12.70	(0.396)	0.466	13.00	(0.396)	0.466	14.38	0.555	(0.255)	0.300	11.91	(0.255)	0.300	12.33	(0.255)	0.300	14.38
External	5.56	0.287	(0.132)	0.155	4.23	(0.132)	0.155	4.33	(0.132)	0.155	4.79	0.185	(0.085)	0.100	3.97	(0.085)	0.100	4.11	(0.085)	0.100	4.79
Internal	11.11	0.575	(0.264)	0.311	8.47	(0.264)	0.311	8.67	(0.264)	0.311	9.58	0.370	(0.170)	0.200	7.94	(0.170)	0.200	8.22	(0.170)	0.200	9.58
THIRD PARTY IMPACT	38.89	2.011	(1.006)	1.006	27.40	(1.012)	1.000	27.87	(1.017)	0.994	30.64	1.294	(0.647)	0.647	25.69	(0.651)	0.643	26.44	(0.655)	0.640	30.64
Anchor Impact	33.33	1.724	(0.862)	0.862	23.48	(0.862)	0.862	24.03	(0.862)	0.862	26.58	1.109	(0.555)	0.555	22.02	(0.555)	0.555	22.80	(0.555)	0.555	26.57
Jackup Rig or Spud Barge																					
Trawl/Fishing Net	5.56	0.287	(0.144)	0.144	3.91	(0.150)	0.138	3.84	(0.155)	0.132	4.07	0.185	(0.092)	0.092	3.67	(0.096)	0.089	3.64	(0.100)	0.085	4.07
OPERATION IMPACT	16.67	0.862	(0.241)	0.621	16.92	(0.241)	0.621	17.32	(0.241)	0.621	19.15	0.555	(0.155)	0.400	15.86	(0.155)	0.400	16.43	(0.155)	0.400	19.15
Rig Anchoring	5.56	0.287	(0.080)	0.207	5.64	(0.080)	0.207	5.77	(0.080)	0.207	6.38	0.185	(0.052)	0.133	5.29	(0.052)	0.133	5.48	(0.052)	0.133	6.38
Work Boat	11.11	0.575	(0.161)	0.414	11.28	(0.161)	0.414	11.54	(0.161)	0.414	12.77	0.370	(0.103)	0.266	10.58	(0.103)	0.266	10.95	(0.103)	0.266	12.76
Anchoring																					
MECHANICAL	11.11	0.575		0.575	15.66		0.575	16.02		0.575	17.72	0.370		0.370	14.68		0.370	15.20		0.370	17.72
Connection Failure	5.56	0.287		0.287	7.83		0.287	8.01		0.287	8.86	0.185		0.185	7.34		0.185	7.60		0.185	8.86
Material Failure	5.56	0.287		0.287	7.83		0.287	8.01		0.287	8.86	0.185		0.185	7.34		0.185	7.60		0.185	8.85
NATURAL HAZARD	11.11	0.575	(0.299)	0.275	7.50	(0.287)	0.287	8.01	(0.275)	0.299	9.23	0.370	(0.193)	0.177	7.04	(0.185)	0.185	7.60	(0.177)	0.193	9.23
Mud Slide	11.11	0.575	(0.299)	0.275	7.50	(0.287)	0.287	8.01	(0.275)	0.299	9.23	0.370	(0.193)	0.177	7.04	(0.185)	0.185	7.60	(0.177)	0.193	9.23
Storm/Hurricane																					
ARCTIC			0.440	0.440	12.00	0.350	0.350	9.77	0.001	0.001	0.02		0.440	0.440	17.48	0.350	0.350	14.40	0.001	0.001	0.04
Ice Gouging			0.3495	0.3495	9.52	0.2795	0.2795	7.80					0.3495	0.3495	13.87	0.2795	0.2795	11.49			
Strudel Scour			0.0021	0.0021	0.06								0.0021	0.0021	0.09						
Upheaval Buckling			0.0004	0.0004	0.01	0.0004	0.0004	0.01	0.0004	0.0004	0.01		0.0004	0.0004	0.02	0.0004	0.0004	0.02	0.0004	0.0004	0.02
Thaw Settlement			0.0002	0.0002	0.01	0.0002	0.0002	0.01	0.0002	0.0002	0.01		0.0002	0.0002	0.01	0.0002	0.0002	0.01	0.0002	0.0002	0.01
Other			0.0681	0.0681	2.40	0.0701	0.0701	1.95	0.0002	0.0002	0.00		0.0681	0.0681	3.50	0.0701	0.0701	2.88	0.0002	0.0002	0.01
UNKNOWN	5.56	0.287	(0.287)	0.287	7.83	(0.287)	0.287	8.01	(0.287)	0.287	8.86	0.185	(0.0881)	0.0881	7.34	(0.0701)	0.0701	7.60	(0.0881)	0.185	8.86
TOTALS	100.00	5.172	(1.501)	3.671	100.00	(1.585)	3.587	100.00	(1.929)	3.243	100.00	3.328	(0.809)	2.519	100.00	(0.895)	2.433	100.00	(1.241)	2.087	100.00

Table 4.7
Arctic Pipeline Medium Spill Frequencies

MEDIUM SPILLS 100-999 bbl

CAUSE CLASSIFICATION	% HISTORICAL DISTRIBUTION	FREQUENCY spills per 10/km-year	Pipelines Diameter<10" Shallow Frequency Change	Shallow New Frequency	Shallow % New Distribution	Medium Frequency Change	Medium New Frequency	Medium % New Distribution	Deep Frequency Change	Deep New Frequency	Deep % New Distribution	FREQUENCY spills per 10/km-year	Pipelines Diameter=10" Shallow Frequency Change	Shallow New Frequency	Shallow % New Distribution	Medium Frequency Change	Medium New Frequency	Medium % New Distribution	Deep Frequency Change	Deep New Frequency	Deep % New Distribution
CORROSION	16.67	1.509	(0.692)	0.816	12.69	(0.692)	0.816	12.99	(0.692)	0.816	14.38	1.387	(0.637)	0.750	12.55	(0.637)	0.750	12.88	(0.637)	0.750	14.38
External	5.56	0.503	(0.231)	0.272	4.23	(0.231)	0.272	4.33	(0.231)	0.272	4.79	0.462	(0.212)	0.250	4.18	(0.212)	0.250	4.29	(0.212)	0.250	4.79
Internal	11.11	1.006	(0.462)	0.544	8.46	(0.462)	0.544	8.66	(0.462)	0.544	9.58	0.924	(0.424)	0.500	8.37	(0.424)	0.500	8.58	(0.424)	0.500	9.58
THIRD PARTY IMPACT	38.89	3.520	(1.760)	1.760	27.36	(1.770)	1.749	27.85	(1.781)	1.739	30.64	3.236	(1.618)	1.618	27.08	(1.627)	1.608	27.61	(1.637)	1.599	30.64
Anchor Impact	33.33	3.017	(1.509)	1.509	23.45	(1.509)	1.509	24.01	(1.509)	1.509	26.58	2.773	(1.387)	1.387	23.21	(1.387)	1.387	23.80	(1.387)	1.387	26.58
Jackup Rig or Spud Barge																					
Trawl/Fishing Net	5.56	0.503	(0.251)	0.251	3.91	(0.262)	0.241	3.84	(0.272)	0.231	4.07	0.462	(0.231)	0.231	3.87	(0.241)	0.222	3.80	(0.250)	0.212	4.07
OPERATION IMPACT	16.67	1.509	(0.422)	1.087	16.90	(0.422)	1.087	17.30	(0.422)	1.087	19.15	1.387	(0.388)	0.999	16.72	(0.388)	0.999	17.15	(0.388)	0.999	19.15
Rig Anchoring	5.56	0.503	(0.141)	0.362	5.63	(0.141)	0.362	5.77	(0.141)	0.362	6.38		(0.129)	0.333	5.57	(0.129)	0.333	5.72	(0.129)	0.333	6.35
Work Boat Anchoring	11.11	1.006	(0.281)	0.725	11.27	(0.281)	0.725	11.53	(0.281)	0.725	12.77		(0.258)	0.666	11.15	(0.258)	0.666	11.43	(0.258)	0.666	12.77
MECHANICAL	11.11	1.006		1.006	15.64		1.006	16.01		1.006	17.72	0.924		0.924	15.47		0.924	15.87		0.924	17.72
Connection Failure	5.56	0.503		0.503	7.82		0.503	8.00		0.503	8.85	0.462		0.462	7.74		0.462	7.93		0.462	8.85
Material Failure	5.56	0.503		0.503	7.82		0.503	8.00		0.503	8.85	0.462		0.462	7.74		0.462	7.93		0.462	8.85
NATURAL HAZARD	11.11	1.006	(0.524)	0.482	7.49	(0.503)	0.503	8.00	(0.482)	0.524	9.23	0.924	(0.481)	0.443	7.42	(0.462)	0.462	7.93	(0.443)	0.481	9.23
Mud Side	11.11	1.006	(0.524)	0.482	7.49	(0.503)	0.503	8.00	(0.482)	0.524	9.23	0.924	(0.481)	0.443	7.42	(0.462)	0.462	7.93	(0.443)	0.481	9.23
Storm/Hurricane																					
ARCTIC			0.778	0.778	12.10	0.619	0.619	9.86	0.001	0.001	0.03		0.778	0.778	13.03	0.619	0.619	10.63	0.001	0.001	0.03
Ice Gouging			0.6178	0.6178	9.61	0.4943	0.4943	7.87					0.6178	0.6178	10.34	0.4943	0.4943	8.48			
Strudel Scour			0.0038	0.0038	0.06								0.0038	0.0038	0.06						
Upheaval Buckling			0.0008	0.0008	0.01	0.0008	0.0008	0.01	0.0008	0.0008	0.01		0.0008	0.0008	0.01	0.0008	0.0008	0.01	0.0008	0.0008	0.01
Thaw Settlement			0.0004	0.0004	0.01	0.0004	0.0004	0.01	0.0004	0.0004	0.01		0.0004	0.0004	0.01	0.0004	0.0004	0.01	0.0004	0.0004	0.01
Other			0.1557	0.1557	2.42	0.1238	0.1238	1.97	0.0003	0.0003	0.01		0.1557	0.1557	2.61	0.1238	0.1238	2.13	0.0003	0.0003	0.01
UNKNOWN	5.56	0.503		0.503	7.82		0.503	8.00		0.503	8.86	0.462		0.462	7.74		0.462	7.93		0.462	8.86
TOTALS	100.00	9.051	(2.619)	6.432	100.00	(2.768)	6.283	100.00	(3.375)	5.676	100.00	8.320	(2.345)	5.975	100.00	(2.495)	5.826	100.00	(3.103)	5.218	100.00

Table 4.8
Arctic Pipeline Large Spill Frequencies

LARGE SPILLS 1000-9999 bbl

CAUSE CLASSIFICATION	HISTORICAL DISTRIBUTION %	Pipelines Diameter <10" FREQUENCY spills per 10⁴km-year	Shallow Frequency Change	Shallow New Frequency	Shallow % New Distribution	Medium Frequency Change	Medium New Frequency	Medium % New Distribution	Deep Frequency Change	Deep New Frequency	Deep % New Distribution	Pipelines Diameter =10" FREQUENCY spills per 10⁴km-year	Shallow Frequency Change	Shallow New Frequency	Shallow % New Distribution	Medium Frequency Change	Medium New Frequency	Medium % New Distribution	Deep Frequency Change	Deep New Frequency	Deep % New Distribution
CORROSION	7.69	0.398	(0.183)	0.215	4.92	(0.183)	0.215	5.38	(0.183)	0.215	8.16	0.768	(0.353)	0.415	6.05	(0.353)	0.415	6.42	(0.353)	0.415	8.17
External	7.69	0.398	(0.183)	0.215	4.92	(0.183)	0.215	5.38	(0.183)	0.215	8.16	0.768	(0.353)	0.415	6.05	(0.353)	0.415	6.42	(0.353)	0.415	8.17
Internal		0.398	(0.183)	0.215	4.92	(0.183)	0.215	5.38	(0.183)	0.215	8.16	0.768	(0.353)	0.415	6.05	(0.353)	0.415	6.42	(0.353)	0.415	8.17
THIRD PARTY IMPACT	69.23	3.581	(1.790)	1.790	40.92	(1.823)	1.757	43.89	(1.856)	1.725	65.44	6.912	(3.456)	3.456	50.31	(3.520)	3.393	52.38	(3.582)	3.330	65.48
Anchor Impact	30.77	1.591	(0.796)	0.796	18.19	(0.796)	0.796	19.87	(0.796)	0.796	30.18	3.072	(1.536)	1.536	22.36	(1.536)	1.536	23.72	(1.536)	1.536	30.20
Jackup Rig or Spud Barge	7.69	0.398	(0.199)	0.199	4.55	(0.199)	0.199	4.97	(0.199)	0.199	7.55	0.768	(0.384)	0.384	5.59	(0.384)	0.384	5.93	(0.384)	0.384	7.55
Trawl/Fishing Net	30.77	1.591	(0.796)	0.796	18.19	(0.829)	0.763	19.05	(0.861)	0.731	27.71	3.072	(1.536)	1.536	22.36	(1.600)	1.472	22.74	(1.662)	1.410	27.3
OPERATION IMPACT	7.69	0.398	(0.111)	0.287	6.55	(0.111)	0.287	7.16	(0.111)	0.287	10.87	0.768	(0.215)	0.553	8.05	(0.215)	0.553	8.54	(0.215)	0.553	10.88
Rig Anchoring																					
Work Boat Anchoring	7.69	0.398	(0.111)	0.287	6.55	(0.111)	0.287	7.16	(0.111)	0.287	10.87	0.768	(0.215)	0.553	8.05	(0.215)	0.553	8.54	(0.215)	0.553	10.88
MECHANICAL																					
Connection Failure																					
Material Failure																					
NATURAL HAZARD	15.38	0.796	(0.406)	0.390	8.91	(0.398)	0.398	9.94	(0.390)	0.406	15.40	1.536	(0.784)	0.752	10.95	(0.768)	0.768	11.86	(0.752)	0.784	15.41
Mud Slide	7.69	0.398	(0.207)	0.191	4.36	(0.199)	0.199	4.97	(0.191)	0.207	7.86	0.768	(0.400)	0.368	5.36	(0.384)	0.384	5.93	(0.368)	0.400	7.86
Stormy Hurricane	7.69	0.398	(0.199)	0.199	4.55	(0.199)	0.199	4.97	(0.199)	0.199	7.55	0.768	(0.384)	0.384	5.59	(0.384)	0.384	5.93	(0.384)	0.384	7.55
ARCTIC			1.693	1.693	38.70	1.347	1.347	33.64	0.003	0.003	0.12		1.693	1.693	24.64	1.347	1.347	20.80	0.003	0.003	0.06
Ice Gouging			1.3438	1.3438	30.72	1.0750	1.0750	26.85					1.3438	1.3438	19.56	1.0750	1.0750	16.60			
Strudel Scour			0.0082	0.0082	0.19								0.0082	0.0016	0.12						
Upheaval Buckling			0.0016	0.0016	0.04	0.0016	0.0016	0.04	0.0016	0.0016	0.06		0.0016	0.0016	0.02	0.0016	0.0016	0.03	0.0016	0.0016	0.03
Thaw Settlement			0.0008	0.0008	0.02	0.0008	0.0008	0.02	0.0008	0.0008	0.03		0.0008	0.0008	0.01	0.0008	0.0008	0.01	0.0008	0.0008	0.02
Other			0.3386	0.3386	7.74	0.2694	0.2694	6.73	0.0006	0.0006	0.02		0.3386	0.3386	4.93	0.2694	0.2694	4.16	0.0006	0.0006	0.01
UNKNOWN																					
TOTALS	100.00	5.172	(0.797)	4.375	100.00	(1.168)	4.004	100.00	(2.536)	2.636	100.00	9.985	(3.114)	6.870	100.00	(3.508)	6.476	100.00	(4.898)	5.086	100.00

Table 4.9
Arctic Pipeline Huge Spill Frequencies

HUGE SPILLS =>10000 bbl

CAUSE CLASSIFICATION	HISTORICAL DISTRIBUTION %	Pipelines Diameter <10" FREQUENCY spills per 10⁴km-year	Shallow Freq Change	Shallow New Freq	Shallow New Dist %	Medium Freq Change	Medium New Freq	Medium New Dist %	Deep Freq Change	Deep New Freq	Deep New Dist %	Pipelines Diameter =10" FREQUENCY spills per 10⁴km-year	Shallow Freq Change	Shallow New Freq	Shallow New Dist %	Medium Freq Change	Medium New Freq	Medium New Dist %	Deep Freq Change	Deep New Freq	Deep New Dist %
CORROSION	7.69	0.099	(0.046)	0.054	4.70	(0.046)	0.054	5.17	(0.046)	0.054	8.16	0.256	(0.118)	0.138	6.30	(0.118)	0.138	6.64	(0.118)	0.138	8.17
External																					
Internal	7.69	0.099	(0.046)	0.054	4.70	(0.046)	0.054	5.17	(0.046)	0.054	8.16	0.256	(0.118)	0.138	6.30	(0.118)	0.138	6.64	(0.118)	0.138	8.17
THIRD PARTY IMPACT	69.23	0.895	(0.448)	0.448	39.11	(0.456)	0.439	42.19	(0.464)	0.431	65.43	2.304	(1.152)	1.152	52.37	(1.173)	1.131	54.19	(1.194)	1.110	65.48
Anchor Impact	30.77	0.338	(0.199)	0.199	17.38	(0.199)	0.199	19.10	(0.199)	0.199	30.18	1.024	(0.512)	0.512	23.28	(0.512)	0.512	24.54	(0.512)	0.512	30.20
Jackup Rig or Spud Barge	7.69	0.099	(0.050)	0.050	4.35	(0.050)	0.050	4.78	(0.050)	0.050	7.54	0.256	(0.128)	0.128	5.82	(0.128)	0.128	6.13	(0.128)	0.128	7.55
Trawl/Fishing Net	30.77	0.338	(0.199)	0.199	17.38	(0.207)	0.191	18.31	(0.215)	0.183	27.71	1.024	(0.512)	0.512	23.28	(0.533)	0.491	23.52	(0.554)	0.470	27.73
OPERATION IMPACT	7.69	0.099	(0.028)	0.072	6.26	(0.028)	0.072	6.88	(0.028)	0.072	10.87	0.256	(0.072)	0.184	8.39	(0.072)	0.184	8.84	(0.072)	0.184	10.88
Rig Anchoring																					
Work Boat Anchoring	7.69	0.099	(0.028)	0.072	6.26	(0.028)	0.072	6.88	(0.028)	0.072	10.87	0.256	(0.072)	0.184	8.39	(0.072)	0.184	8.84	(0.072)	0.184	10.88
MECHANICAL																					
Connection Failure																					
Material Failure																					
NATURAL HAZARD	15.38	0.199	(0.102)	0.097	8.51	(0.099)	0.099	9.55	(0.097)	0.102	15.40	0.512	(0.261)	0.251	11.40	(0.256)	0.256	12.27	(0.251)	0.261	15.41
Mud Slide	7.69	0.099	(0.052)	0.048	4.17	(0.050)	0.050	4.78	(0.048)	0.052	7.86	0.256	(0.133)	0.123	5.58	(0.128)	0.128	6.13	(0.128)	0.133	7.86
Stormy Hurricane	7.69	0.099	(0.050)	0.050	4.35	(0.050)	0.050	4.78	(0.050)	0.050	7.54	0.256	(0.128)	0.128	5.82	(0.128)	0.128	6.13	(0.128)	0.128	7.55
ARCTIC			0.474	0.474	41.42	0.377	0.377	36.21	0.001	0.001	0.13		0.474	0.474	21.55	0.377	0.377	18.07	0.001	0.001	0.05
Ice Gouging			0.3762	0.3762	32.87	0.3010	0.3010	28.90					0.3762	0.3762	17.10	0.3010	0.3010	14.42			
Strudel Scour			0.0023	0.0023	0.20								0.0023	0.0023	0.10						
Upheaval Buckling			0.0005	0.0005	0.04	0.0005	0.0005	0.04	0.0005	0.0005	0.07		0.0005	0.0005	0.02	0.0005	0.0005	0.02	0.0005	0.0005	0.03
Thaw Settlement			0.0002	0.0002	0.02	0.0002	0.0002	0.02	0.0002	0.0002	0.03		0.0002	0.0002	0.01	0.0002	0.0002	0.01	0.0002	0.0002	0.01
Other			0.0948	0.0948	8.28	0.0754	0.0754	7.24	0.0002	0.0002	0.03		0.0948	0.0948	4.31	0.0754	0.0754	3.61	0.0002	0.0002	0.01
UNKNOWN																					
TOTALS	100.00	1.293	(0.149)	1.144	100.00	(0.252)	1.041	100.00	(0.534)	0.659	100.00	3.328	(1.128)	2.200	100.00	(1.241)	2.087	100.00	(1.633)	1.695	100.00

Table 4.10
Arctic Pipeline Spill Frequencies Expected Value Summary

Pipeline Spill Size	Pipeline Diameter <10"				Pipeline Diameter =10"			
	Historical Frequency spills per 10^5km-year	Arctic Frequency			Historical Frequency spills per 10^5km-year	Arctic Frequency		
		Shallow	Medium	Deep		Shallow	Medium	Deep
SMALL SPILLS 50-99 bbl	5.172	3.671	3.587	3.243	3.328	2.519	2.433	2.087
MEDIUM SPILLS 100-999 bbl	9.051	6.432	6.283	5.676	8.320	5.975	5.826	5.218
LARGE SPILLS 1000-9999 bbl	5.172	4.375	4.004	2.636	9.985	6.870	6.476	5.086
HUGE SPILLS =10000 bbl	1.293	1.144	1.041	0.659	3.328	2.200	2.087	1.695

4.4   Platform Fault Tree Analysis

4.4.1   Platform First Order Arctic Effects

Table 4.11 summarizes the variations in the modified and unique Arctic effect inputs for platforms. As for pipeline unique effects, both the Triangular Distribution expected and modal values are given.

The first three modified cause classifications, the process facility release, storage tank release, and structural failure were reduced by 30 to 50% primarily as a result of the state-of-the-art engineering, construction, and operational standards and practices expected. As before, storms tend to be less severe in the Arctic, and certainly during the ice season would have limited impact on the facility. Due to the extremely low traffic density, as for the case of pipelines, the ship collision cause has been reduced by 50 percent.

Unique effects are also included. Increments in facility spills were attributed to ice force, low temperature effects, and unknown effects which were taken as a percentage of the other unique Arctic effects. Ice force effect calculations were based on the 1/10,000 year ice force causing spills, predominantly small and medium. Ice forces are also considered to increase as a contributor to oil spill occurrences with water depth, due to the increasing severity of ice loads as one moves towards the edge of the landfast ice zone with increasing water depth. Increase of low temperature effects with water depth was estimated as 10% of historical process facility spill rates.

4.4.2   Platform Second Order Arctic Effects

Changes in frequency distribution attributable to Arctic effects were calculated using the second order effect probability distribution, as was done for pipelines. Table 4.12 summarizes the principal distribution parameters for both the Arctic modified and Arctic unique effect distributions.

4.4.3   Arctic Platform Fault Tree Spill Frequency Calculations

Figure 4.5 shows the fault tree developed for Arctic platform spills for the different water depth zones for large and huge spill sizes, which were grouped together as described for platforms in Chapter 2. Again, the fault tree gives the historical value, together with the calculated values for shallow, medium, and deep water. In the case of this particular fault tree, there was room to represent both the small and medium or less than 1,000 bbl and the large and huge or greater than 1,000 bbl spills. Like pipelines, it is evident that platforms manifest a somewhat lower frequency for both spill size categories for the Arctic conditions. Tables 4.13 and 4.14 show the frequency calculations for platforms for small and medium and large and huge spill sizes, respectively. Table 4.15 summarizes the historical and derived Arctic expected values of platform spill frequencies.

Table 4.11
Platform First Order Arctic Effect Summary

CAUSE CLASSIFICATION	Spill Size	Historical Expected Frequency Change %			Reason
		Shallow	Medium	Deep	
PROCESS FACILITY RLS.	All	(30)	(30)	(30)	State of the art now, High QC, High Inspection and Maintenance Requirements
STORAGE TANK RLS.	All	(30)	(30)	(30)	State of the art now, High QC, High Inspection and Maintenance Requirements
STRUCTURAL FAILURE	All	(20)	(20)	(20)	High safety factor, Monitoring Programs
HURRICANE/STORM	All	(50)	(40)	(30)	Less severe storms. More intensity in deep water.
COLLISION	All	(50)	(50)	(50)	Very low traffic density.
		Freq. Increment per 10^4 well-year			
		Expected	Expected	Expected	
		Mode	Mode	Mode	
ARCTIC					
Ice Force	SM	0.1447	0.2170	0.3256	Assumed 10,000 year return period ice force causes spill 4% of occurrences (96% reliability). 85% of the spills are SM.
		0.0340	0.0510	0.0765	
	LH	0.0255	0.0383	0.0575	
		0.0060	0.0090	0.0135	
Facility Low Temperature	SM	0.1000	0.1000	0.1000	Assumed fraction of Historical Process Facilities release frequency with 6% SM and 3% for LH spill sizes.
		0.1000	0.1000	0.1000	
	LH	0.0080	0.0080	0.0080	
		0.0080	0.0080	0.0080	
Other	SM	0.0244	0.0316	0.0424	10% of sum of above.
		0.0134	0.0151	0.0177	
	LH	0.0033	0.0046	0.0065	
		0.0014	0.0017	0.0022	

Table 4.12

Platform First and Second Order Arctic Effects Distribution Summary

CAUSE CLASSIFICATION	Spill Size	Shallow			Medium			Deep		
		Min	Mode	Max	Min	Mode	Max	Min	Mode	Max
		Frequency Change %								
PROCESS FACILITY RLS.	All	(60)	(30)	(10)	(60)	(30)	(10)	(60)	(30)	(10)
STORAGE TANK RLS.	All	(60)	(30)	(10)	(60)	(30)	(10)	(60)	(30)	(10)
STRUCTURAL FAILURE	All	(60)	(20)	(10)	(60)	(20)	(10)	(60)	(20)	(10)
HURRICANE/STORM	All	(90)	(50)	(10)	(90)	(40)	(10)	(90)	(30)	(10)
COLLISION	All	(90)	(50)	(10)	(90)	(50)	(10)	(90)	(50)	(10)
		Frequency Increment per 10^4 well-year								
ARCTIC										
Ice Force	SM	0.003	0.034	0.340	0.005	0.051	0.510	0.008	0.077	0.765
	LH	0.001	0.006	0.060	0.001	0.009	0.090	0.001	0.014	0.135
Facility Low Temperature	SM	0.050	0.100	0.150	0.050	0.100	0.150	0.050	0.100	0.150
	LH	0.004	0.008	0.012	0.004	0.008	0.012	0.004	0.008	0.012
Other	SM	0.005	0.013	0.049	0.006	0.015	0.066	0.006	0.018	0.092
	LH	0.000	0.001	0.007	0.000	0.002	0.010	0.001	0.002	0.015

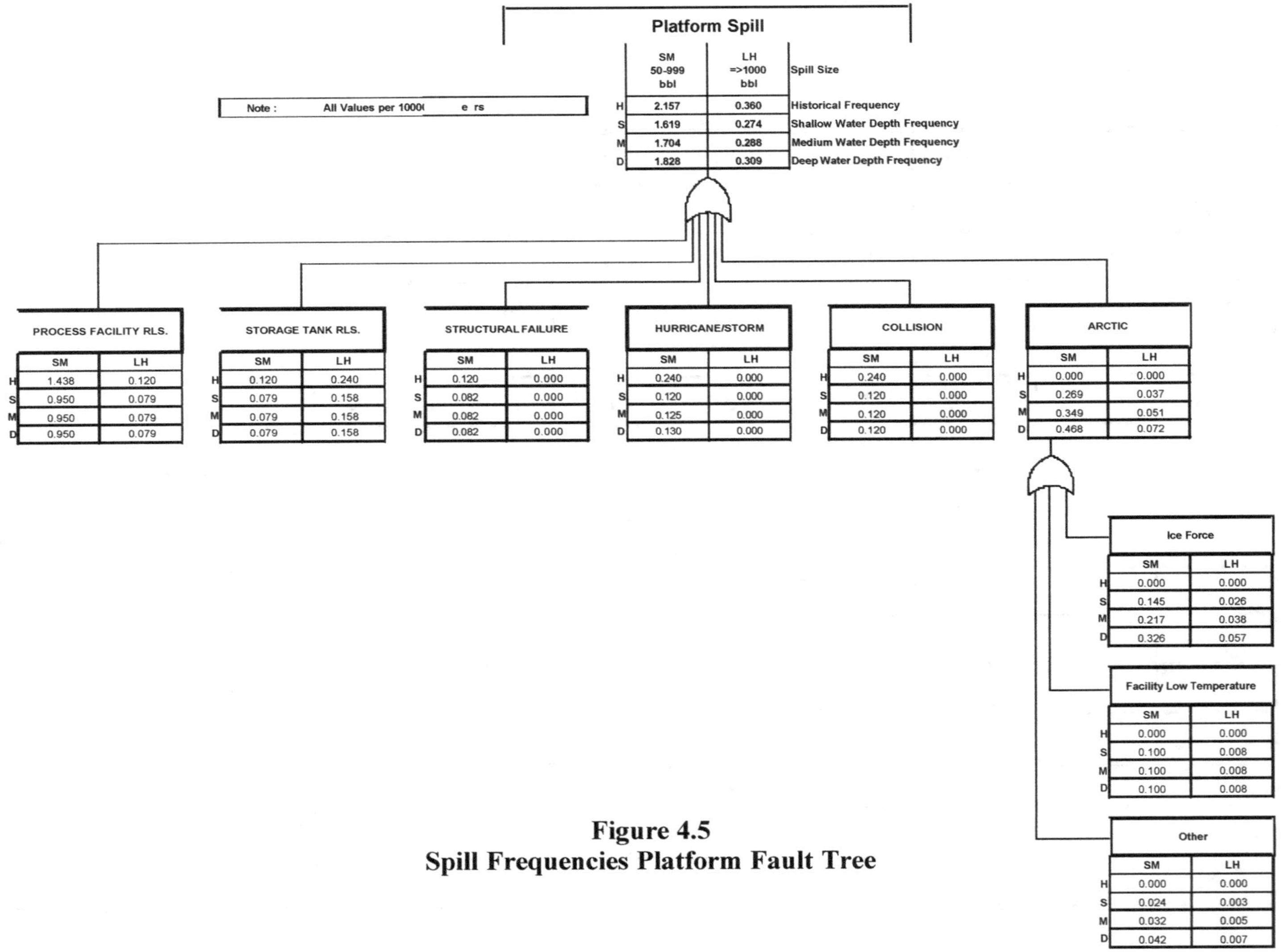

Platform Spill

	SM 50-999 bbl	LH =>1000 bbl	Spill Size
H	2.157	0.360	Historical Frequency
S	1.619	0.274	Shallow Water Depth Frequency
M	1.704	0.288	Medium Water Depth Frequency
D	1.826	0.309	Deep Water Depth Frequency

Note: All Values per 1000   e rs

PROCESS FACILITY RLS.

	SM	LH
H	1.438	0.120
S	0.950	0.079
M	0.950	0.079
D	0.950	0.079

STORAGE TANK RLS.

	SM	LH
H	0.120	0.240
S	0.079	0.158
M	0.079	0.158
D	0.079	0.158

STRUCTURAL FAILURE

	SM	LH
H	0.120	0.000
S	0.082	0.000
M	0.082	0.000
D	0.082	0.000

HURRICANE/STORM

	SM	LH
H	0.240	0.000
S	0.120	0.000
M	0.125	0.000
D	0.130	0.000

COLLISION

	SM	LH
H	0.240	0.000
S	0.120	0.000
M	0.120	0.000
D	0.120	0.000

ARCTIC

	SM	LH
H	0.000	0.000
S	0.269	0.037
M	0.349	0.051
D	0.468	0.072

Ice Force

	SM	LH
H	0.000	0.000
S	0.145	0.026
M	0.217	0.038
D	0.326	0.057

Facility Low Temperature

	SM	LH
H	0.000	0.000
S	0.100	0.008
M	0.100	0.008
D	0.100	0.008

Other

	SM	LH
H	0.000	0.000
S	0.024	0.003
M	0.032	0.005
D	0.042	0.007

Figure 4.5
Spill Frequencies Platform Fault Tree

Table 4.13
Platform Small and Medium Spill Frequencies

CAUSE CLASSIFICATION	HISTORICAL DISTRIBUTION %	FREQUENCY spills per 10⁴ well-year	SMALL AND MEDIUM SPILLS 50-999 bbl								
			Shallow			Medium			Deep		
			Frequency Change	New Frequency	% New Distribution	Frequency Change	New Frequency	% New Distribution	Frequency Change	New Frequency	% New Distribution
PROCESS FACILITY RLS.	66.67	1.438	(0.488)	0.950	58.65	(0.488)	0.950	55.74	(0.488)	0.950	51.96
STORAGE TANK RLS.	5.56	0.120	(0.041)	0.079	4.89	(0.041)	0.079	4.65	(0.041)	0.079	4.33
STRUCTURAL FAILURE	5.56	0.120	(0.038)	0.082	5.04	(0.038)	0.082	4.79	(0.038)	0.082	4.46
HURRICANE/STORM	11.11	0.240	(0.120)	0.120	7.40	(0.115)	0.125	7.33	(0.110)	0.130	7.09
COLLISION	11.11	0.240	(0.120)	0.120	7.40	(0.120)	0.120	7.03	(0.120)	0.120	6.56
ARCTIC			0.269	0.269	16.62	0.349	0.349	20.46	0.468	0.468	25.60
Ice Force			0.145	0.145	8.94	0.217	0.217	12.74	0.326	0.326	17.81
Facility Low Temperature			0.100	0.100	6.18	0.100	0.100	5.87	0.100	0.100	5.47
Other			0.024	0.024	1.51	0.032	0.032	1.86	0.042	0.042	2.32
TOTALS	100.00	2.157	(0.538)	1.619	100.00	(0.453)	1.704	100.00	(0.329)	1.828	100.00

Table 4.14
Platform Large and Huge Spill Frequencies

CAUSE CLASSIFICATION	HISTORICAL DISTRIBUTION %	FREQUENCY spills per 10^4 well-year	LARGE AND HUGE SPILLS =1000 bbl								
			Shallow			Medium			Deep		
			Frequency Change	New Frequency	New Distribution %	Frequency Change	New Frequency	New Distribution %	Frequency Change	New Frequency	New Distribution %
PROCESS FACILITY RLS.	33.33	0.120	(0.041)	0.079	28.85	(0.041)	0.079	27.45	(0.041)	0.079	25.58
STORAGE TANK RLS.	66.67	0.240	(0.081)	0.158	57.70	(0.081)	0.158	54.89	(0.081)	0.158	51.16
STRUCTURAL FAILURE											
HURRICANE/STORM											
COLLISION											
ARCTIC			0.037	0.037	13.44	0.051	0.051	17.66	0.072	0.072	23.27
Ice Force			0.026	0.026	9.31	0.038	0.038	13.28	0.057	0.057	18.57
Facility Low Temperature			0.008	0.008	2.92	0.008	0.008	2.77	0.008	0.008	2.59
Other			0.003	0.003	1.22	0.005	0.005	1.60	0.007	0.007	2.11
TOTALS	100.00	0.360	(0.085)	0.274	100.00	(0.071)	0.288	100.00	(0.050)	0.309	100.00

Table 4.15
Arctic Platforms Spill Frequency Expected Value Summary

Platform Spill Size	Historical Frequency spills per 10^4 well-year	Arctic Frequency		
		Shallow	Medium	Deep
SMALL AND MEDIUM SPILLS 50-999 bbl	2.157	1.619	1.703	1.828
LARGE AND HUGE SPILLS =1000 bbl	.359	.274	.288	.309

4.5　Blowout Frequency Analysis

4.5.1　Well Blowout First Order Arctic Effects

The historical data, as described in Chapter 2, was modified for each well type, spill size, and water depth range, as described in Table 4.16. No Arctic unique effects or second order effects were introduced for well blowouts.

4.5.2　Arctic Well Blowout Spill Frequency Calculation

Table 4.17 gives the details of the frequency calculation for well blowouts. No fault tree was required here, as only base events with no causal distributions were modeled for each case. The modifications given in Table 4.16 were applied to all three values (minimum, mode, maximum) to yield the values summarized in Table 4.17.

4.6　Spill Volume Distributions

Table 4.18 summarizes the spill volume distribution parameters for each facility type, including the expected value that was calculated utilizing a Monte Carlo calculation. The spill volume parameters were derived from the historical data as described in Section 2.7.

Table 4.16
Well Fault Tree Analysis Arctic Effect Summary

EVENT	FREQUENCY UNIT	Historical Expected Frequency Change %			Reason
		Shallow	Medium	Deep	
		Small and Medium Spills 50-999 bbl			
PRODUCTION WELL	spill per 10⁴ well-year	(30)	(30)	(30)	State of the art now, High QC, High Inspection and Maintenance Requirements
EXPLORATION WELL DRILLING	spill per 10⁴ wells	(30)	(20)	(10)	Highly qualified drilling contractor. Better logistics support in shallow water.
DEVELOPMENT WELL DRILLING	spill per 10⁴ wells	(30)	(20)	(10)	Highly qualified drilling contractor. Better logistics support in shallow water.
		Large Spills 1000-9999 bbl			
PRODUCTION WELL	spill per 10⁴ well-year	(30)	(30)	(30)	State of the art now, High QC, High Inspection and Maintenance Requirements
EXPLORATION WELL DRILLING	spill per 10⁴ wells	(30)	(20)	(10)	Highly qualified drilling contractor. Better logistics support in shallow water.
DEVELOPMENT WELL DRILLING	spill per 10⁴ wells	(30)	(20)	(10)	Highly qualified drilling contractor. Better logistics support in shallow water.
		Spill 10000-149999 bbl			
PRODUCTION WELL	spill per 10⁴ well-year	(30)	(30)	(30)	State of the art now, High QC, High Inspection and Maintenance Requirements
EXPLORATION WELL DRILLING	spill per 10⁴ wells	(30)	(20)	(10)	Highly qualified drilling contractor. Better logistics support in shallow water.
DEVELOPMENT WELL DRILLING	spill per 10⁴ wells	(30)	(20)	(10)	Highly qualified drilling contractor. Better logistics support in shallow water.
		Spill =150000 bbl			
PRODUCTION WELL	spill per 10⁴ well-year	(30)	(30)	(30)	State of the art now, High QC, High Inspection and Maintenance Requirements
EXPLORATION WELL DRILLING	spill per 10⁴ wells	(30)	(20)	(10)	Highly qualified drilling contractor. Better logistics support in shallow water.
DEVELOPMENT WELL DRILLING	spill per 10⁴ wells	(30)	(20)	(10)	Highly qualified drilling contractor. Better logistics support in shallow water.

Table 4.17
Arctic Well Blowout Frequencies

EVENT	FREQUENCY UNIT	HISTORICAL FREQUENCY	Shallow		Medium		Deep	
			Frequency Change	New Frequency	Frequency Change	New Frequency	Frequency Change	New Frequency
Small and Medium Spills 50-999 bbl								
PRODUCTION WELL	spill per 10^4 well-year	0.147	-0.044	0.103	-0.044	0.103	-0.044	0.103
EXPLORATION WELL DRILLING	spill per 10^4 wells	2.262	-0.678	1.583	-0.452	1.809	-0.226	2.035
DEVELOPMENT WELL DRILLING	spill per 10^4 wells	0.692	-0.208	0.484	-0.138	0.554	-0.069	0.623
Large Spills 1000-9999 bbl								
PRODUCTION WELL	spill per 10^4 well-year	1.026	-0.308	0.718	-0.308	0.718	-0.308	0.718
EXPLORATION WELL DRILLING	spill per 10^4 wells	15.824	-4.747	11.077	-3.165	12.659	-1.582	14.242
DEVELOPMENT WELL DRILLING	spill per 10^4 wells	4.833	-1.450	3.383	-0.967	3.867	-0.483	4.350
Spills 10000-149999 bbl								
PRODUCTION WELL	spill per 10^4 well-year	0.440	-0.132	0.308	-0.132	0.308	-0.132	0.308
EXPLORATION WELL DRILLING	spill per 10^4 wells	6.799	-2.040	4.759	-1.360	5.439	-0.680	6.119
DEVELOPMENT WELL DRILLING	spill per 10^4 wells	2.076	-0.623	1.453	-0.415	1.661	-0.208	1.868
Spills =150000 bbl								
PRODUCTION WELL	spill per 10^4 well-year	0.293	-0.088	0.205	-0.088	0.205	-0.088	0.205
EXPLORATION WELL DRILLING	spill per 10^4 wells	3.936	-1.181	2.755	-0.787	3.149	-0.394	3.543
DEVELOPMENT WELL DRILLING	spill per 10^4 wells	2.076	-0.623	1.453	-0.415	1.661	-0.208	1.868

Table 4.18
Summary of Spill Size Distribution Parameters

PIPELINE SPILL VOLUMES

Spill Size	Small Spills 50-999 bbl				Medium Spills 100-999 bbl				Large Spills 1000-9999 bbl				Huge Spills ≥10000 bbl			
Spill Expectation	Low	Mode	High	Expected	Low	Mode	High	Expected	Low	Mode	High	Expected	Low	Mode	High	Expected
Pipelines Diameter 10" Spill	50	58	99	71	100	226	999	485	1000	4436	9999	5279	10000	14423	20000	14880
Pipelines Diameter 10" Spill	50	58	99	71	100	387	999	516	1000	3932	9999	5176	10000	17705	20000	15552

PLATFORM SPILL VOLUMES

Spill Size	Small and Medium Spills 50-999 bbl				Large and Huge Spills ≥1000 bbl			
Spill Expectation	Low	Mode	High	Expected	Low	Mode	High	Expected
Platform Spill	50	158	999	452	1000	6130	10000	5631

WELL SPILL VOLUMES

Spill Size	Small and Medium Spills 50-999 bbl				Large Spills 1000-9999 bbl				Spills 10000-149999 bbl				Spills ≥150000 bbl			
Spill Expectation	Low	Mode	High	Expected	Low	Mode	High	Expected	Low	Mode	High	Expected	Low	Mode	High	Expected
Well Spill	50	500	999	519	1000	4500	9999	5292	10000	20000	150000	68349	150000	200000	250000	200000

BERCHA GROUP

MMS

CHAPTER 5

OIL SPILL OCCURRENCE INDICATOR QUANTIFICATION

5.1   Definition of Oil Spill Occurrence Indicators

Three primary oil spill occurrence indicators (generally referred to as "spill indicators" after this) were quantified in this study. These are as follows:

- Frequency in spills per year.
- Frequency in spills per barrel produced in each year.
- Spill index, the product of spill frequency and associated average spill size.
- Life of field indicator.

The spill indicators defined above are subdivided as follows for this study:

- By scenario (five scenarios).
- By water depth (three ranges).
- By facility type (six types).
- By spill size (four sizes).
- By year (average of 35 years).

There are a total of five scenarios that are four Arctic scenarios – Sales 1, 2, and 3, and their composite (Sale All) – and the fifth scenario, the non-Arctic version of Sale All. The five scenarios are shown in Figure 5.1.

The above combinations translate into 360 sets of spill indicators, for a total of 1,080 individual indicators. Given that these are calculated for each year, this gives 43,740 indicators. In this chapter, we will try to summarize only the salient results of the indicators; the appendices give the full calculation printouts for the Monte Carlo results used in this report.

5.2   Oil Spill Occurrence Indicator Calculation Process

The oil spill occurrence indicator calculation process is shown in the flow chart originally given in Figure 1.2, and again presented as Figure 5.1. This chapter deals with the spill occurrence indicator calculations as shown in the shaded rectangle in Figure 5.1. Previous chapters covered the balance of the items in that figure.

Essentially, this chapter addresses the combining of the development scenarios described in Chapter 3 with the unit-spill frequency distributions presented in Chapter 4 to provide measures of oil spill occurrence, the oil spill indicators. Although the calculation is complex because of the many combinations considered (approximately 5,000), in principle, it is a simple process of accounting. Essentially, the quantities of potential oil spill sources are multiplied by their appropriate unit oil spill frequency to give the total expected spill distributions. To develop the probability distributions by the Monte Carlo process, each of the 5,000 combinations needs to be sampled, in this case a sampling of 5,000 iterations was carried out for each combination studied. This translates into roughly 25 million arithmetic operations to generate the Monte Carlo results.

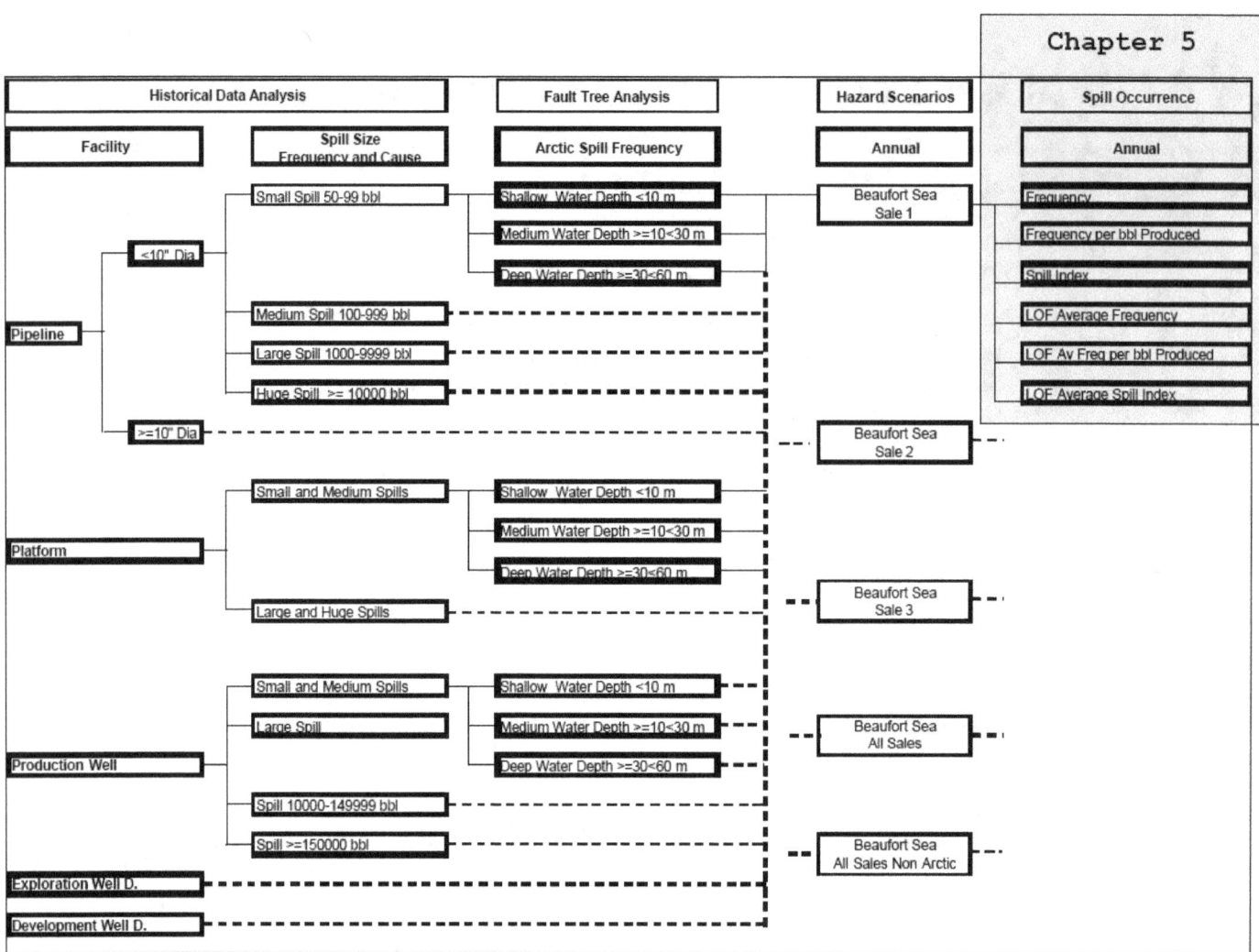

Figure 5.1
Calculation Flow Chart

5.3   Summary of Beaufort Sea Oil Spill Occurrence Indicators

5.3.1   Sale 1 Oil Spill Occurrence Indicators

Each of the principal oil spill occurrence indicators calculated for the pipelines, platforms, and wells under Sale 1 for each year is given in Figures 5.2, 5.3, and 5.4.

As can be seen, each of these figures spans the development scenario to year 2033 as described in Appendix 3. Further, each of the indicators has been subdivided into three segments for each year, those corresponding to spills < 1,000 bbl (small and medium), spills = 1,000 < 10,000 bbl (large), and spills =10,000 bbl (huge). It should be noted that the spill frequency associated with each spill size is only the increment shown in each of the bars. Thus, for example, for the year 2020, small and medium spills are approximately 18.0 per thousand years. Next, in that year, large spills are approximately 6.0 per thousand years, as shown in the second bar increment (i.e., 24.0 – 18.0 = 6.0). Finally, the top increment corresponds to huge spills, and is approximately 4.0 per thousand years. The same form of presentation applies for spills per barrel produced and for the spill index shown in Figures 5.3 and 5.4. Clearly, the spill index is dominated by the huge spills, which have an average spill size of 15,000 bbl. The spills per barrel produced continue to rise to the peak production year of 2016, because the facility quantities (and hence spill rate) remain relatively high, while production volumes decrease significantly each year. The reader should note that following this detailed presentation of the spill indicators in separate figures, all three spill indicators will be given in one figure in order to conserve space and make the report a little more concise.

Spill indicators by facility type were also quantified. All three spill indicators for pipelines for Sale 1 are shown in Figure 5.5. Figure 5.6 shows the spill indicators for platforms and Figure 5.7 shows the spill indicators for drilling of wells and producing wells. The graph ordinate axes have intentionally been kept the same to facilitate comparison. Numerous conclusions can be drawn from the comparison of these spill indicators. For example, it can be seen that the major contributors to spill frequency are platforms. The largest of the facility spill expectations, as represented by spill index, are the wells, simply because they have the potential to release the largest amounts of oil in blowouts.

Finally, as part of the assessment of each lease sale or development scenario, a Monte Carlo analysis was carried out for each year, with the distributed inputs described earlier. For Lease Sale 1, tabular results of the Monte Carlo simulation of 5,000 iterations, is summarized in Table 5.1. This table gives the statistical characteristics of the calculated indicators for each of three spill size ranges, as well as a tabular summary of their cumulative distribution curves for a representative production year (2016). Figure 5.8 shows graphs of the calculated cumulative distribution functions. Basically, the vertical axis gives the probability in percent that the corresponding value on the horizontal axis will not be exceeded. Thus, for example, referring to the central graph, for significant spills = 1,000 bbl (large and huge), there is a 40% probability that a spill frequency will be no more than 0.28 per billion barrels produced.

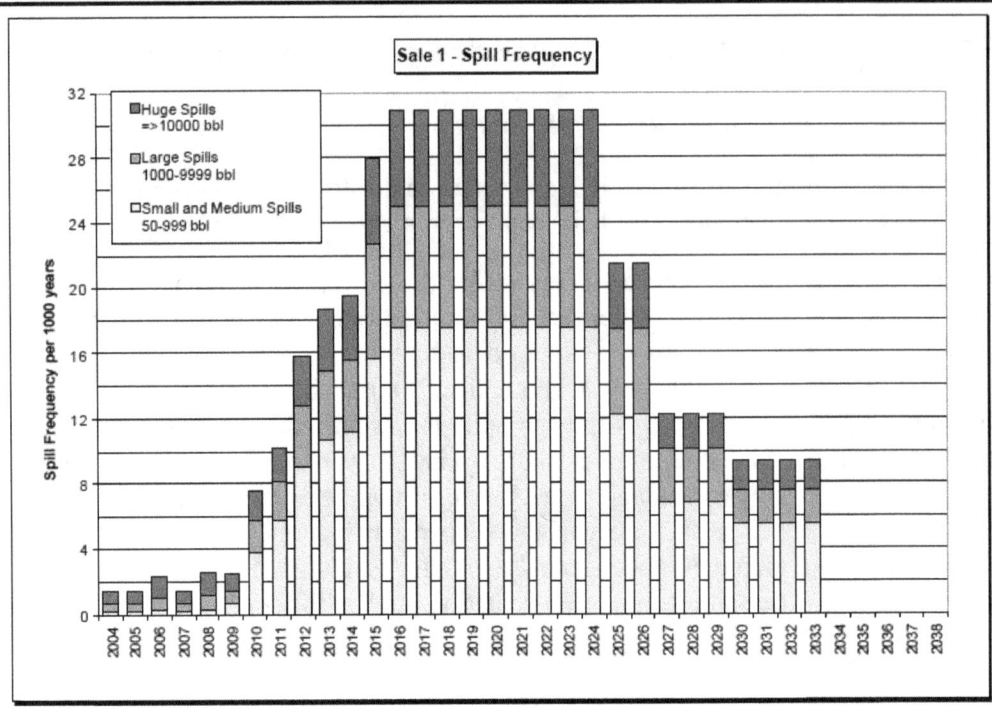

Figure 5.2
Sale 1 Spill Frequency per 1,000 Years

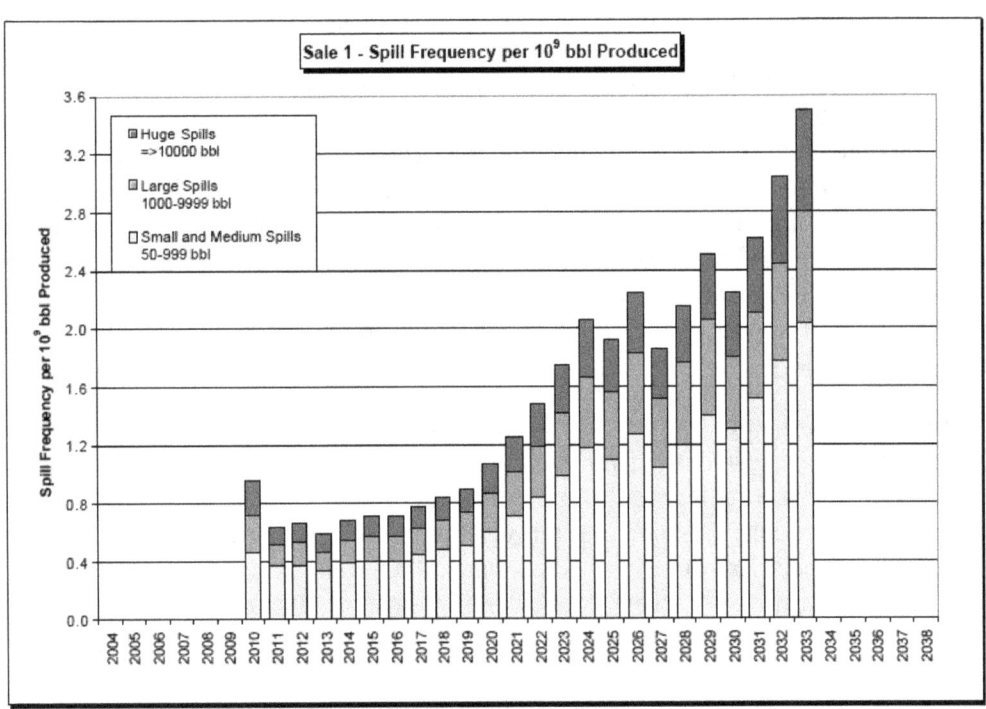

Figure 5.3
Sale 1 Spill Frequency per 10⁹ Barrels Produced

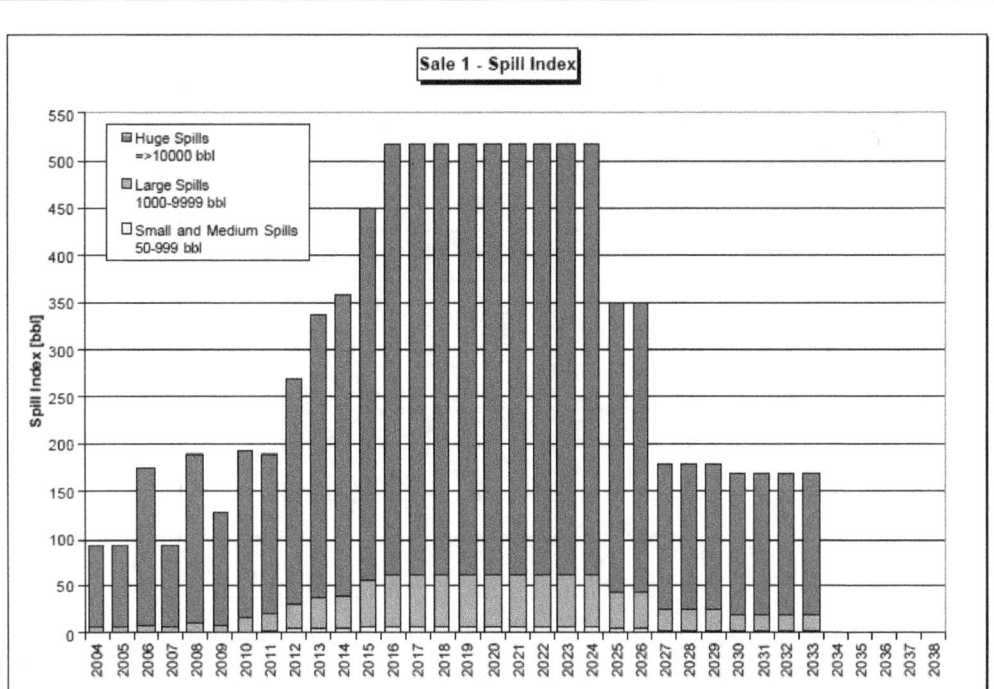

Figure 5.4
Sale 1 Spill Index

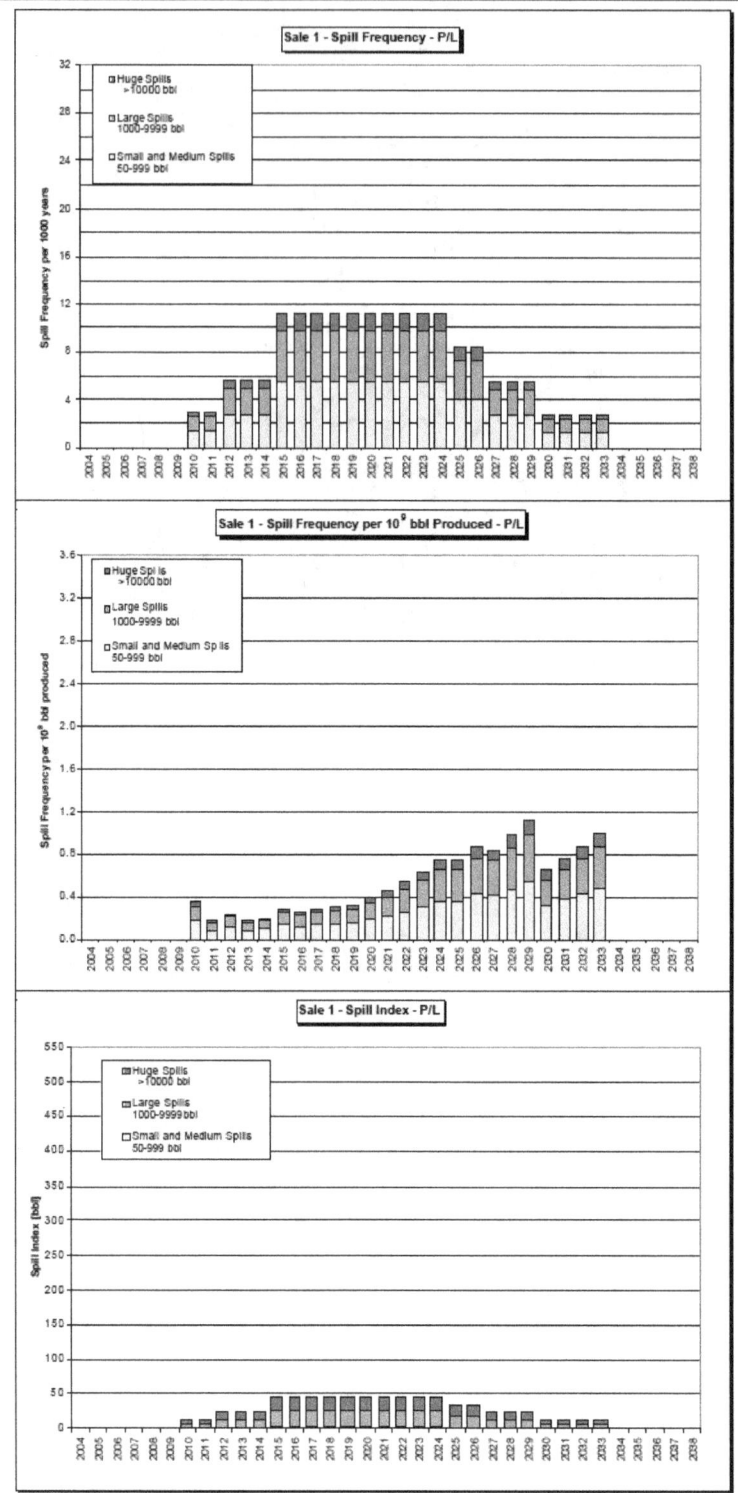

Figure 5.5
Sale 1 Indicators – Pipeline – Spill Frequency per 1,000 Years

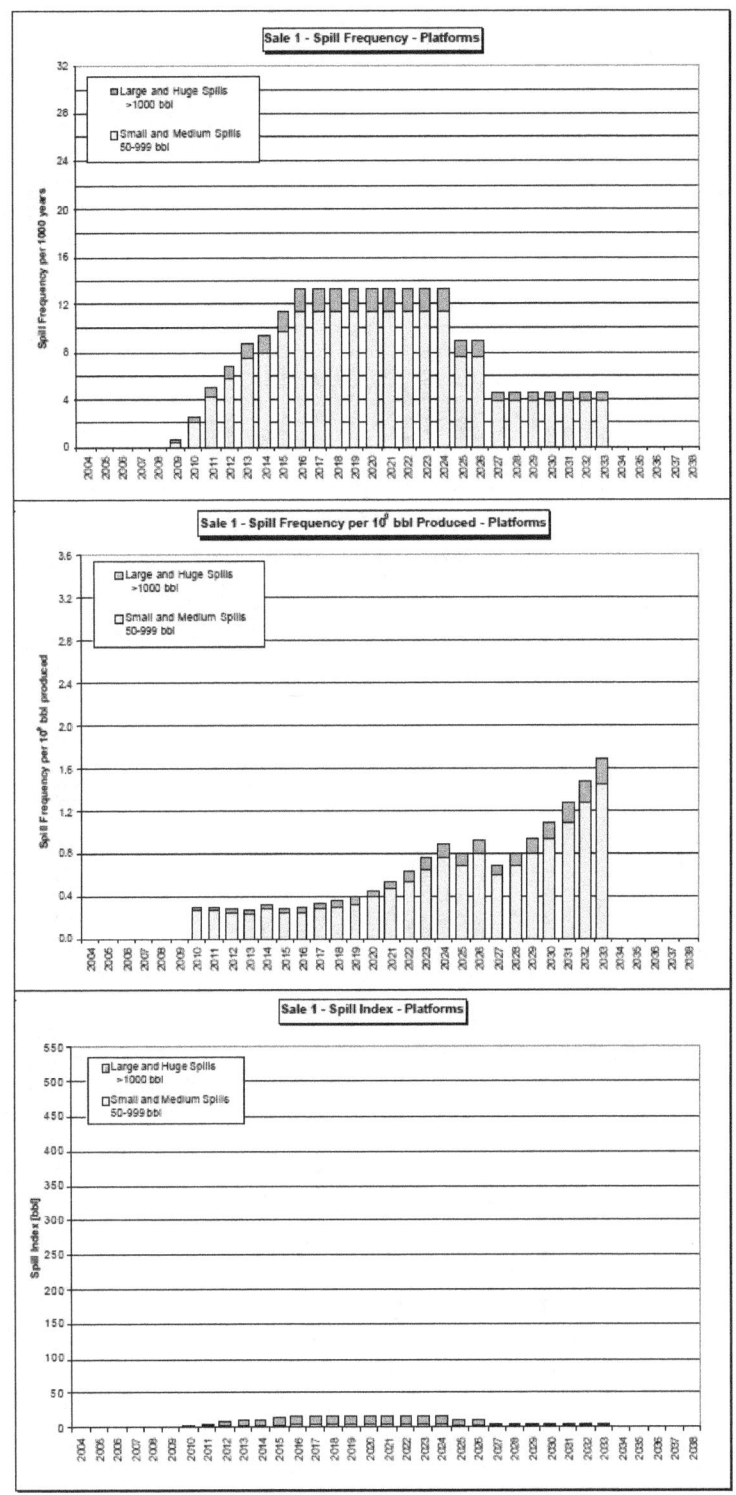

Figure 5.6
Sale 1 Indicators – Platforms – Spill Frequency per 1,000 Years

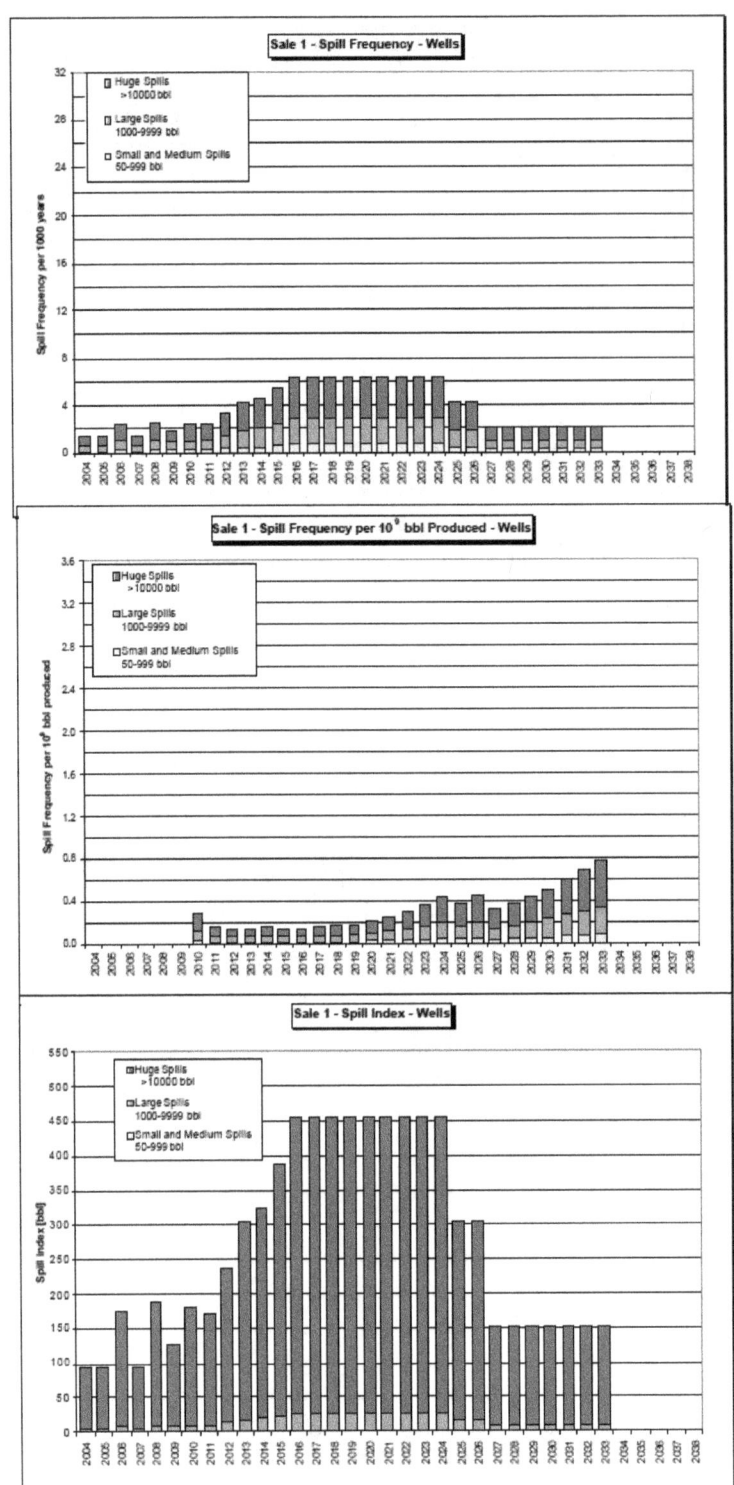

Figure 5.7
Sale 1 Indicators – Wells – Spill Frequency per 1,000 Years

Table 5.1
Sale 1 Year 2016 – Monte Carlo Results

Frequency — Spills per 10 years

SALE 1 Year 2016	Small and Medium Spills 50-999 bbl	Large Spills 1000-9999 bbl	Huge Spills =10000 bbl	Significant Spills =1000 bbl	All Spills
Mean =	17.50	7.45	5.90	13.35	30.85
Std Deviation =	6.85	2.38	1.38	3.12	7.58
Variance =	46.991	5.654	1.903	9.706	57.430
Skewness =	0.57	0.49	0.18	0.25	0.45
Kurtosis =	2.81	2.93	2.83	2.90	2.82
Mode =	14.87	6.40	6.33	11.98	33.42
Minimum =	3.665	1.394	2.076	4.074	12.206
5% Perc =	8.076	3.992	3.705	8.488	19.551
10% Perc =	9.265	4.598	4.127	9.457	21.641
15% Perc =	10.270	5.022	4.439	10.087	22.946
20% Perc =	11.235	5.354	4.707	10.666	24.124
25% Perc =	12.128	5.670	4.941	11.157	25.226
30% Perc =	12.989	5.971	5.116	11.576	26.248
35% Perc =	13.921	6.282	5.311	11.995	27.182
40% Perc =	14.716	6.555	5.506	12.425	28.082
45% Perc =	15.575	6.863	5.681	12.802	28.931
50% Perc =	16.524	7.166	5.858	13.237	29.860
55% Perc =	17.509	7.483	6.045	13.634	31.058
60% Perc =	18.530	7.825	6.241	13.987	32.172
65% Perc =	19.589	8.174	6.404	14.414	33.330
70% Perc =	20.739	8.559	6.598	14.840	34.578
75% Perc =	22.154	9.023	6.828	15.352	35.978
80% Perc =	23.441	9.480	7.073	15.948	37.394
85% Perc =	24.998	10.051	7.342	16.611	39.225
90% Perc =	27.201	10.754	7.710	17.483	41.113
95% Perc =	30.205	11.653	8.247	18.771	44.481
Maximum =	45.353	17.402	10.734	24.254	58.144

Frequency — Spills per 10^9 bbl Produced

	Small and Medium Spills 50-999 bbl	Large Spills 1000-9999 bbl	Huge Spills =10000 bbl	Significant Spills =1000 bbl	All Spills
Mean =	0.40	0.17	0.13	0.30	0.70
Std Deviation =	0.16	0.05	0.03	0.07	0.17
Variance =	0.024	0.003	0.001	0.005	0.030
Skewness =	0.57	0.49	0.18	0.25	0.45
Kurtosis =	2.81	2.93	2.83	2.90	2.82
Mode =	0.61	0.15	0.16	0.27	0.76
Minimum =	0.084	0.032	0.047	0.093	0.279
5% Perc =	0.184	0.091	0.085	0.194	0.446
10% Perc =	0.212	0.105	0.094	0.216	0.494
15% Perc =	0.234	0.115	0.101	0.230	0.524
20% Perc =	0.257	0.122	0.107	0.244	0.551
25% Perc =	0.277	0.129	0.113	0.255	0.576
30% Perc =	0.297	0.136	0.117	0.264	0.599
35% Perc =	0.318	0.143	0.121	0.274	0.621
40% Perc =	0.336	0.150	0.126	0.284	0.641
45% Perc =	0.356	0.157	0.130	0.292	0.661
50% Perc =	0.377	0.164	0.134	0.302	0.682
55% Perc =	0.400	0.171	0.138	0.311	0.709
60% Perc =	0.423	0.179	0.142	0.319	0.735
65% Perc =	0.447	0.187	0.146	0.329	0.761
70% Perc =	0.473	0.195	0.151	0.339	0.789
75% Perc =	0.506	0.206	0.156	0.350	0.821
80% Perc =	0.535	0.216	0.161	0.364	0.854
85% Perc =	0.571	0.229	0.168	0.379	0.896
90% Perc =	0.621	0.246	0.176	0.399	0.939
95% Perc =	0.690	0.266	0.188	0.429	1.016
Maximum =	1.035	0.397	0.245	0.554	1.327

Spill Index [bbl]

	Small and Medium Spills 50-999 bbl	Large Spills 1000-9999 bbl	Huge Spills =10000 bbl	Significant Spills =1000 bbl	All Spills
Mean =	7.58	54.14	453.92	508.06	515.64
Std Deviation =	5.09	25.33	166.83	168.75	168.83
Variance =	25.875	641.728	27830.730	28477.370	28504.210
Skewness =	1.51	0.75	0.47	0.47	0.47
Kurtosis =	5.90	3.49	3.15	3.18	3.17
Mode =	3.99	38.10	336.73	403.87	238.43
Minimum =	0.048	-5.653	57.627	89.063	100.160
5% Perc =	1.930	19.473	203.555	254.737	261.714
10% Perc =	2.578	24.401	247.551	300.820	308.648
15% Perc =	3.060	28.576	280.502	332.078	339.452
20% Perc =	3.527	31.871	309.260	359.667	367.135
25% Perc =	3.959	35.321	334.223	386.799	393.868
30% Perc =	4.390	38.345	355.170	410.086	418.341
35% Perc =	4.842	41.377	378.285	431.522	439.141
40% Perc =	5.303	44.483	400.053	452.817	460.282
45% Perc =	5.786	47.460	420.241	475.868	483.356
50% Perc =	6.233	50.572	440.511	495.134	503.779
55% Perc =	6.822	53.834	460.705	516.303	524.229
60% Perc =	7.465	57.228	482.578	537.060	545.385
65% Perc =	8.144	60.767	505.826	561.518	566.816
70% Perc =	8.864	65.029	532.804	587.964	596.134
75% Perc =	9.854	69.273	559.280	615.176	621.757
80% Perc =	10.915	74.410	591.103	646.552	653.645
85% Perc =	12.365	80.256	628.854	685.742	693.119
90% Perc =	14.407	88.387	676.355	732.058	740.066
95% Perc =	17.787	102.136	746.994	804.537	811.342
Maximum =	34.668	159.414	1141.096	1187.318	1190.433

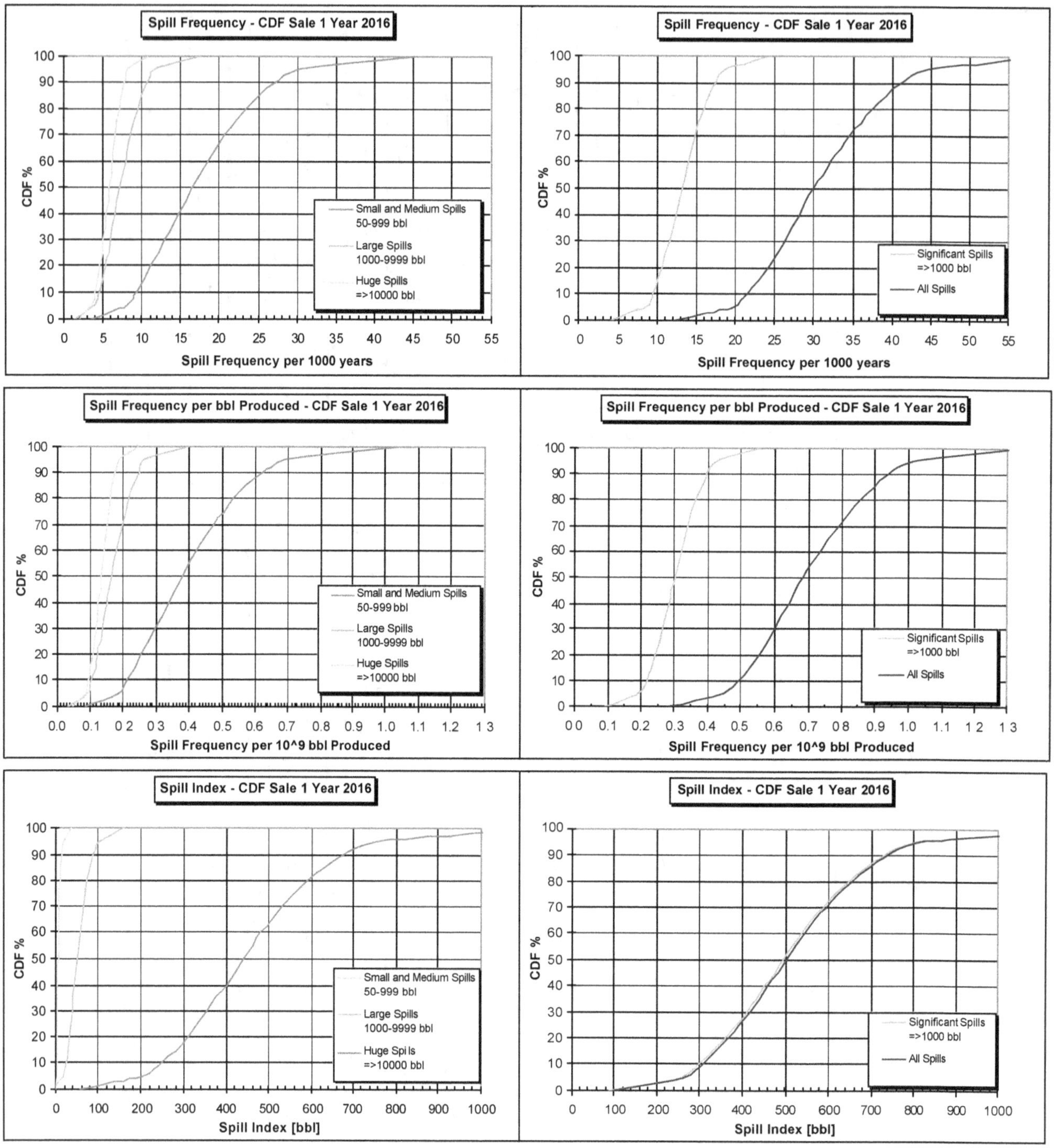

Figure 5.8
Sale 1 Spill Indicator Distributions – Year 2016 – Spill Frequency per 1,000 Years

In other words, there is a 40% chance that large and huge spills will occur at a rate of 0.28 per billion or less. Conversely, there is a 60% chance that the small and medium spill rate will be greater than 0.28 per billion.

The frequency spill indicator variability can be estimated from the upper (95%) and lower (5%) bound values. For example, for large spill frequency (from Table 5.1), the lower bound (3.992) is 55% of the mean (7.166); the upper bound (11.653), 160% of the mean.

In addition, since the Life of Field (LOF) averages were calculated, results from these are available for each scenario. Only selected ones are given in the text, with the balance given in the appendix. Table 5.2 shows the composition of the spill indicators for the Sale 1 Life of Field average. The composition both by spill size (on the left hand side of the table) and by facility contribution (on the right hand side of the table). The variability of the spill frequencies Life of Field averages is shown in the following figures: Figure 5.9 illustrates the variability of the spill frequency, while Figure 5.10 shows variabiltiy of frequency per billion barrels produced.

5.3.2   Sale 2 Oil Spill Occurrence Indicators

Figure 5.11 summarizes the three oil spill occurrence indicators for Sale 2. The primary difference is one of scheduling with some differences in magnitude of the indicators, although they are not substantially different from those of Sale 1.

5.3.3   Sale 3 Oil Spill Occurrence Indicators

Figure 5.12 summarizes all three of the Sale 3 oil spill occurrence indicators. Again, these are not substantially different from the Sale 1 and 2 indicators.

5.3.4   Sale All Oil Spill Occurrence Indicators

The oil spill occurrence indicators for the composite or total of all three Beaufort Sea Sale development scenarios are summarized in Figure 5.13. As one would expect, the absolute values of spill frequencies are significantly higher than any of the sales, essentially because they are the sum, through the Monte Carlo iteration process, of the three sales spill frequencies. Spills per barrel produced tend to be the same as those of the individual sales. Finally, the spill index, which is the product of the frequency and average spill size, as one would expect, is significantly higher for the composite scenario, roughly three times the average value for the three sales. Naturally, the spill by facility breakdowns, the Monte Carlo results, and all the details of the calculations for the composite scenario as well as each individual sale scenario are given in Appendix 3.

Table 5.2
Composition of Spill Indicators – Sale 1 – Life of Field Average

Spill Source

Sale 1 - Life of Field Average Spill Frequency per 10^3 years

Spill Size	Pipelines		Platforms		Wells		Platforms and Wells		All	
Small and Medium Spills 50-999 bbl	2.892	49%	6.090	86%	0.422	11%	6.512	60%	9.404	56%
Large Spills 1000-9999 bbl	2.318	39%	0.516	7%	1.265	33%	1.781	16%	4.099	24%
Huge Spills =>10000 bbl	0.744	12%	0.516	7%	2.110	56%	2.626	24%	3.369	20%
Significant Spills =>1000 bbl	3.062	51%	1.031	14%	3.375	89%	4.406	40%	7.468	44%
All Spills	5.953	100%	7.122	100%	3.797	100%	10.918	100%	16.872	100%

Sale 1 - Life of Field Average Spill Frequency per 10^9 bbl produced

Spill Size	Pipelines		Platforms		Wells		Platforms and Wells		All	
Small and Medium Spills 50-999 bbl	0.188	49%	0.397	86%	0.027	11%	0.424	60%	0.612	56%
Large Spills 1000-9999 bbl	0.151	39%	0.034	7%	0.082	33%	0.116	16%	0.267	24%
Huge Spills =>10000 bbl	0.048	12%	0.034	7%	0.137	56%	0.171	24%	0.219	20%
Significant Spills =>1000 bbl	0.199	51%	0.067	14%	0.220	89%	0.287	40%	0.486	44%
All Spills	0.388	100%	0.464	100%	0.247	100%	0.711	100%	1.098	100%

Sale 1 - Life of Field Average Spill Index [bbl]

Spill Size	Pipelines		Platforms		Wells		Platforms and Wells		All	
Small and Medium Spills 50-999 bbl	1	5%	3	32%	0	0%	3	1%	4	1%
Large Spills 1000-9999 bbl	12	49%	3	34%	16	6%	19	7%	31	10%
Huge Spills =>10000 bbl	12	47%	3	34%	255	94%	258	92%	270	89%
Significant Spills =>1000 bbl	24	95%	6	68%	271	100%	277	99%	300	99%
All Spills	25	100%	9	100%	271	100%	280	100%	304	100%

Spill Size

Sale 1 - Life of Field Average Spill Frequency per 10^3 years

Spill Source	S+M 50-999 bbl		Large 1000-9999 bbl		Huge =>10000 bbl		Significant =>1000 bbl		All Spills	
Pipelines	2.892	31%	2.318	57%	0.744	22%	3.062	41%	5.953	35%
Platforms	6.090	65%	0.516	13%	0.516	15%	1.031	14%	7.122	42%
Wells	0.422	4%	1.265	31%	2.110	63%	3.375	45%	3.797	23%
Platforms and Wells	6.512	69%	1.781	43%	2.626	78%	4.406	59%	10.918	65%
All	9.404	100%	4.099	100%	3.369	100%	7.468	100%	16.872	100%

Sale 1 - Life of Field Average Spill Frequency per 10^9 bbl produced

Spill Source	S+M 50-999 bbl		Large 1000-9999 bbl		Huge =>10000 bbl		Significant =>1000 bbl		All Spills	
Pipelines	0.188	31%	0.151	57%	0.048	22%	0.199	41%	0.388	35%
Platforms	0.397	65%	0.034	13%	0.034	15%	0.067	14%	0.464	42%
Wells	0.027	4%	0.082	31%	0.137	63%	0.220	45%	0.247	23%
Platforms and Wells	0.424	69%	0.116	43%	0.171	78%	0.287	59%	0.711	65%
All	0.612	100%	0.267	100%	0.219	100%	0.486	100%	1.098	100%

Sale 1 - Life of Field Average Spill Index [bbl]

Spill Source	S+M 50-999 bbl		Large 1000-9999 bbl		Huge =>10000 bbl		Significant =>1000 bbl		All Spills	
Pipelines	1	27%	12	39%	12	4%	24	8%	25	8%
Platforms	3	67%	3	10%	3	1%	6	2%	9	3%
Wells	0	5%	16	51%	255	95%	271	90%	271	89%
Platforms and Wells	3	73%	19	61%	258	96%	277	92%	280	92%
All	4	100%	31	100%	270	100%	300	100%	304	100%

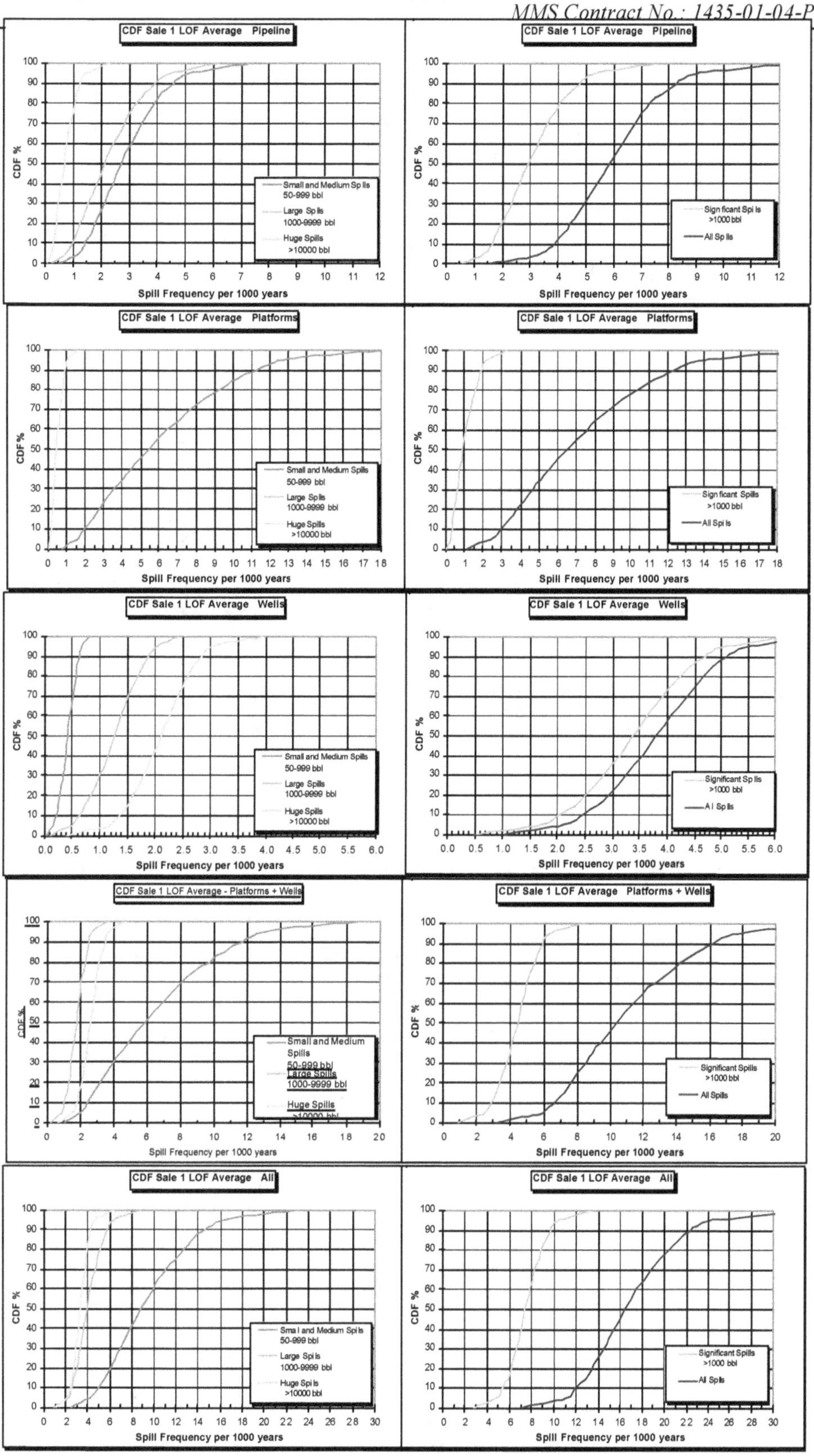

Figure 5.9
Sale 1 Life of Field Average Spill Frequency

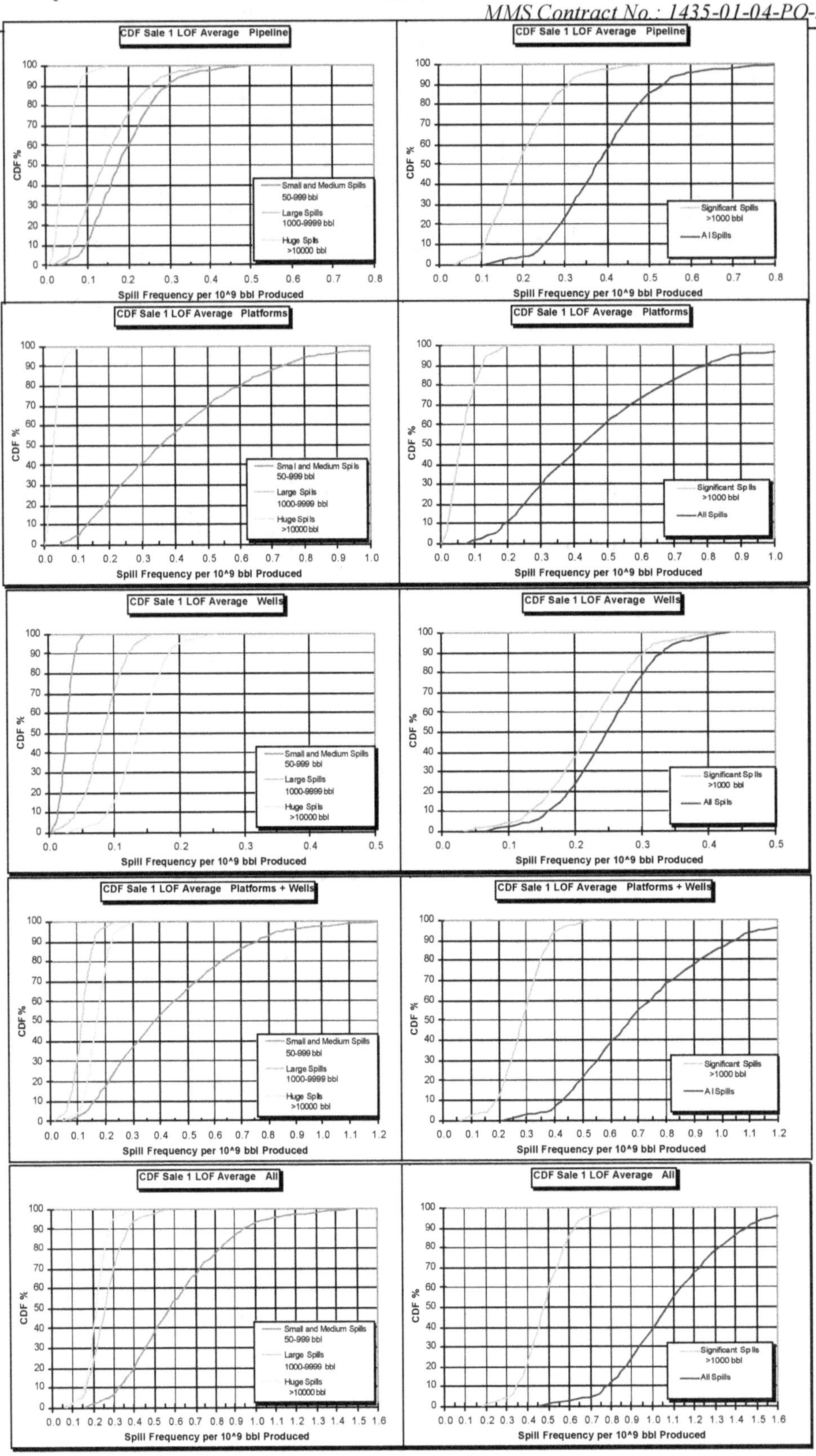

Figure 5.10
Sale 1 Life of Field Average Spills per Barrel Produced

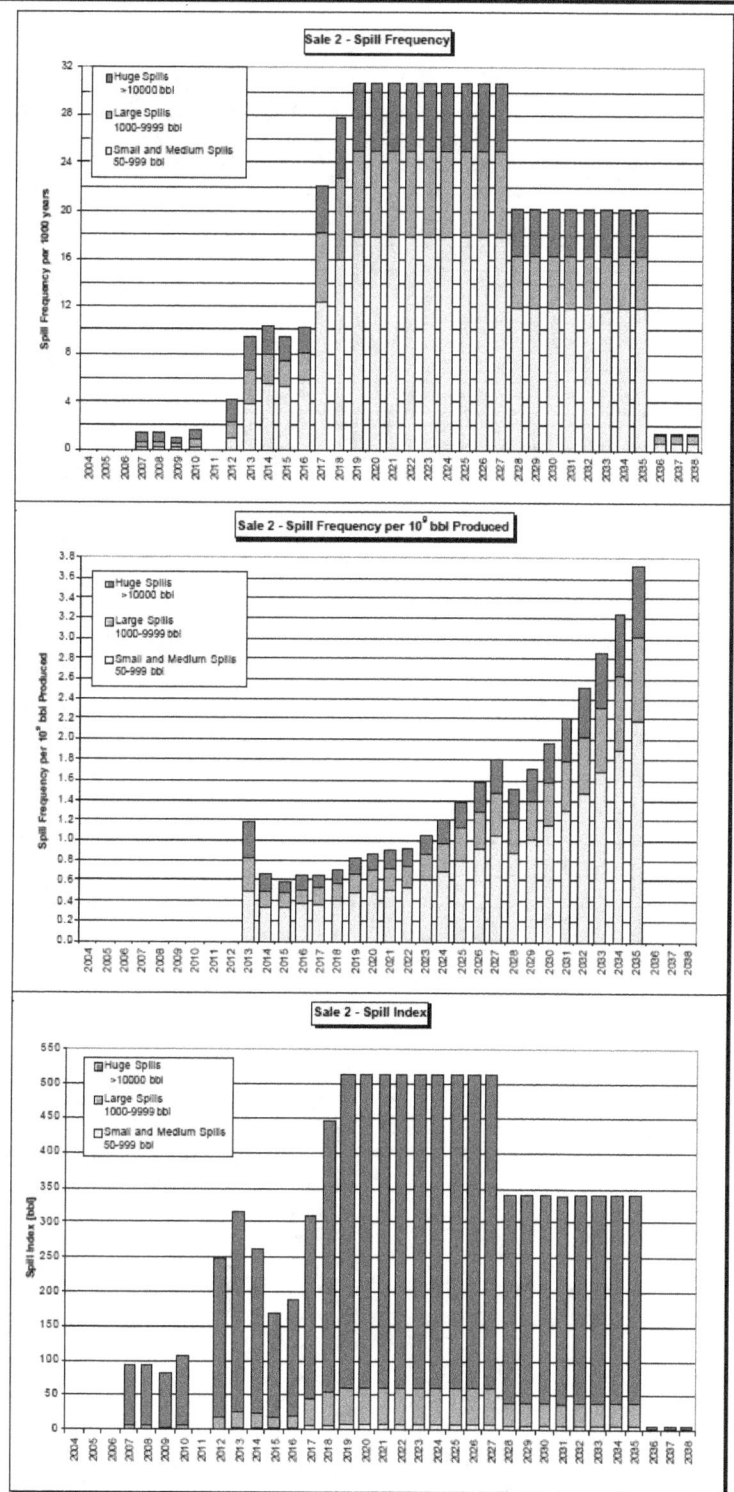

Figure 5.11
Sale 2 Spill Indicators

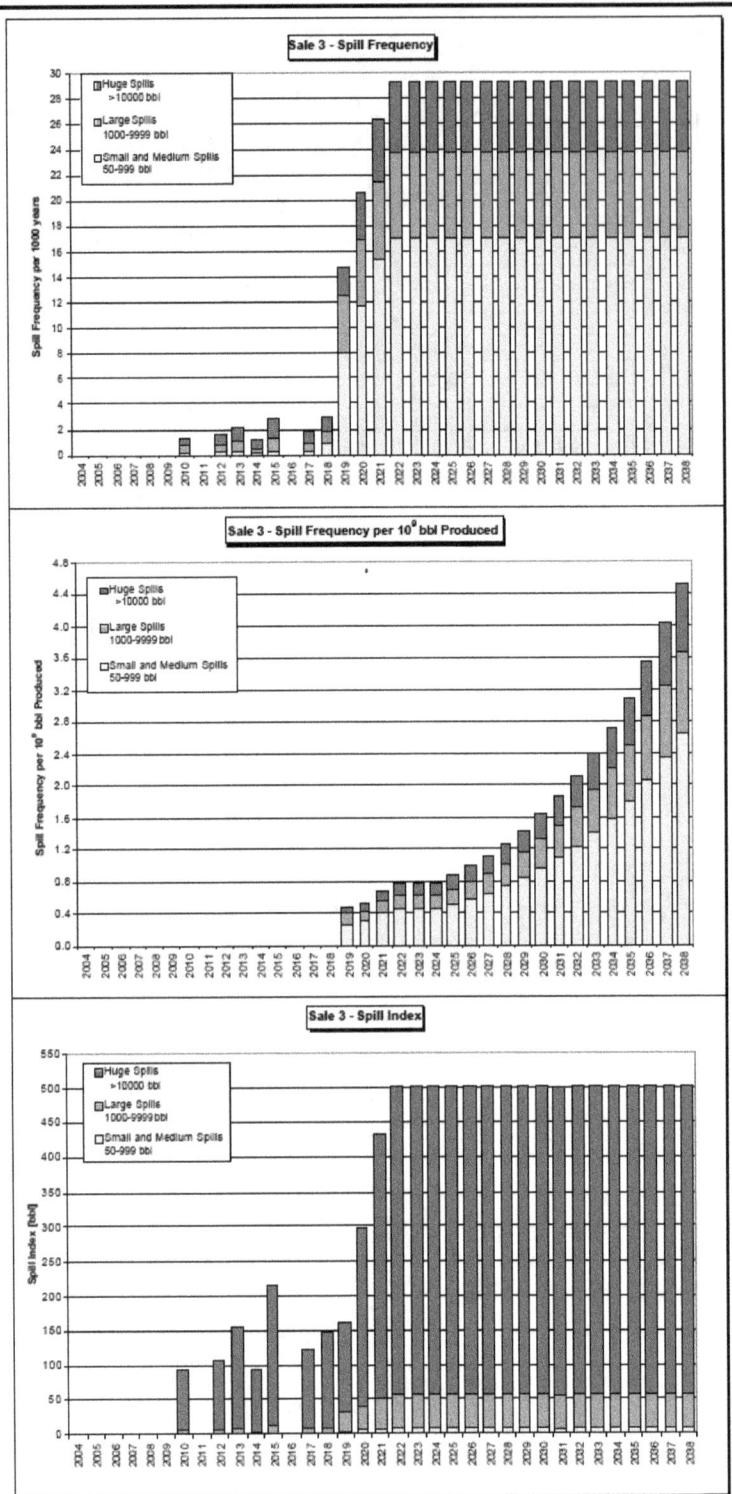

Figure 5.12
Sale 3 Spill Indicators

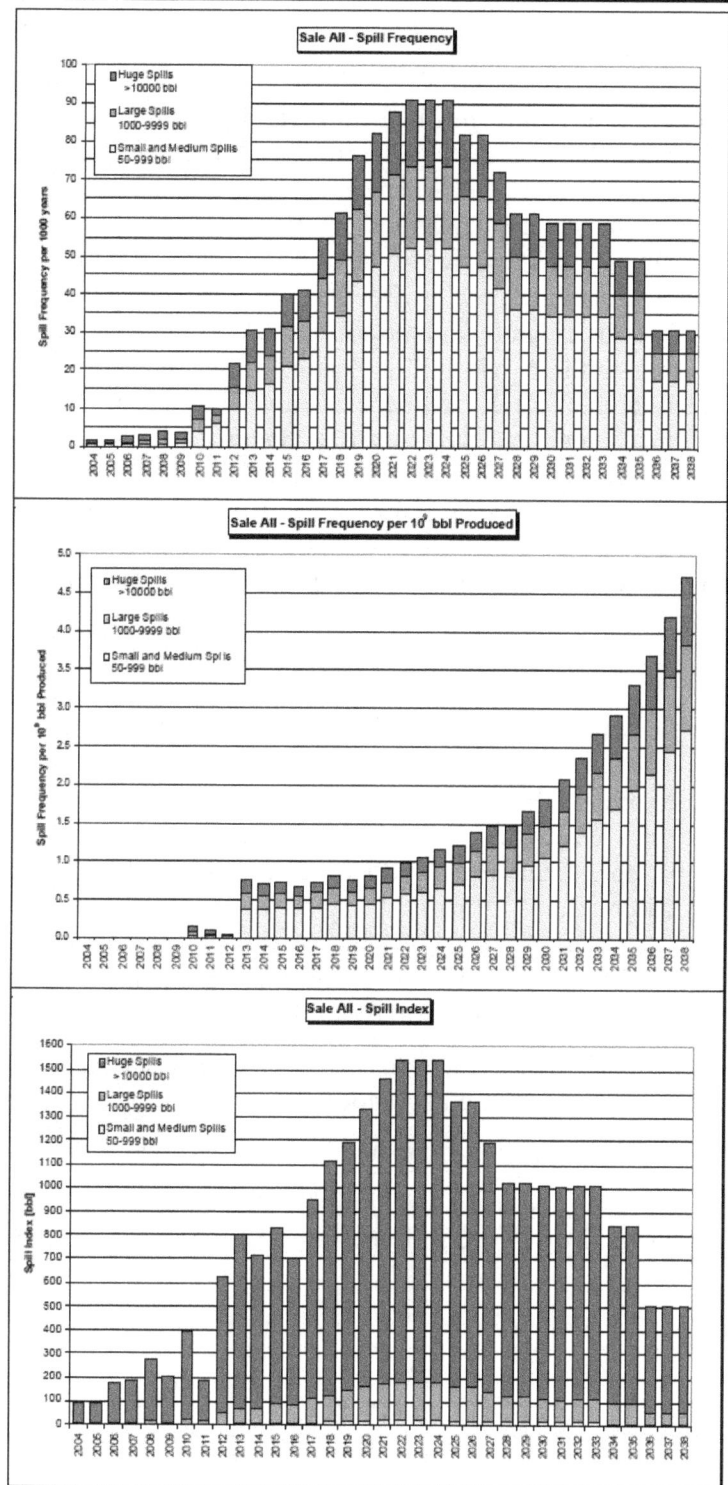

Figure 5.13
Sale All Spill Indicators

5.3.5   *Sale All Comparative Non-Arctic Indicator Assessment*

To give an idea of the effect of the frequency variations introduced in Chapter 4, the composite (Sale All) Beaufort Sea scenario was also modeled utilizing unaltered historical frequencies. That is, no changes to incorporate the Arctic effects were introduced in the spill indicator calculations. Put yet another way, it was assumed that the facilities of the composite scenario would behave as if they were in the Gulf of Mexico environment rather than in the Arctic environment. Figures 5.14, 5.15, and 5.16 show the total values calculated for each of the three spill indicators. The dark histogram bar on the right side corresponds to the Arctic spill indicator, while that, on the left, corresponds to the computation based on historical frequencies only. Spill frequency in an absolute sense is significantly reduced for the Arctic situation roughly by 30%. The spills per barrel produced are also significantly reduced, as can be seen in Figure 5.15. However, the spill index, because of the disproportionate effect of large spills, shows only a reduction of approximately 40%. What the comparison shows is that the Arctic development scenarios can be expected to have a lower oil spill occurrence than similar development scenarios in the GOM.

5.4   Summary of Representative Oil Spill Occurrence Indicator Results

How do spill indicators for the different scenarios and for their non-Arctic counterparts vary by spill size and location? Table 5.3 summarizes the Life of Field average spill indicator values for representative years. Figure 5.17 illustrates these. The following can be observed from Table 5.3.

- Each spill indicator for Sale 1, 2, and 3 is similar in value. The indicators are higher for the composite "Sale All" scenario.

- Spill frequency per year and per barrel-year decreases significantly with increasing spill size for all scenarios.

- The spill index increases dramatically with spill size for all scenarios.

- All non-Arctic scenario spill indicators are greater than their Arctic counterparts. Non-Arctic spill indicators are approximately 40% greater.

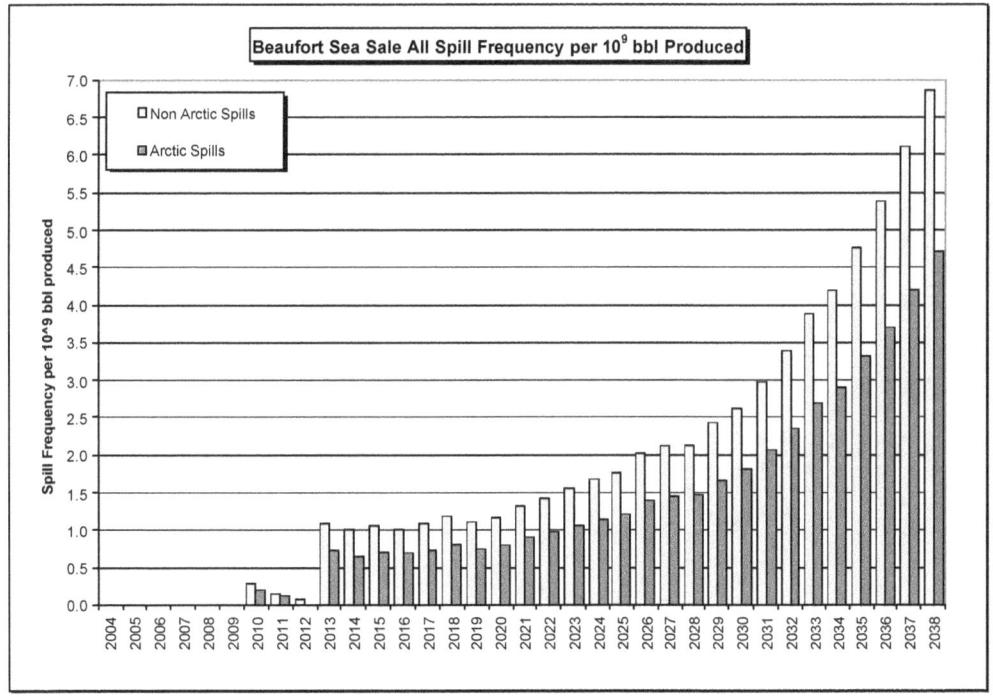

Figure 5.14
Beaufort Sea Sale All Spill Frequency – Arctic and Non-Arctic

Figure 5.15
Beaufort Sea Sale All Spill Frequency per 10⁹ Barrels Produced –
Arctic and Non-Arctic

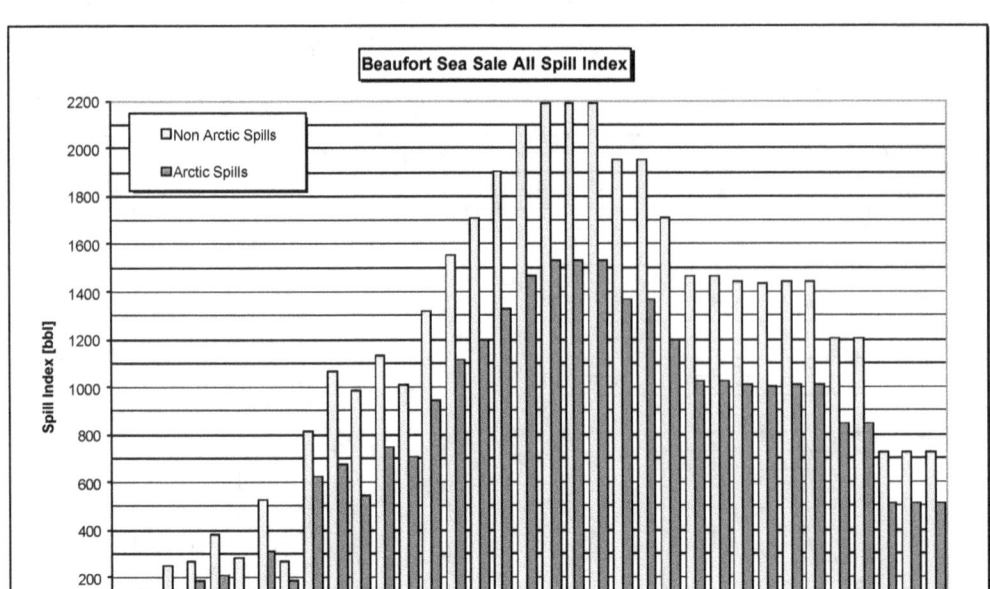

Figure 5.16
Beaufort Sea Sale All Spill Index – Arctic and Non-Arctic

5.21

Table 5.3
Summary of Average Spill Indicators for All Scenarios

Spill Indicators Life of Field Average	SALE 1 Spill Frequency per 10^3 years	SALE 1 Spill Frequency per 10^9 bbl produced	SALE 1 Spill Index [bbl]	SALE 2 Spill Frequency per 10^3 years	SALE 2 Spill Frequency per 10^9 bbl produced	SALE 2 Spill Index [bbl]	SALE 3 Spill Frequency per 10^3 years	SALE 3 Spill Frequency per 10^9 bbl produced	SALE 3 Spill Index [bbl]	SALE All Spill Frequency per 10^3 years	SALE All Spill Frequency per 10^9 bbl produced	SALE All Spill Index [bbl]	SALE All non Arctic Spill Frequency per 10^3 years	SALE All non Arctic Spill Frequency per 10^9 bbl produced	SALE All non Arctic
Small and Medium Spills 50-999 bbl	9.404 / 56%	0.612 / 56%	4 / 1%	9.586 / 57%	0.674 / 57%	4 / 1%	11.320 / 57%	0.714 / 57%	5 / 1%	26.204 / 57%	0.667 / 57%	11 / 1%	38.900 / 58%	0.990 / 58%	15 / 1%
Large Spills 1000-9999 bbl	4.099 / 24%	0.267 / 24%	31 / 10%	3.989 / 24%	0.281 / 24%	30 / 10%	4.575 / 23%	0.289 / 23%	35 / 10%	10.951 / 24%	0.279 / 24%	82 / 10%	15.653 / 23%	0.398 / 23%	117 / 10%
Huge Spills =>10000 bbl	3.369 / 20%	0.219 / 20%	270 / 89%	3.323 / 20%	0.234 / 20%	268 / 89%	3.901 / 20%	0.246 / 20%	317 / 89%	9.158 / 20%	0.233 / 20%	740 / 89%	12.956 / 19%	0.330 / 19%	1048 / 89%
Significant Spills =>1000 bbl	7.468 / 44%	0.486 / 44%	300 / 99%	7.312 / 43%	0.514 / 43%	298 / 99%	8.476 / 43%	0.535 / 43%	352 / 99%	20.109 / 43%	0.512 / 43%	822 / 99%	28.608 / 42%	0.728 / 42%	1165 / 99%
All Spills	16.872 / 100%	1.098 / 100%	304 / 100%	16.897 / 100%	1.188 / 100%	302 / 100%	19.796 / 100%	1.249 / 100%	357 / 100%	46.313 / 100%	1.178 / 100%	833 / 100%	67.508 / 100%	1.718 / 100%	1180 / 100%
Pipeline Spills	5.953 / 35%	0.388 / 35%	25 / 8%	5.899 / 35%	0.415 / 35%	23 / 8%	6.551 / 33%	0.413 / 33%	26 / 7%	15.925 / 34%	0.405 / 34%	64 / 8%	27.192 / 40%	0.692 / 40%	96 / 8%
Platform Spills	7.122 / 42%	0.464 / 42%	9 / 3%	7.210 / 43%	0.507 / 43%	9 / 3%	8.751 / 44%	0.552 / 44%	11 / 3%	19.947 / 43%	0.508 / 43%	24 / 3%	25.562 / 38%	0.650 / 38%	30 / 3%
Well Spills	3.797 / 23%	0.247 / 23%	271 / 89%	3.787 / 22%	0.266 / 22%	271 / 89%	4.494 / 23%	0.283 / 23%	321 / 90%	10.441 / 23%	0.266 / 23%	746 / 89%	14.755 / 22%	0.375 / 22%	1054 / 89%
Platform and Well Spills	10.918 / 65%	0.711 / 65%	280 / 92%	10.998 / 65%	0.773 / 65%	279 / 92%	13.245 / 67%	0.835 / 67%	331 / 93%	30.388 / 66%	0.773 / 66%	770 / 92%	40.317 / 60%	1.026 / 60%	1084 / 92%
All Spills	16.872 / 100%	1.098 / 100%	304 / 100%	16.897 / 100%	1.188 / 100%	302 / 100%	19.796 / 100%	1.249 / 100%	357 / 100%	46.313 / 100%	1.178 / 100%	833 / 100%	67.508 / 100%	1.718 / 100%	1180 / 100%

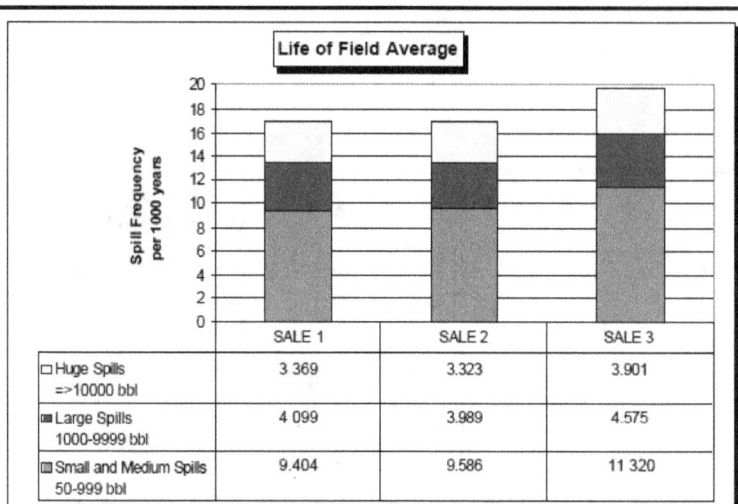

	SALE 1	SALE 2	SALE 3
□ Huge Spills =>10000 bbl	3 369	3.323	3.901
▦ Large Spills 1000-9999 bbl	4 099	3.989	4.575
▦ Small and Medium Spills 50-999 bbl	9.404	9.586	11 320

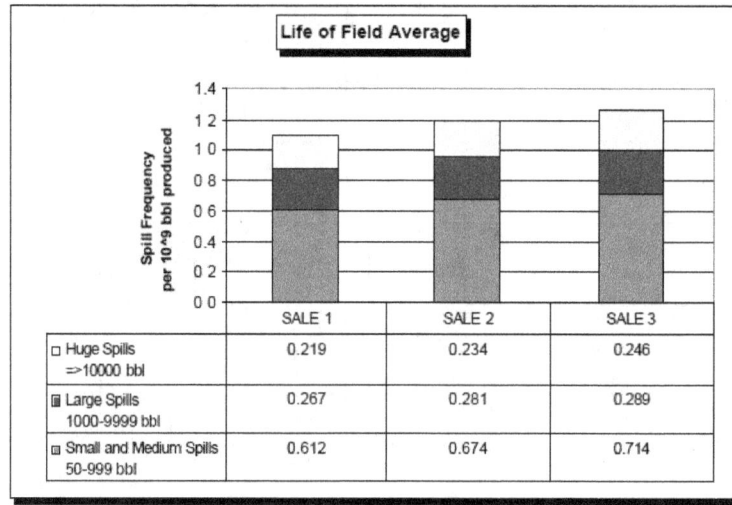

	SALE 1	SALE 2	SALE 3
□ Huge Spills =>10000 bbl	0.219	0.234	0.246
▦ Large Spills 1000-9999 bbl	0.267	0.281	0.289
▦ Small and Medium Spills 50-999 bbl	0.612	0.674	0.714

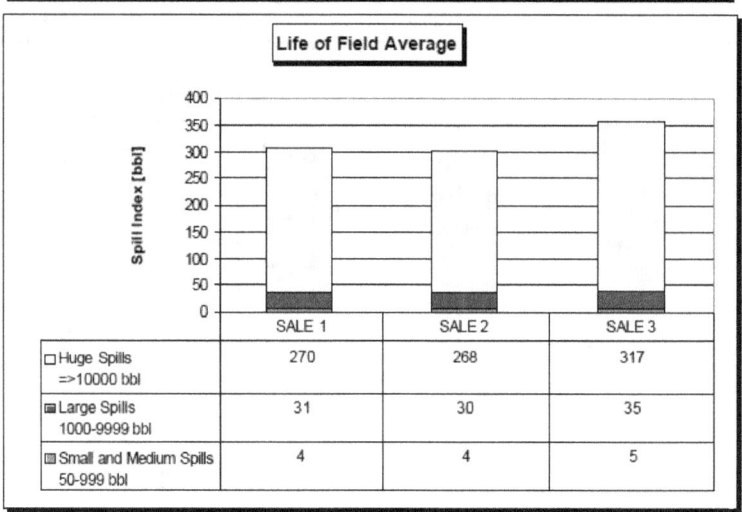

	SALE 1	SALE 2	SALE 3
□ Huge Spills =>10000 bbl	270	268	317
▦ Large Spills 1000-9999 bbl	31	30	35
▦ Small and Medium Spills 50-999 bbl	4	4	5

Figure 5.17
Life of Field Spill Indicators – By Spill Size

How do the spill indicators vary by facility type for representative scenarios? The contributions of spill indicators by facility have been summarized by representative scenario years, again, in Table 5.3 and also in Figure 5.18. Table 5.3 and Figure 5.18 give the component contributions, in absolute value and percent, for each of the main facility types; namely, pipelines (P/L), platforms, and wells. The following may be noted from Table 5.3:

- Platforms contribute the most (43%) to the two spill frequency indicators, but the least (3%) to the spill index.

- Pipelines are next in relative contribution to spill frequencies (34%) and intermediate in contribution to spill index (8%).

- Wells are by far (at 89%) the highest contributors to spill index, while platforms and wells together are responsible for a 92% contribution to the spill index.

- It can be concluded that platforms are likely to have the most, but smaller spills, while wells will have the least number, but largest spills. Pipelines will be in between, with a tendency towards more spills than wells, but less or about the same number as platforms.

Figures 5.19 and 5.20 show relative contributions by facility and spill size to the maximum production year 2024 and Life of Field average spill indicators, respectively. Although Life of Field average absolute values are significantly smaller than the maximum production year values, the proportional contributions by spill facility source and spill size are almost identical.

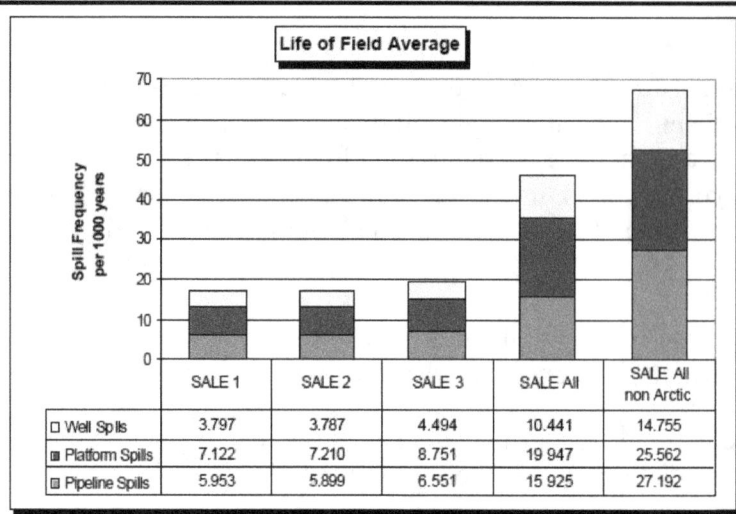

	SALE 1	SALE 2	SALE 3	SALE All	SALE All non Arctic
Well Spills	3.797	3.787	4.494	10.441	14.755
Platform Spills	7.122	7.210	8.751	19 947	25.562
Pipeline Spills	5.953	5.899	6.551	15 925	27.192

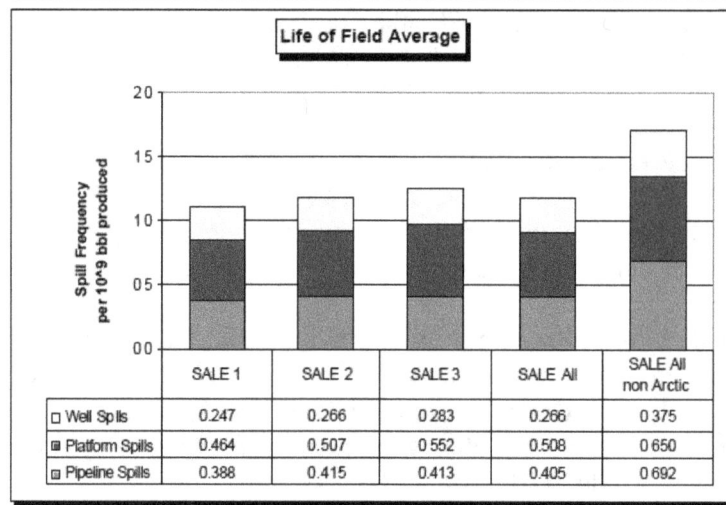

	SALE 1	SALE 2	SALE 3	SALE All	SALE All non Arctic
Well Spills	0.247	0.266	0 283	0.266	0 375
Platform Spills	0.464	0.507	0 552	0.508	0 650
Pipeline Spills	0.388	0.415	0.413	0.405	0 692

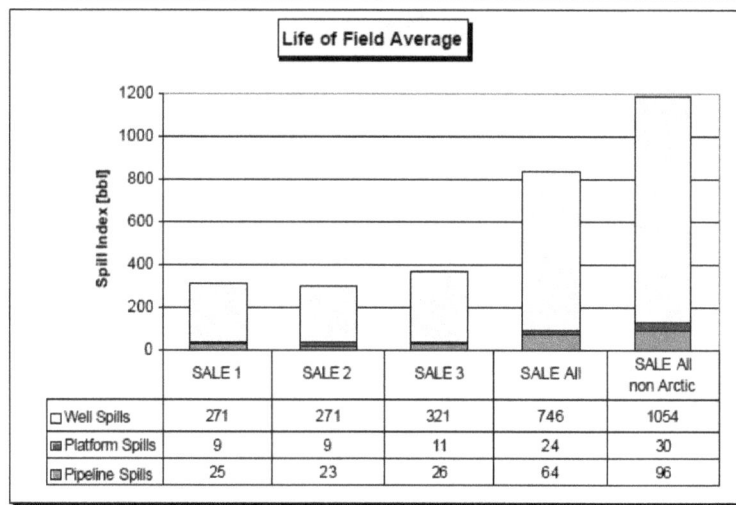

	SALE 1	SALE 2	SALE 3	SALE All	SALE All non Arctic
Well Spills	271	271	321	746	1054
Platform Spills	9	9	11	24	30
Pipeline Spills	25	23	26	64	96

Figure 5.18
Life of Field Spill Indicators – By Source Composition

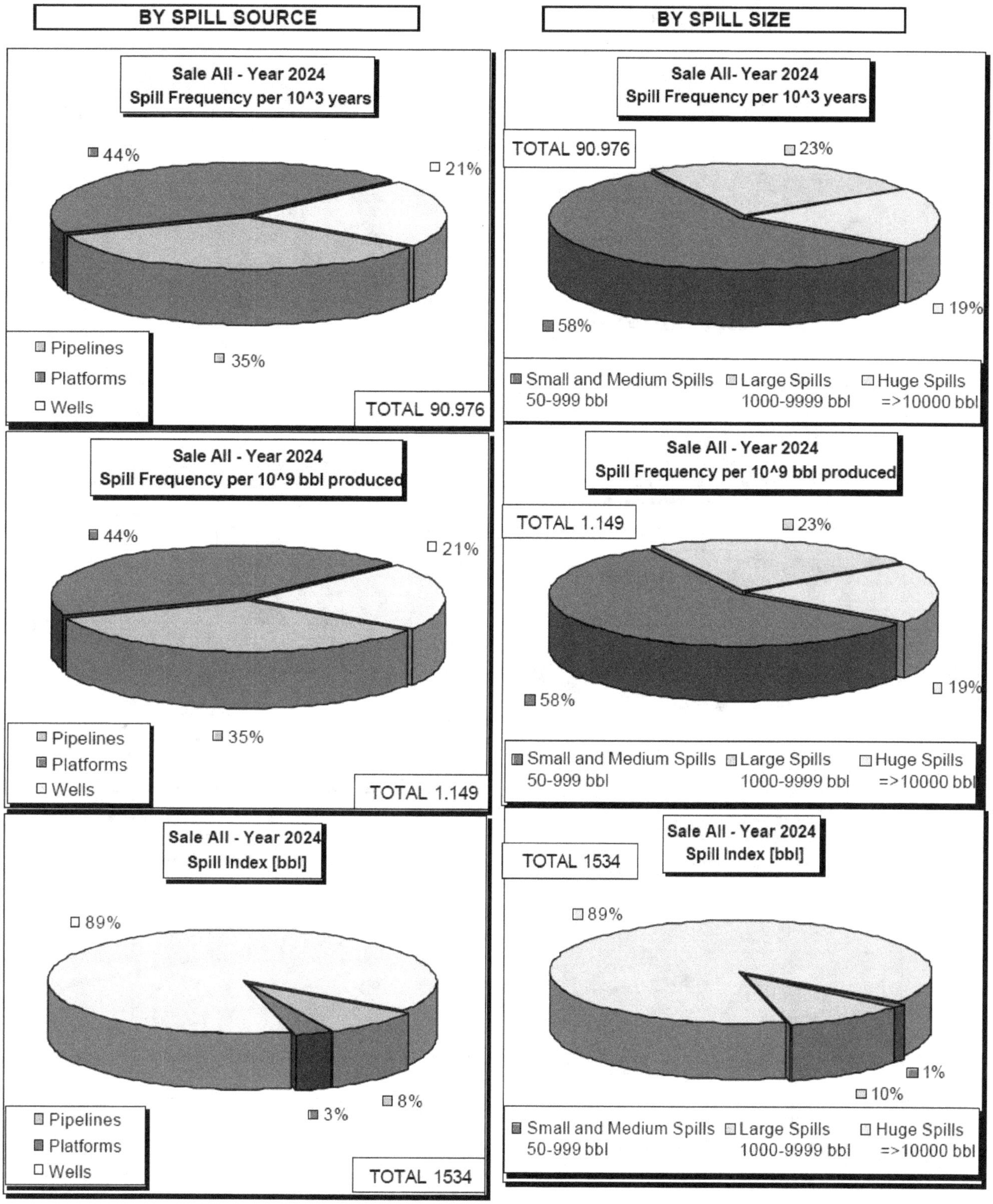

BY SPILL SOURCE

Sale All - Year 2024
Spill Frequency per 10^3 years

44%
21%
35%

□ Pipelines
■ Platforms
□ Wells

TOTAL 90.976

Sale All - Year 2024
Spill Frequency per 10^9 bbl produced

44%
21%
35%

□ Pipelines
■ Platforms
□ Wells

TOTAL 1.149

Sale All - Year 2024
Spill Index [bbl]

89%
3%
8%

□ Pipelines
■ Platforms
□ Wells

TOTAL 1534

BY SPILL SIZE

Sale All- Year 2024
Spill Frequency per 10^3 years

TOTAL 90.976
23%
58%
19%

■ Small and Medium Spills   □ Large Spills   □ Huge Spills
50-999 bbl   1000-9999 bbl   =>10000 bbl

Sale All - Year 2024
Spill Frequency per 10^9 bbl produced

TOTAL 1.149
23%
58%
19%

■ Small and Medium Spills   □ Large Spills   □ Huge Spills
50-999 bbl   1000-9999 bbl   =>10000 bbl

Sale All - Year 2024
Spill Index [bbl]

TOTAL 1534
89%
1%
10%

■ Small and Medium Spills   □ Large Spills   □ Huge Spills
50-999 bbl   1000-9999 bbl   =>10000 bbl

Figure 5.19
Sale All – Year 2024 – Spill Indicator Composition by Source and Spill Size

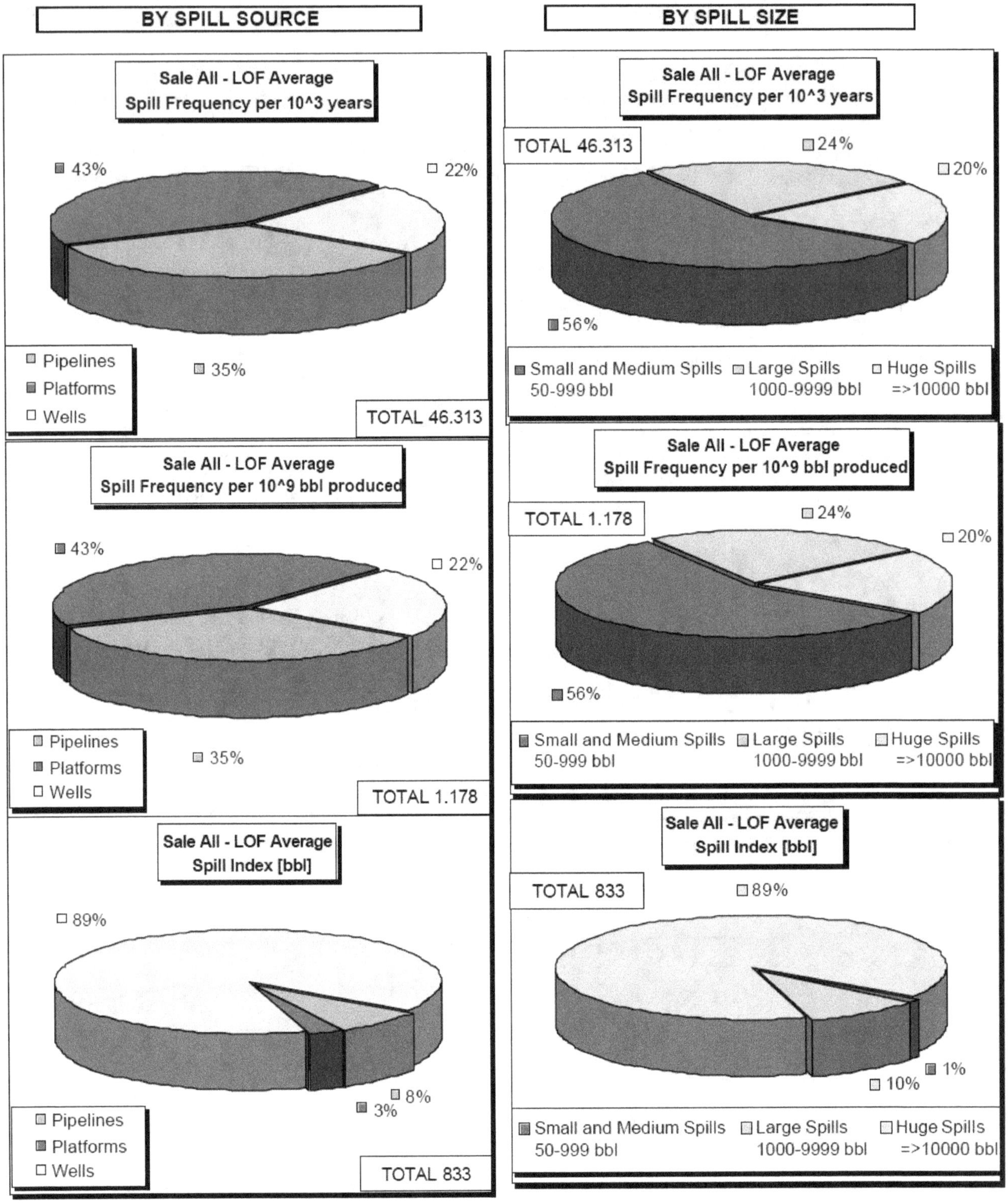

BY SPILL SOURCE

BY SPILL SIZE

Sale All - LOF Average
Spill Frequency per 10^3 years

■ 43% □ 22%

□ Pipelines
■ Platforms
□ Wells

■ 35%

TOTAL 46.313

Sale All - LOF Average
Spill Frequency per 10^3 years

TOTAL 46.313 □ 24% □ 20%

■ 56%

■ Small and Medium Spills   □ Large Spills   □ Huge Spills
   50-999 bbl   1000-9999 bbl   =>10000 bbl

Sale All - LOF Average
Spill Frequency per 10^9 bbl produced

■ 43% □ 22%

□ Pipelines
■ Platforms
□ Wells

■ 35%

TOTAL 1.178

Sale All - LOF Average
Spill Frequency per 10^9 bbl produced

TOTAL 1.178 □ 24% □ 20%

■ 56%

■ Small and Medium Spills   □ Large Spills   □ Huge Spills
   50-999 bbl   1000-9999 bbl   =>10000 bbl

Sale All - LOF Average
Spill Index [bbl]

□ 89%

□ Pipelines
■ Platforms
□ Wells

■ 3% ■ 8%

TOTAL 833

Sale All - LOF Average
Spill Index [bbl]

TOTAL 833 □ 89%

■ 1%
□ 10%

■ Small and Medium Spills   □ Large Spills   □ Huge Spills
   50-999 bbl   1000-9999 bbl   =>10000 bbl

Figure 5.20
Sale All – Life of Field Average Spill Indicator Composition by Source and Spill Size

Figures 5.21, 5.22, and 5.23 show the CDFs for the Beaufort Sea Sale All Life of Field average spill indicators. The variability of these indicators is fairly representative of the trends in variability for spill indicators for all sales and locations studied. Generally, the following can be observed from the figures:

- The variance of the frequency spill indicators (Figures 5.21 and 5.22) decreases as spill size increases. In other words, small and medium spills illustrate the largest variability; huge spills show the least variability for facilities.

- The variability of the spill index (Figure 5.23) shows the same trend for pipelines and platforms, but the opposite trend for wells.

From Figure 5.21, it can be seen, for significant spills, that the Life of Field average mean value of 20 (spills per 1,000 years) ranges between 30 and 12 at the upper and lower 95% confidence intervals. A similar percentage variation is shown for the Life of Field average spill frequency per barrel produced in Figure 5.22. The spill index variability shown in Figure 5.23 is proportionally higher. For example, in Figure 5.23, the mean value of the significant spills index of 800 per billion barrels produced ranges from 1,300 to 400– a somewhat larger proportion of mean than that of the spill frequency indicators.

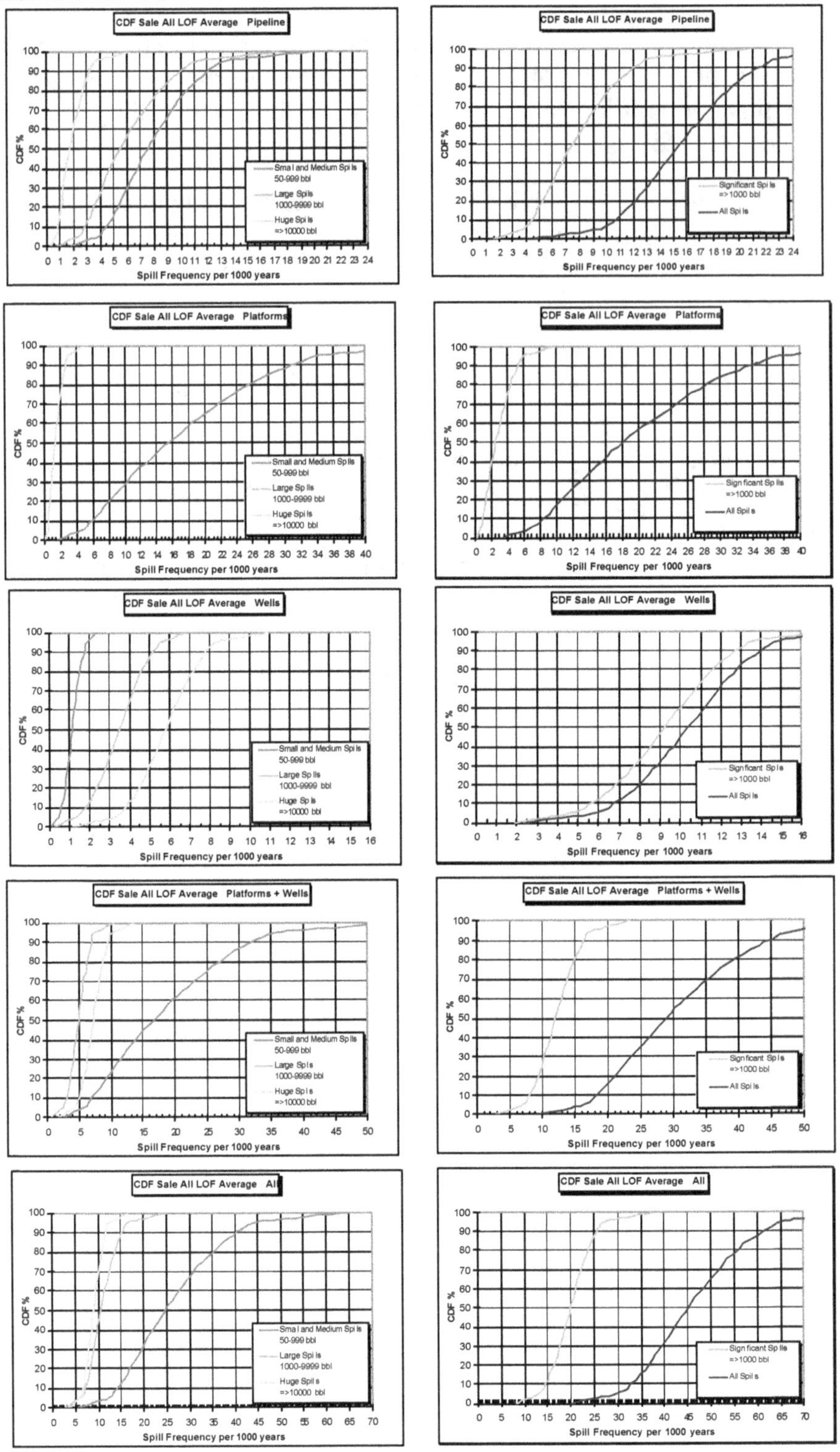

Figure 5.21
Life of Field Average Spill Frequency – CDF – Sale All

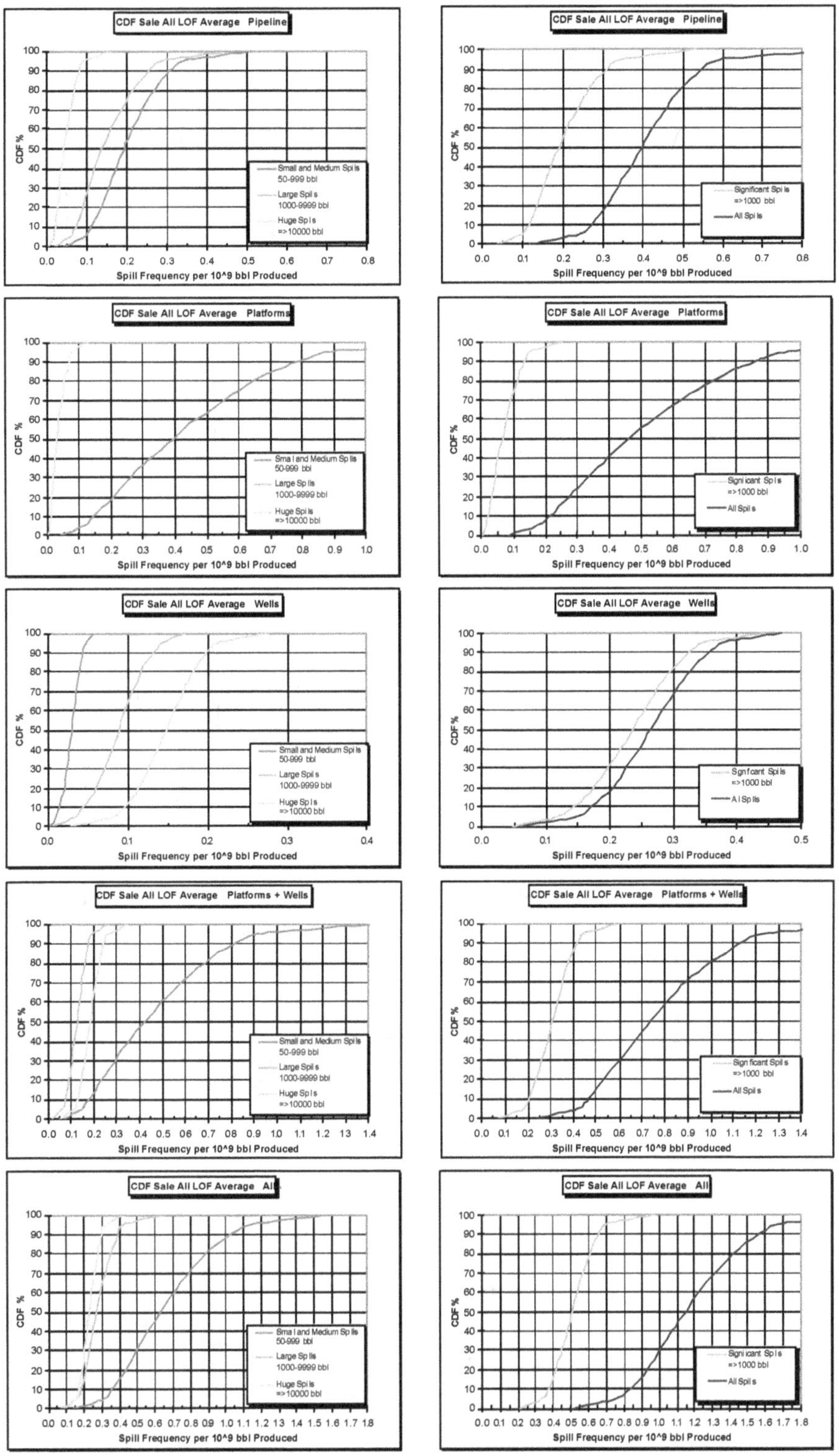

Figure 5.22
Life of Field Average Spill Frequency per Barrel Produced – CDF – Sale All

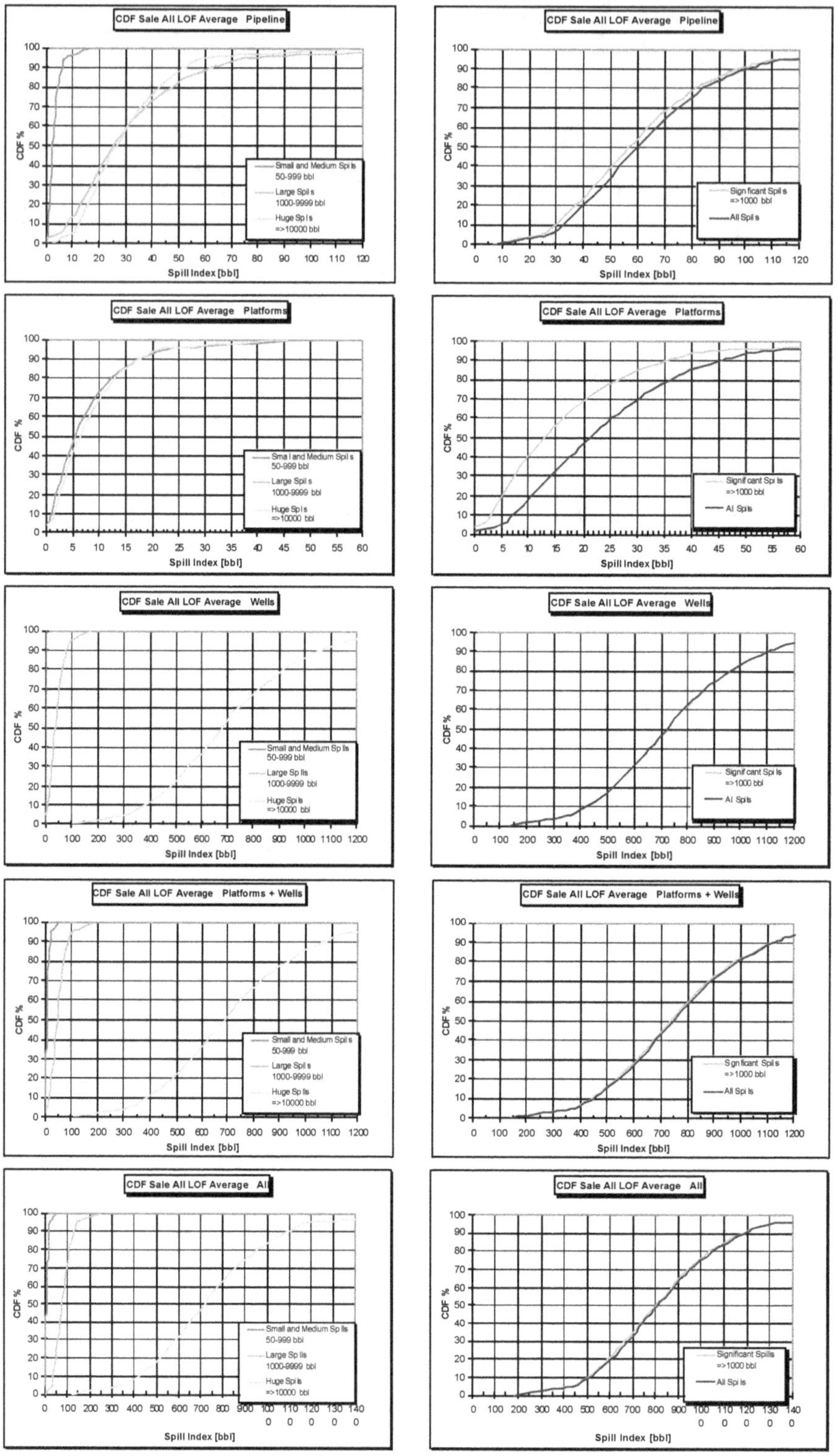

Figure 5.23
Life of Field Average Spill Index (bbl) – CDF – Sale All

CHAPTER 6

CONCLUSIONS AND RECOMMENDATIONS

6.1   Conclusions

6.1.1   General Conclusions

Oil spill occurrence indicators were quantified for future offshore development scenarios in the south Beaufort Sea in the area of MMS jurisdiction. The quantification included the consideration of the variability of historical data as well as the expected variability of Arctic effects on oil spill occurrence indicators. Consideration of the variability of all input data yields both higher variability and higher expected value of the spill occurrence indicators. The three types of spill occurrence indicators were: annual oil spill frequency, annual oil spill frequency per barrel produced, and annual spill index – and, additionally, the life of field averages for each of these three oil spill indicators were assessed.

6.1.2   Oil Spill Occurrence Indicators by Spill Size

How do spill indicators for the different scenarios and for their non-Arctic counterparts vary by spill size and source? Table 6.1 summarizes the Life of Field (LOF) average spill indicator values. Figure 6.1 illustrates these for Sale 1, 2, and 3. The following can be observed from Table 6.1.

- Each spill indicator for Sale 1, 2, and 3 is similar in value. The indicators are higher for the composite "Sale All" scenario.

- Spill frequency per year and per barrel decreases significantly with increasing spill size for all scenarios.

- The spill index increases dramatically with spill size for all scenarios.

- All non-Arctic scenario spill indicators are greater than their Arctic counterparts. Non-Arctic spill indicators are approximately 40% greater.

Table 6.1
Summary of Average Spill Indicators for All Scenarios

Spill Indicators Life of Field Average	SALE 1 Spill Frequency per 10^3 years	SALE 1 Spill Frequency per 10^9 bbl produced	SALE 1 Spill Index [bbl]	SALE 2 Spill Frequency per 10^3 years	SALE 2 Spill Frequency per 10^9 bbl produced	SALE 2 Spill Index [bbl]	SALE 3 Spill Frequency per 10^3 years	SALE 3 Spill Frequency per 10^9 bbl produced	SALE 3 Spill Index [bbl]	SALE All Spill Frequency per 10^3 years	SALE All Spill Frequency per 10^9 bbl produced	SALE All Spill Index [bbl]	SALE All non Arctic Spill Frequency per 10^3 years	SALE All non Arctic Spill Frequency per 10^9 bbl produced	SALE All non Arctic Spill Index [bbl]
Small and Medium Spills 50-999 bbl	9.404 / 56%	0.612 / 56%	4 / 1%	9.586 / 57%	0.674 / 57%	4 / 1%	11.320 / 57%	0.714 / 57%	5 / 1%	26.204 / 57%	0.667 / 57%	11 / 1%	38.900 / 58%	0.990 / 58%	15 / 1%
Large Spills 1000-9999 bbl	4.099 / 24%	0.267 / 24%	31 / 10%	3.989 / 24%	0.281 / 24%	30 / 10%	4.575 / 23%	0.289 / 23%	35 / 10%	10.951 / 24%	0.279 / 24%	82 / 10%	15.653 / 23%	0.398 / 23%	117 / 10%
Huge Spills =>10000 bbl	3.369 / 20%	0.219 / 20%	270 / 89%	3.323 / 20%	0.234 / 20%	268 / 89%	3.901 / 20%	0.246 / 20%	317 / 89%	9.158 / 20%	0.233 / 20%	740 / 89%	12.956 / 19%	0.330 / 19%	1048 / 89%
Significant Spills =>1000 bbl	7.468 / 44%	0.486 / 44%	300 / 99%	7.312 / 43%	0.514 / 43%	298 / 99%	8.476 / 43%	0.535 / 43%	352 / 99%	20.109 / 43%	0.512 / 43%	822 / 99%	28.608 / 42%	0.728 / 42%	1165 / 99%
All Spills	16.872 / 100%	1.098 / 100%	304 / 100%	16.897 / 100%	1.188 / 100%	302 / 100%	19.796 / 100%	1.249 / 100%	357 / 100%	46.313 / 100%	1.178 / 100%	833 / 100%	67.508 / 100%	1.718 / 100%	1180 / 100%
Pipeline Spills	5.953 / 35%	0.388 / 35%	25 / 8%	5.899 / 35%	0.415 / 35%	23 / 8%	6.551 / 33%	0.413 / 33%	26 / 7%	15.925 / 34%	0.405 / 34%	64 / 8%	27.192 / 40%	0.692 / 40%	96 / 8%
Platform Spills	7.122 / 42%	0.464 / 42%	9 / 3%	7.210 / 43%	0.507 / 43%	9 / 3%	8.751 / 44%	0.552 / 44%	11 / 3%	19.947 / 43%	0.508 / 43%	24 / 3%	25.562 / 38%	0.650 / 38%	30 / 3%
Well Spills	3.797 / 23%	0.247 / 23%	271 / 89%	3.787 / 22%	0.266 / 22%	271 / 89%	4.494 / 23%	0.283 / 23%	321 / 90%	10.441 / 23%	0.266 / 23%	746 / 89%	14.755 / 22%	0.375 / 22%	1054 / 89%
Platform and Well Spills	10.918 / 65%	0.711 / 65%	280 / 92%	10.998 / 65%	0.773 / 65%	279 / 92%	13.245 / 67%	0.835 / 67%	331 / 93%	30.388 / 66%	0.773 / 66%	770 / 92%	40.317 / 60%	1.026 / 60%	1084 / 92%
All Spills	16.872 / 100%	1.098 / 100%	304 / 100%	16.897 / 100%	1.188 / 100%	302 / 100%	19.796 / 100%	1.249 / 100%	357 / 100%	46.313 / 100%	1.178 / 100%	833 / 100%	67.508 / 100%	1.718 / 100%	1180 / 100%

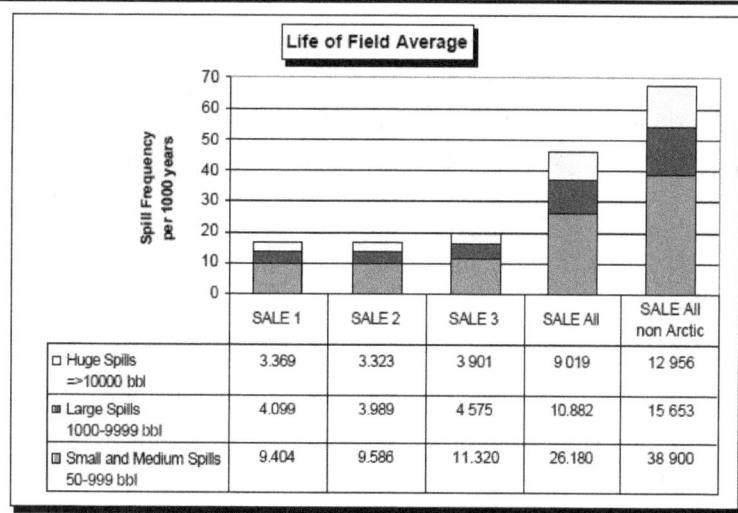

	SALE 1	SALE 2	SALE 3	SALE All	SALE All non Arctic
□ Huge Spills =>10000 bbl	3.369	3.323	3 901	9 019	12 956
▨ Large Spills 1000-9999 bbl	4.099	3.989	4 575	10.882	15 653
▨ Small and Medium Spills 50-999 bbl	9.404	9.586	11.320	26.180	38 900

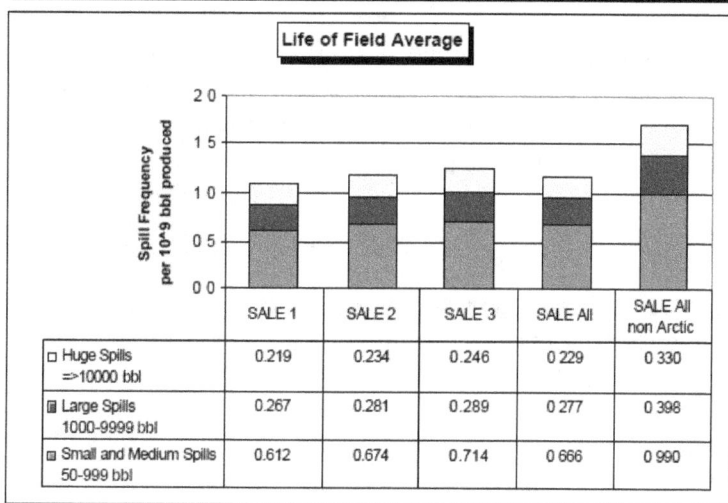

	SALE 1	SALE 2	SALE 3	SALE All	SALE All non Arctic
□ Huge Spills =>10000 bbl	0.219	0.234	0.246	0 229	0 330
▨ Large Spills 1000-9999 bbl	0.267	0.281	0.289	0 277	0 398
▨ Small and Medium Spills 50-999 bbl	0.612	0.674	0.714	0 666	0 990

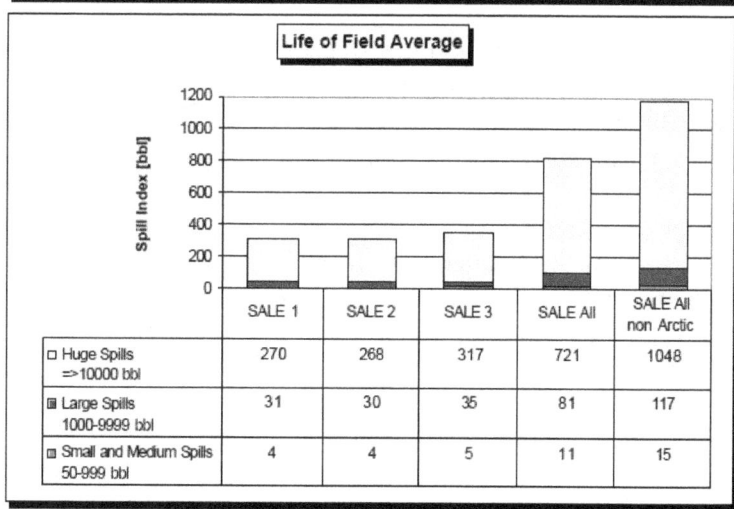

	SALE 1	SALE 2	SALE 3	SALE All	SALE All non Arctic
□ Huge Spills =>10000 bbl	270	268	317	721	1048
▨ Large Spills 1000-9999 bbl	31	30	35	81	117
▨ Small and Medium Spills 50-999 bbl	4	4	5	11	15

Figure 6.1
Life of Field Spill Indicators – By Spill Size

6.1.3   Oil Spill Occurrence Indicators by Spill Source

How do the spill indicators vary by spill source facility type for representative scenarios? The contributions of spill indicators by source facility have been summarized by representative scenario years, again, in Table 6.1 and also in Figure 6.2. Table 6.1 and Figure 6.2 give the component contributions, in absolute value and percent, for each of the main facility types; namely, pipelines (P/L), platforms, and wells. The following may be noted from Table 6.1:

- Platforms contribute the most (43%) to the two spill frequency indicators, but the least (3%) to the spill index.

- Pipelines are next in relative contribution to spill frequencies (34%) and intermediate in contribution to spill index (8%).

- Wells are by far (at 89%) the highest contributors to spill index.

- It can be concluded that platforms are likely to have the most, but smaller spills, while wells will have the least number, but largest spills. Pipelines will be in between, with a tendency towards more spills than wells, but less or about the same number as platforms.

Figures 6.3 and 6.4 show relative contributions by facility and spill size to the maximum production year 2024 and Life of Field average spill indicators, respectively. Although Life of Field average spill indicator absolute values are significantly smaller than the maximum production year values, the proportional contributions by spill facility source and spill size are almost identical.

6.1.4   Variability of Oil Spill Occurrence Indicators

Figures 6.5, 6.6, and 6.7 show the Cumulative Distribution Functions for each of the Beaufort Sea Sale All Life of Field average spill indicators by spill size and source. The variability of these indicators is fairly representative of the trends in variability for spill indicators for all scenarios modeled. Generally, the following can be observed from the figures:

- The variance of the frequency spill indicators (Figures 6.5 and 6.6) decreases as spill size increases. In other words, small and medium spills illustrate the largest variability; huge spills show the least variability for facilities.

- The variability of the spill index (Figure 6.7) shows the same trend for pipelines and platforms, but the opposite trend for wells.

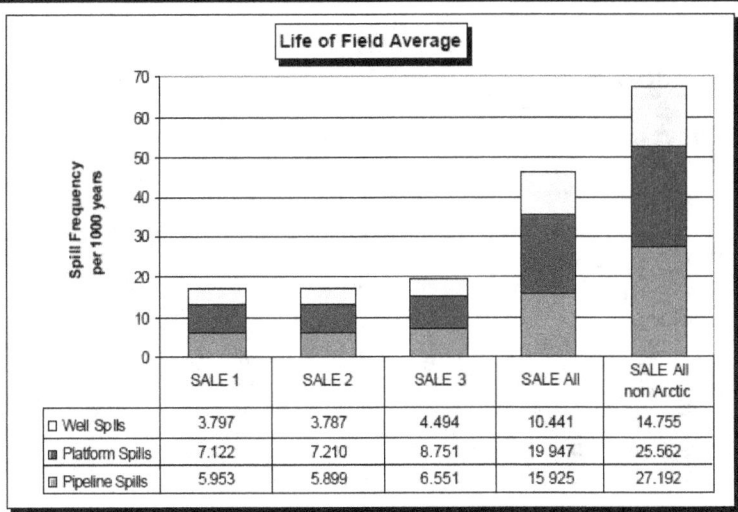

	SALE 1	SALE 2	SALE 3	SALE All	SALE All non Arctic
□ Well Spills	3.797	3.787	4.494	10.441	14.755
▨ Platform Spills	7.122	7.210	8.751	19 947	25.562
▨ Pipeline Spills	5.953	5.899	6.551	15 925	27.192

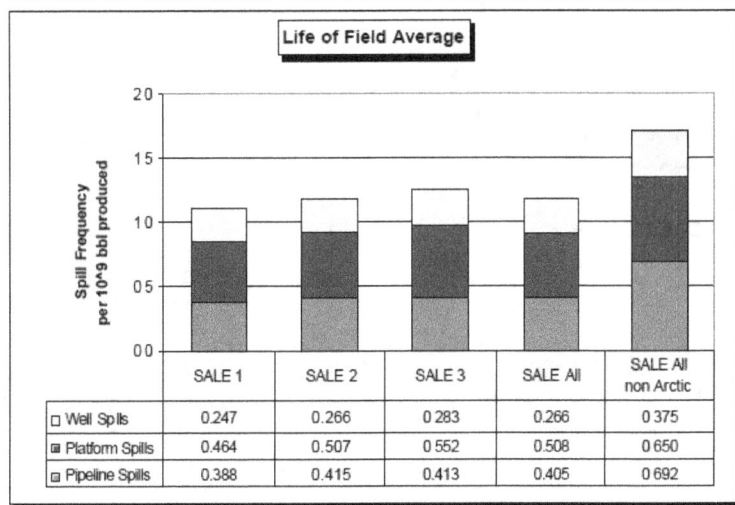

	SALE 1	SALE 2	SALE 3	SALE All	SALE All non Arctic
□ Well Spills	0.247	0.266	0 283	0.266	0 375
▨ Platform Spills	0.464	0.507	0 552	0.508	0 650
▨ Pipeline Spills	0.388	0.415	0.413	0.405	0 692

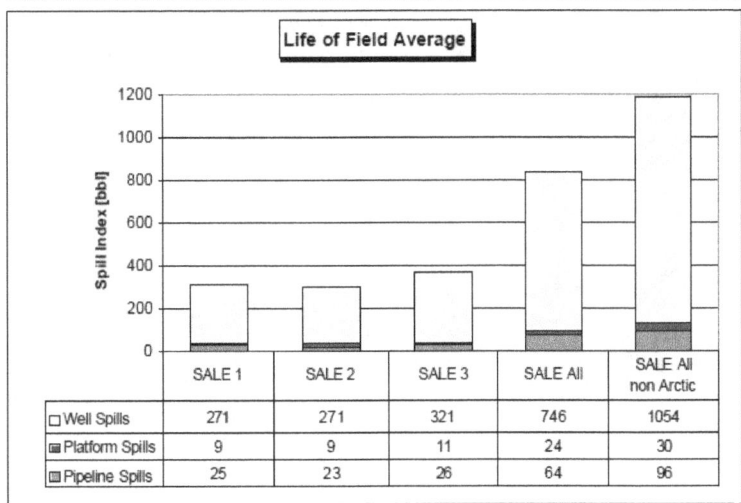

	SALE 1	SALE 2	SALE 3	SALE All	SALE All non Arctic
□ Well Spills	271	271	321	746	1054
▨ Platform Spills	9	9	11	24	30
▨ Pipeline Spills	25	23	26	64	96

Figure 6.2
Life of Field Spill Indicators – By Source Composition

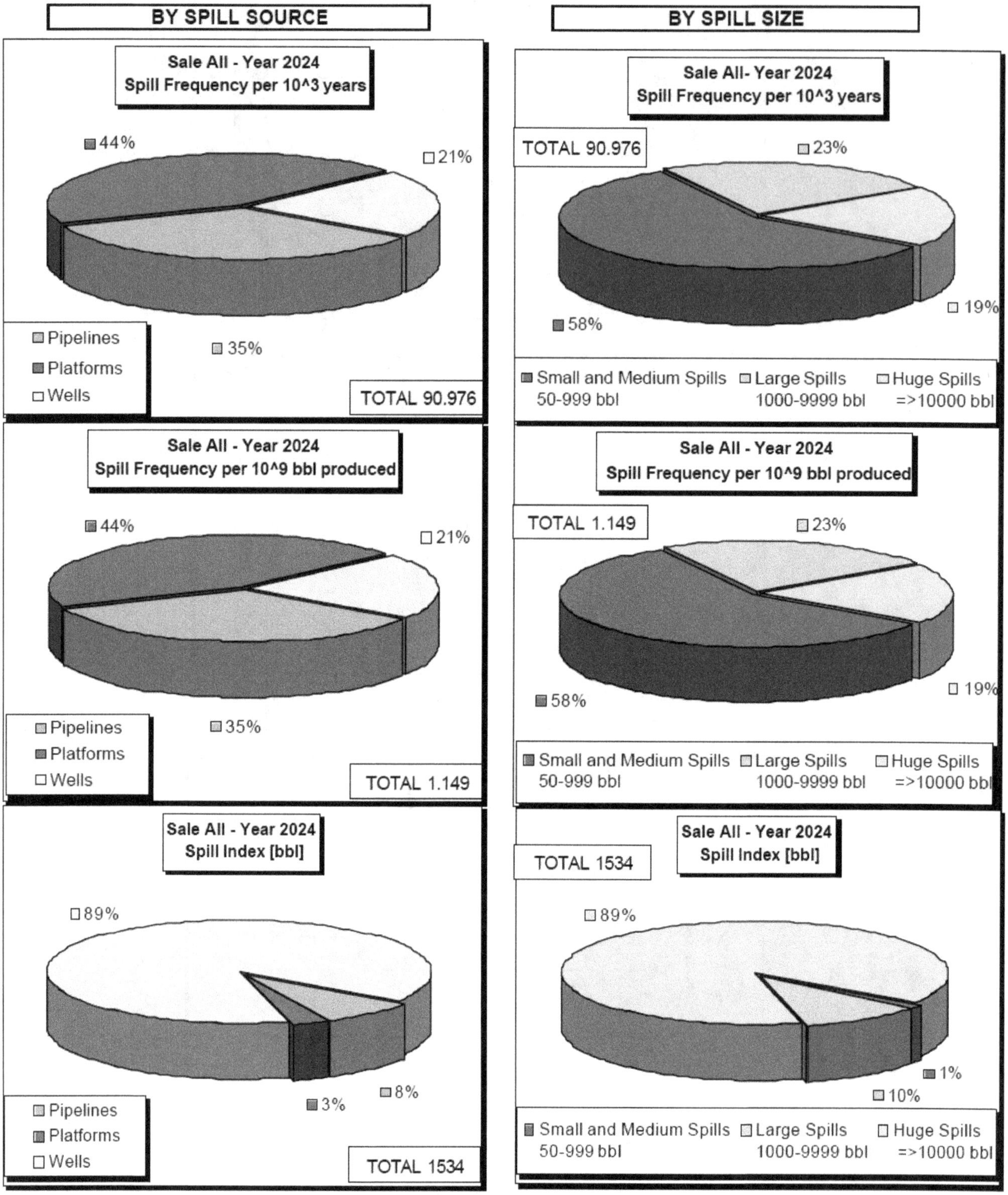

BY SPILL SOURCE

Sale All - Year 2024
Spill Frequency per 10^3 years

- ■44%
- □21%
- ☐35%

Legend:
- ☐ Pipelines
- ■ Platforms
- □ Wells

TOTAL 90.976

Sale All - Year 2024
Spill Frequency per 10^9 bbl produced

- ■44%
- □21%
- ☐35%

Legend:
- ☐ Pipelines
- ■ Platforms
- □ Wells

TOTAL 1.149

Sale All - Year 2024
Spill Index [bbl]

- □89%
- ■3%
- ☐8%

Legend:
- ☐ Pipelines
- ■ Platforms
- □ Wells

TOTAL 1534

BY SPILL SIZE

Sale All- Year 2024
Spill Frequency per 10^3 years

TOTAL 90.976

- ☐23%
- □19%
- ■58%

Legend:
- ■ Small and Medium Spills 50-999 bbl
- ☐ Large Spills 1000-9999 bbl
- ☐ Huge Spills =>10000 bbl

Sale All - Year 2024
Spill Frequency per 10^9 bbl produced

TOTAL 1.149

- ☐23%
- □19%
- ■58%

Legend:
- ■ Small and Medium Spills 50-999 bbl
- ☐ Large Spills 1000-9999 bbl
- □ Huge Spills =>10000 bbl

Sale All - Year 2024
Spill Index [bbl]

TOTAL 1534

- □89%
- ■1%
- □10%

Legend:
- ■ Small and Medium Spills 50-999 bbl
- ☐ Large Spills 1000-9999 bbl
- □ Huge Spills =>10000 bbl

Figure 6.3
Sale All – Year 2024 – Spill Indicator Composition by Source and Spill Size

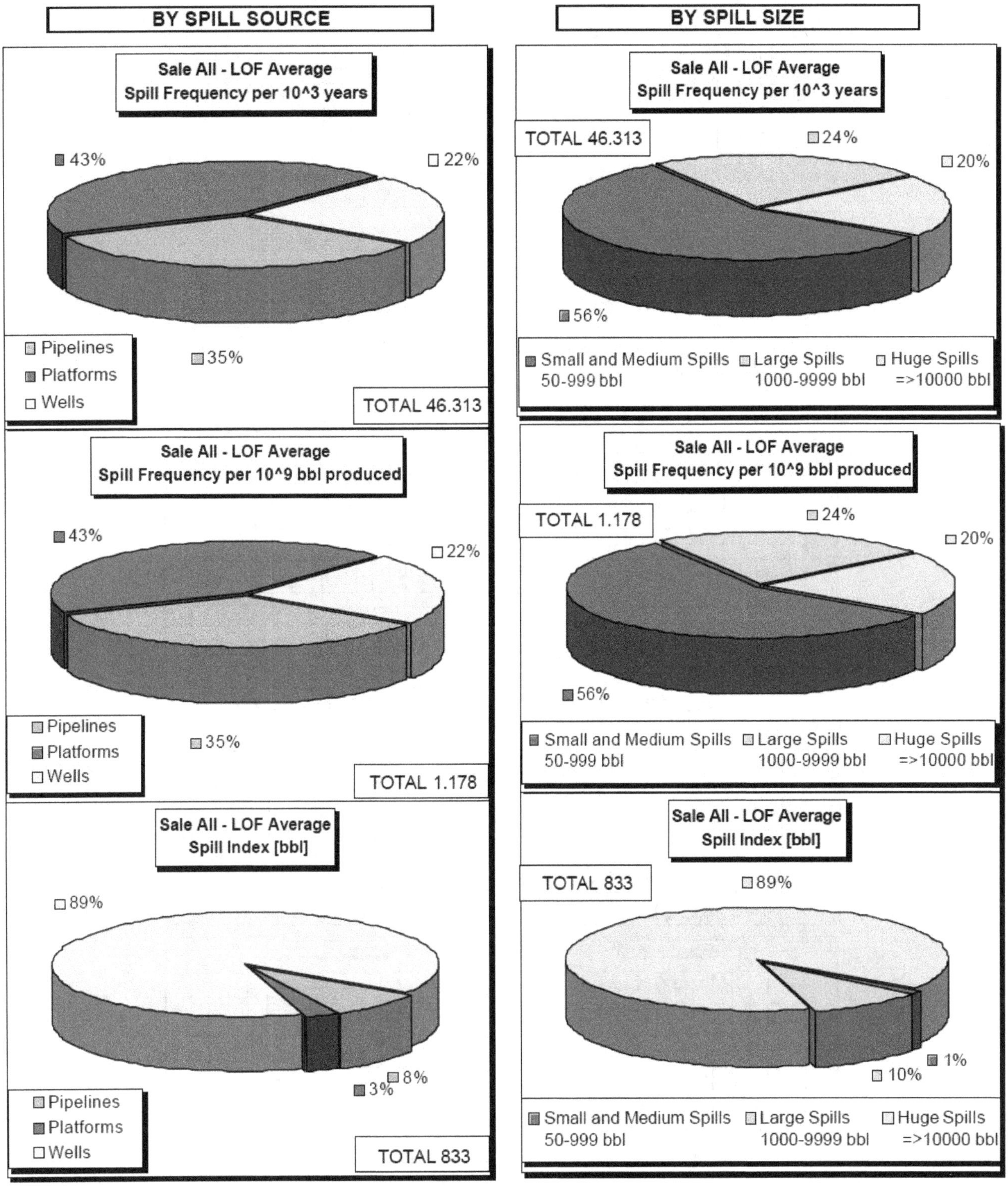

BY SPILL SOURCE

Sale All - LOF Average
Spill Frequency per 10^3 years

■ 43%   □ 22%

□ Pipelines
■ Platforms   ■35%
□ Wells

TOTAL 46.313

Sale All - LOF Average
Spill Frequency per 10^9 bbl produced

■ 43%   □ 22%

□ Pipelines   ■35%
■ Platforms
□ Wells

TOTAL 1.178

Sale All - LOF Average
Spill Index [bbl]

□ 89%

□ Pipelines
■ Platforms   ■3% ■8%
□ Wells

TOTAL 833

BY SPILL SIZE

Sale All - LOF Average
Spill Frequency per 10^3 years

TOTAL 46.313   □24%   □20%

■56%

■ Small and Medium Spills   □ Large Spills   □ Huge Spills
50-999 bbl   1000-9999 bbl   =>10000 bbl

Sale All - LOF Average
Spill Frequency per 10^9 bbl produced

TOTAL 1.178   □24%   □20%

■56%

■ Small and Medium Spills   □ Large Spills   □ Huge Spills
50-999 bbl   1000-9999 bbl   =>10000 bbl

Sale All - LOF Average
Spill Index [bbl]

TOTAL 833   □89%

■ 1%
□ 10%

■ Small and Medium Spills   □ Large Spills   □ Huge Spills
50-999 bbl   1000-9999 bbl   =>10000 bbl

Figure 6.4
Sale All – Life of Field Average Spill Indicator Composition by Source and Spill Size

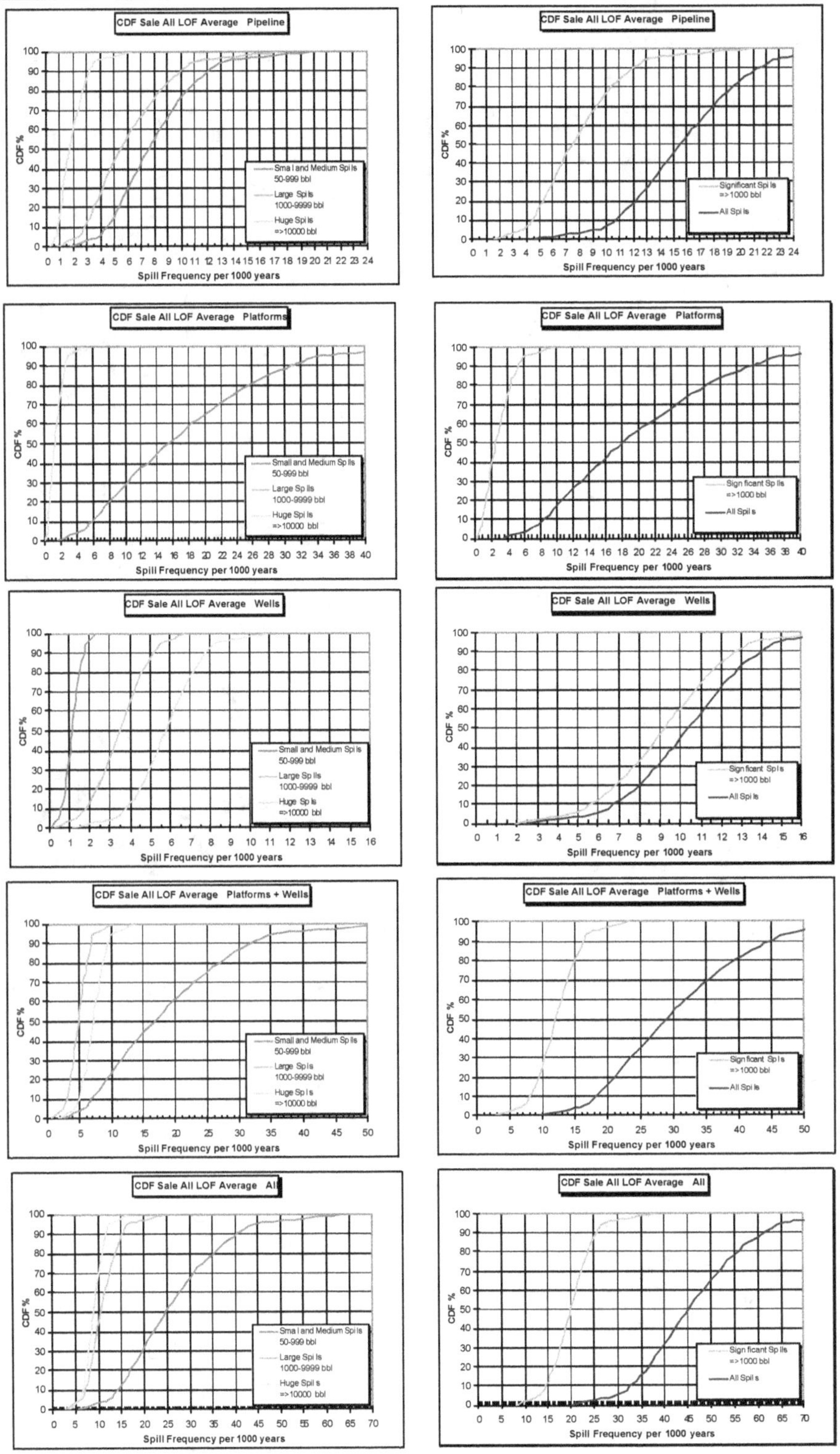

Figure 6.5
Life of Field Average Spill Frequency – Cumulative Distribution Functions – Sale All

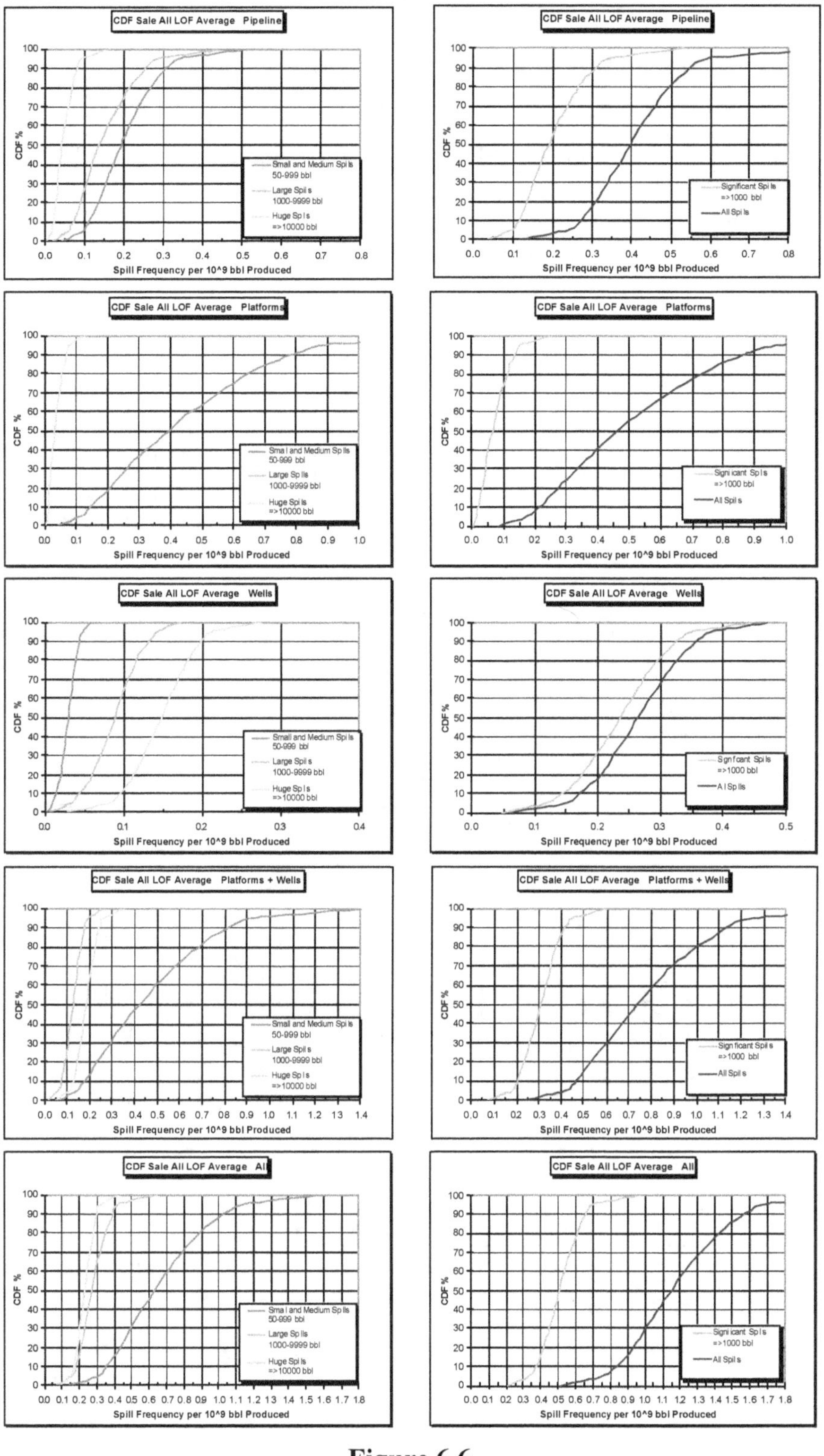

Figure 6.6
Life of Field Average Spill Frequency per Barrel Produced – Cumulative
Distribution Functions – Sale All

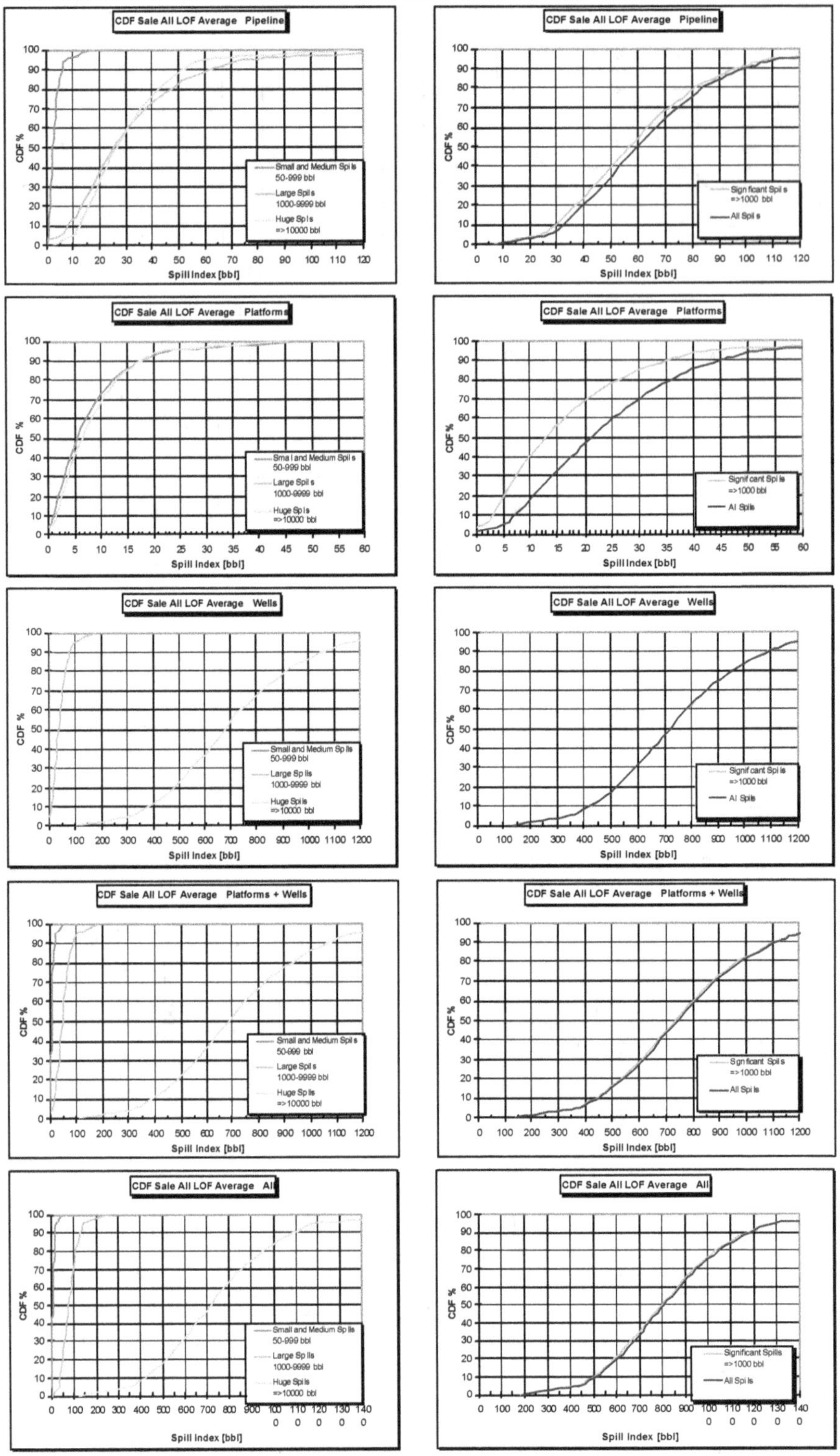

Figure 6.7
Life of Field Average Spill Index (bbl) – Cumulative Distribution Functions – Sale All

The Cumulative Distribution Functions contain extensive information on the statistical properties of the spill indicators. For example, from Figure 6.5, it can be seen, for significant spills, that the Life of Field average mean (50%) value of 20 (spills per 1,000 years) ranges between 30 and 12 at the upper and lower 95% confidence intervals. A similar percentage variation is shown for the Life of Field average spill frequency per barrel produced in Figure 6.6. The spill index variability shown in Figure 6.7 is proportionally higher. For example, in Figure 6.7, the mean value of the significant spills index of 800 per billion barrels produced ranges from 1,300 to 400 – a somewhat larger proportion of mean than that of the spill frequency indicators.

6.2.   Conclusions on the Methodology and its Applicability

An analytical tool for the prediction of oil spill occurrence indicators for systems without history has been developed based on the utilization of fault tree methodology. Although the results generated are voluminous, they are essentially transparent, simple, and easy to understand. The analytical tool developed is also quite transparent, very efficient in terms of computer time and input-output capability. In addition, the basic model is setup so that any input variables can be entered as distributions.

A wealth of information that can be utilized for the optimal planning and regulation of future developments is generated by the analytical tool. Key aspects of the analytical tool capability may be summarized as follows:

- Ability to generate expected and mean values as well as their variability in rigorous numerical statistical format.

- Use of verifiable input data based on MMS or other historical spill data and statistics.

- Ability to independently vary the impacts of different causes on the spill occurrences as well as add new causes such as some of those that may be expected for the Arctic or other new environments.

- Ability to generate spill occurrence indicator characteristics such as annual variations, facility contributions, spill size distributions, and spill causes, and life of field (Life of Field) averages.

- Ability to generate comparative spill occurrence indicators such as those of comparable scenarios in more temperate regions. The model developed provides a basis for estimating each Arctic effect's importance through sensitivity analysis as well as propagation of uncertainties.

- Capability to quantify uncertainties rigorously, together with their measures of variability.

6.3.   Limitations of the Methodology and Results

During the work, a number of limitations in the input data, the scenarios, the application of the fault tree methodology, and finally the oil spill occurrence indicators themselves have been identified. These shortcomings are summarized in the following paragraphs.

Two categories of input data were used; namely the historical spill data and the Arctic effect data. Although a verifiable and optimal historical spill data set has been used, the following shortcomings may be noted:

- Gulf of Mexico (OCS) historical data bases were provided by MMS for pipelines and facilities, and were used as a starting point for the fault tree analysis. Although these data are adequate, a broader population base would give more robust statistics. Unfortunately, data from a broader population base, such as the North Sea, do not contain the level of detail provided in the GOM data.

- The Arctic effects include modifications in causes associated with the historical data set as well as additions of spill causes unique to the Arctic environment. Quantification of existing causes for Arctic effects was done in a relative cursory way restricted to engineering judgment.

- Upheaval buckling and thaw settlement effect assessments were included on the basis of an educated guess; no engineering analysis was carried out for the assessment of frequencies to be expected for these effects.

- A reproducible but relatively elementary analysis of gouging and scour effects was carried out.

The scenarios are those developed for use in the MMS Alaska OCS Region Environmental Impact Statements for Oil and Gas Lease Sales. As estimated they appear reasonable and were incorporated in the form provided. There are two possible shortcomings of the scenarios as follows:

- Distributed values for the key quantities were not provided, thus precluding their incorporation as distributions in the Monte Carlo analysis.

- The facility abandonment rate appears to be significantly lower than the rate of decline in production.

Generally, the fault tree methodology was limited primarily by the shortcomings in input data discussed above.

The following comments can be made on limitations associated with the indicators that have been generated.

- The indicators have inherited the deficiencies of the input and scenario data noted above.

- The model generating the indicators is fundamentally a linear model which ignores the effects of scale, of time variations such as the learning and wear-out curves (Bathtub curve), and production volume non-linear effects.

6.4　Recommendations

The following recommendations based on the work may be made:

- Continue to utilize the Monte Carlo spill occurrence indicator model for new scenarios to support MMS needs, as it is currently the best predictive spill occurrence model available.

- Utilize the oil spill occurrence indicator model to generate additional model validation information, including direct application to specific non-Arctic scenarios, such as GOM projects, which have an oil spill statistical history.

- Utilize the oil spill occurrence indicator model in a sensitivity mode to identify the importance of different Arctic effect variables introduced to provide a prioritized list of those items having the highest potential impact on Arctic oil spills. These effects are incorporated to the extent that they are represented in spill databases used.

- Generalize the model so that it can be run both in an adjusted expected value and a distributed value (Monte Carlo) form with the intent that expected value form can be utilized without the Monte Carlo add-in for preliminary estimates and sensitivity analyses, while for more comprehensive rigorous studies, the Monte Carlo version can be used.

- Develop an adjusted expected value oil spill occurrence indicator model as a user friendly software package, which can be used for the assessment of oil spill occurrence indicators and their characteristics for any designated scenario. The software package should include the following:
  - Modular structure
  - User manual
  - Online help
  - Password protected parameters and algorithms
  - Extensive tabular and graphical outputs

REFERENCES

1. AIChE, "Guidelines for Chemical Process Quantitative Risk Analysis", 2nd Edition, Center for Chemical Process Safety, NY, 2000.

2. Anderson, Cheryl McMahon, and Robert P. LaBelle, "Update of Comparative Occurrence Rates for Offshore Oil Spills", Spill Science & Technology Bulletin, Vol. 6., No. 5/6, pp. 303-321, 2000.

3. Beaumont, S., "Refinery Construction in Arctic Weather Conditions – Some Construction, Inspection, and Corrosion Concerns", in Material Performance, Vol. 26:8, pp 53-56, 01 August 1987.

4. Bercha F.G., "Special Problems in Pipeline Risk Assessment", Proceedings of IPC 2000, International Pipeline Conference, Calgary, AB, October 1-5, 2000.

5. Bercha, F.G., A.C. Churcher, and M. Cerovšek, "Escape, Evacuation, and Rescue Modeling for Frontier Offshore Installations", Offshore Technology Conference, Houston, Texas, USA, 2000.

6. Bercha, F.G., and M. Cerovšek, Large Arctic Offshore Project Risk Analysis" Proceeding of Russian Arctic Offshore Conference, St. Petersburg, Russia, 1997.

7. Bercha, F.G., "Fault Trees for Everyday Risk Analysis", Proceedings of Canadian Society for Chemical Engineering, Risk Analysis Seminar, Edmonton, 1990.

8. Bercha, F.G., and Associates (Alberta) Limited, "Ice Scour Methodology Study", Final Report to Gulf Canada Resources, Calgary, AB, March 1986.

9. Bercha, F.G., "Application of Risk Analysis to Offshore Drilling and Risk Mitigation," Proceedings, Risk Analysis Seminar, Royal Commission of the Ocean Ranger Marine Disaster, Toronto, 1984.

10. Bercha, F.G., "Probabilities of Blowouts in the Canadian Arctic", North Sea Offshore Conference, Stavanger, Norway, 1978.

11. Bercha, F.G., and Associates Limited, "Probabilties of Blowouts in Canadian Arctic Waters", Final Report, Fisheries and Environment Canada, Report #EPS 3-EC-78-12, October 1978.

12. Bercha International Inc., "Alternative Oil Spill Occurrence Estimators for the Beaufort and Chukchi Seas – Fault Tree Method", Volumes I and II, OCS Study MMS 2002-047, Final Report to US Department of the Interior, Minerals Management Service, Alaska Outer Continental Shelf Region, August 2002..

13. Brighton Webs Ltd., "BW D-Calc 1.0 Distribution Calculator", www.brighton-webs.co.uk/distributions/, 22 July 2005.

14. Doelp, L.C., G.K. Lee, R.E Linney, and R.W. Ormsby, "Quantitative Fault Tree Analysis: Gate-by-Gate Method", in Plant/Operations Progress, 4(3) 227-238, 1984.

15. Energy Resources Conservation Board of Alberta, "GASRISK – A Model to Estimate Risk to Public Safety for Uncontrolled Sour Gas Releases", Volume 6, April 1990.

16. E&P Forum, Quantitative Risk Assessment (QRA) Data Sheet Directory, The Oil Industry International Exploration and Production Forum, 25-28 Old Burlington Street, London, 1996.

17. Fairweather E&P Services, Inc., "Historical Blowout Study, North Slope, Alaska", Study for BP-Amoco Exploration (Alaska), Anchorage, AK, June 2000.

18. Fussell, J.B., "How to Hand Calculate System Reliability and Safety Characteristics", in IEEE Transactions on Reliability, R-24(3), 169-174, 1975.

19. Gadd, P.E., G. Hearon, C.B. Leidersdorf, W.G. McDougal, J. Ellsworth, and D. Thomas, "Slope Armor Design and Construction Northstar Production Island", in Proceedings, Volume 1, 16th International Conference on Port and Ocean Engineering under Arctic Conditions (POAC), Ottawa, ON, August 12-17, 2001.

20. Goff, R., J. Hammond, and A.C. Nogueira, "Northstar Sub Sea Pipeline Design of Metallurgy, Weldability, and Supporting Full Scale Bending Tests", in Proceedings, Volume 1, 16th International Conference on Port and Ocean Engineering under Arctic Conditions (POAC), Ottawa, ON, August 12-17, 2001.

21. Gulf Canada, "Analysis of Accidents in Offshore Operations Where Hydrocarbons Were Lost", Report by the Houston Technical Services Center of Gulf Research and Development Company for Gulf Canada Resources, Inc., Calgary, AB, 1981.

22. Hart Crowser Inc., "Estimation of Oil Spill Risk From Alaska North Slope, Trans-Alaskan Pipeline, and Arctic Canada Oil Spill Data Sets", OCS Study MMS 2000-007, Study for US Department of the Interior, Minerals Management Service, Alaska Outer Continental Shelf Region, Anchorage, AK, April 2000.

23. Henley, E.J., and H. Kumamoto, "Reliability Engineering and Risk Assessment", Printice-Hall, Englewood Cliffs, NJ, (ISBN 0-13-772251-6), 1981.

24. Hnatiuk, J., and K.D. Brown, "Sea Bottom Scouring in the Canadian Beaufort Sea", 9th Annual OTC, Houston, TX, May 2-5, 1983.

25. Holand, Per, Offshore Blowouts, Causes and Control, Gulf Publishing, Houston, Texas, USA, 1997.

26. Hoyland, A., and M. Rausand, "System Reliability Theory: Models and Statistical Methods", John Wiley and Sons, New York, NY, 1994.

27. Hunt, D.M., K.R. McClusky, R. Shirley, and R. Spitzenberger, "Facility Engineering for Arctic Conditions", in Proceedings, Volume 1, 16th International Conference on Port and Ocean Engineering under Arctic Conditions (POAC), Ottawa, ON, August 12-17, 2001.

28. Kato, S., and N.J. Adams, "Quantitative Assessment of Blowout Data as It Relates to Pollution Potential", SPE 23289, First International Conference on Health, Safety and Environment, the Netherlands, November 10-14, 1991.

29. Lanan, G.A., and J.O. Ennis, "Northstar Offshore Arctic Pipeline Project", in Proceedings, Volume 1, 16th International Conference on Port and Ocean Engineering under Arctic Conditions (POAC), Ottawa, ON, August 12-17, 2001.

30. Leidersdorf, C.B., G.E. Hearon, R.C. Hollar, P.E. Gadd, and T.C. Sullivan, "Ice Gouge and Strudel Scour Data for the Northstar Pipelines", in Proceedings, Volume 1, 16th International Conference on Port and Ocean Engineering under Arctic Conditions (POAC), Ottawa, ON, August 12-17, 2001.

31. Lowrance, W.W., "Of Acceptable Risk", Kaufmann Inc., 1976.

32. Masterson, D.M., A.B. Christopherson, and J.W. Pickering, "Sheet Pile Design for Offshore Gravel Islands", in Proceedings, Volume 1, 16th International Conference on Port and Ocean Engineering under Arctic Conditions (POAC), Ottawa, ON, August 12-17, 2001.

33. Miller, D.L., "Hypersaline Permafrost under a Lagoon of the Arctic Ocean", in Proceedings, Volume 1, 16th International Conference on Port and Ocean Engineering under Arctic Conditions (POAC), Ottawa, ON, August 12-17, 2001.

34. MMS (Minerals Management Service), "Accidents Associated with Oil and Gas Operations: Outer Continental Shelf 1956-1990", OCS Report MMS 92-0058, 1992.

35. MMS (Minerals Management Service), "Federal Offshore Statistics: 1995. Leasing, exploration, production and revenues to December 31, 1995", US Department of the Interior, Mineral Management Service, Operations and Safety Management, OCS Report MMS 97-0007, 1997.

36. MMS (US Department of the Interior, Minerals Management Service, Alaska OCS Region), "Alaska Outer Continental Shelf - Beaufort Sea Planning Area Oil and Gas Lease Sale 144 - Final Environmental Impact Statement", Vol. II, OCS EIS/EA MMS 96-0012, May 1996.

37. MMS (US Department of the Interior, Minerals Management Service, Alaska OCS Region), "Alaska Outer Continental Shelf - Beaufort Sea Planning Area Oil and Gas Lease Sale 170 - Final Environmental Impact Statement", OCS EIS/EA MMS 98-0007, February 1998.

38. MMS (US Department of the Interior, Minerals Management Service, Alaska OCS Region), "Alaska Outer Continental Shelf - Chukchi Sea Oil & Gas Lease Sale 126 - Final Environmental Impact Statement", Vol. II, OCS EIS/EA MMS 90-0095, Anchorage, AK, January 1991.

39. MMS (US Department of the Interior, Minerals Management Service, Alaska OCS Region), "Undiscovered Oil and Gas Resources, Alaska Federal Offshore", OCS Monograph MMS 98-0054, Anchorage, AK, 1998.

40. MMS (US Department of the Interior, Minerals Management Service, Gulf of Mexico OCS Region), "Investigation of Shell Offshore Inc., Hobbit Pipeline Leak Ship Shoal Block 281, January 24, 1990, Gulf of Mexico, Offshore Louisiana", OCS Report MMS 91-0025, New Orleans, March 1991.

41. MMS (US Department of the Interior, Minerals Management Service, Gulf of Mexico OCS Region), "Investigation of the Exxon Company USA Pipeline Leak /Eugene Island Block 314, May 6, 1990, Gulf of Mexico, Offshore Louisiana", OCS Report MMS 91-0066, New Orleans, November 1991.

42. MMS (US Department of the Interior, Minerals Management Service, Gulf of Mexico OCS Regional Office), "Investigation of Chevron Pipe Line Company Pipeline Leak, South Pass Block 38, September 29, 1998, Gulf of Mexico Off the Louisiana Coast", OCS Report MMS 99-0053, New Orleans, September 1999.

43. MMS (US Department of the Interior, Minerals Management Service, Gulf of Mexico OCS Regional Office), "Investigation of Shell Offshore Inc., Hobbit Pipeline Leak, Ship Shoal Block 281, November 16, 1994, Gulf of Mexico, Off the Louisiana Coast", OCS Report MMS 97-0031, New Orleans, August 1997.

44. MMS (US Department of the Interior, Minerals Management Service, Gulf of Mexico OCS Regional Office), "Investigation of Shell Pipe Line Corporation Pipeline Leak South Pass Block 65 December 30, 1986, Gulf of Mexico off the Louisiana Coast", OCS Report MMS 87-0114, December 1987.

45. Modarres, M., M. Kaminsky, and V. Krisvtsov, "Reliability Engineering and Risk Analysis", Marcel Deker Inc., 1999.

46. O'Connor, M.J, and Associates Ltd., Preliminary Ice Keel/Seabed Interaction Study", Final Report to GCRI, March 1984.

47. Offshore Technology Research Center, "Comparative Risk Analysis for Deepwater Production Systems", Final Project Report for Minerals Management Service, January 2001.

48. OPL, "Field Development Concepts of the World", 1990.

49. Owen, L., D. Blanchet, and P. Flones, "The Northstar Project - Year-Round Production in the Alaskan Beaufort Sea", in Proceedings, Volume 1, 16th International Conference on Port and Ocean Engineering under Arctic Conditions (POAC), Ottawa, ON, August 12-17, 2001.

50. Paulin, M.J., D. Nixon, G.A. Lanan, and B. McShane, "Environmental Loadings & Geotechnical Considerations for the Northstar Offshore Pipelines", in Proceedings, Volume 1, 16th International Conference on Port and Ocean Engineering under Arctic Conditions (POAC), Ottawa, ON, August 12-17, 2001.

51. Roberts, N.H., W.E. Veseley, D.F. Haasl, and F.F. Goldberg, "Fault Tree Handbook", NUREG-0492, US Nuclear Regulatory Commission, Washington, DC, 1985.

52. S.L. Ross Environmental Research Ltd., "Blowout and Spill Probability Assessment for the Northstar and Liberty Oil Development Projects in the Alaska North Slope", Report to BP Exploration (Alaska), Inc., November 1998.

53. Ross, S.L., c.W. Ross, F. Lepine, and K.E. Langtry, "*Ixtoc I* Oil Blowout", Environment Canada E.P.S. Spill Technology Newsletter, pp. 245-256, July-August 1979.

54. S.L. Ross Environmental Research Ltd., "Blowout and Spill Probability Assessment for the Sable Offshore Energy Project", Report to Mobil Oil Canada Properties, November 1995.

55. S.L. Ross Environmental Research Ltd., "Contingency Plans to Monitor and Clean Up Large Spills from SOEP Offshore Facilities", Prepared for Sable Offshore Energy Project, Halifax, NS, March 31, 1998.

56. S.L. Ross Environmental Research Ltd., "Large Oil Spills and Blowouts from Exploration Drilling on Georges Bank: An Analysis of their Probability, Behaviour, Control and Environmental Effects", Chevron Canada Resources and Texaco Canada Petroleum Inc., submitted to the Georges Bank Review Panel, January 1999.

57. S.L. Ross Environmental Research Ltd., "Oil Spills Associated with the Terra Nova Development Project off Newfoundland: Risk Assessment; Spill Fate, Behaviour and Impact; Countermeasures; and Contingency Planning", Report to Petro-Canada Inc., December 1996.

58. S.L. Ross Environmental Research Ltd., "Panuke/Cohasset Field Development Project: Risk, Behaviour and Effects of Oil Spills", Report to IONA Resources Ltd. and Nova Scotia Resources Ltd., July 1989.

59. ScanPower A.S., "Blowout Frequency Assessment of Northstar", Report to BP Exploration (Alaska), Report No. 27.83.01/R1, Kjeller, Norway, July 2, 2001.

60. Sefton, A.D., "The Development of the U.K. Safety Case Regime: A Shift in Responsibility from Government to Industry", Offshore Technology Conference, Houston, USA, 1994.

61. Shared Services Drilling, "A Review of Alaska North Slope Blowouts, 1974-1997", June 30, 1998.

62. Sharples, B.P.M., J.J. Stiff, D.W. Kalinowski and W.G. Tidmarsh, "Statistical Risk Methodology: Application for Pollution Risks from Canadian Georges Bank Drilling Program", 21st Annual Offshore Technology Conference, Houston, TX, May 1-4, 1989.

63. Southwest Research Institute, "New Methods for Rapid Leak Detection in Offshore Pipelines", Final Report to Minerals management Service, US Department of the Interior, SwRI Project No. 04-4558, April 1992.

64. System Safety and Reliability Committee, Santa Barbara County, Energy Division, "Risk Matrix Guidelines", 1998.

65. U.S. Nuclear Regulatory Commission, "Reactor Safety Study", WASH-1400, NUREG-75/014, Appendix I – IV, October 1975.

66. Upstream Technology Group, "Analysis of Strudel Scours and Ice Gouges for the Liberty Development Pipeline", Final Draft, *no date*.

67. Weeks, W.F., P.W. Barnes, D.M. Rearic, and E. Reimnitz, "Some Probabilistic Aspects of Ice Gouging on the Alaskan Shelf of the Beaufort Sea", US Army Cold Regions Research and Engineering Laboratory, June 7, 1983.

68. Weeks, W.F., P.W. Barnes, D.M. Rearic, and E. Reimnitz, "Statistical Aspects of Ice Gouging on the Alaskan Shelf of the Beaufort Sea", US Army Cold Regions Research and Engineering Laboratory, 1982.

69. Wylie, W.W., and A.B. Visram, "Drilling Kick Statistics", Proceedings, IADC/SPE Drilling Conference, Houston, TX, February 27-March 2, 1980.

The Department of the Interior Mission

As the Nation's principal conservation agency, the Department of the Interior has responsibility for most of our nationally owned public lands and natural resources. This includes fostering sound use of our land and water resources; protecting our fish, wildlife, and biological diversity; preserving the environmental and cultural values of our national parks and historical places; and providing for the enjoyment of life through outdoor recreation. The Department assesses our energy and mineral resources and works to ensure that their development is in the best interests of all our people by encouraging stewardship and citizen participation in their care. The Department also has a major responsibility for American Indian reservation communities and for people who live in island territories under U.S. administration.

The Minerals Management Service Mission

As a bureau of the Department of the Interior, the Minerals Management Service's (MMS) primary responsibilities are to manage the mineral resources located on the Nation's Outer Continental Shelf (OCS), collect revenue from the Federal OCS and onshore Federal and Indian lands, and distribute those revenues.

Moreover, in working to meet its responsibilities, the **Offshore Minerals Management Program** administers the OCS competitive leasing program and oversees the safe and environmentally sound exploration and production of our Nation's offshore natural gas, oil and other mineral resources. The MMS **Royalty Management Program** meets its responsibilities by ensuring the efficient, timely and accurate collection and disbursement of revenue from mineral leasing and production due to Indian tribes and allottees, States and the U.S. Treasury.

The MMS strives to fulfill its responsibilities through the general guiding principles of: (1) being responsive to the public's concerns and interests by maintaining a dialogue with all potentially affected parties and (2) carrying out its programs with an emphasis on working to enhance the quality of life for all Americans by lending MMS assistance and expertise to economic development and environmental protection.